Growing Up Gay in Urban India

Ketki Ranade

# Growing Up Gay in Urban India

## A Critical Psychosocial Perspective

 Springer

Ketki Ranade
Tata Institute of Social Sciences
Mumbai, Maharashtra
India

ISBN 978-981-10-8365-5     ISBN 978-981-10-8366-2    (eBook)
https://doi.org/10.1007/978-981-10-8366-2

Library of Congress Control Number: 2018935876

Printed on acid-free paper

This Springer imprint is published by the registered company Springer Nature Singapore Pte Ltd.
part of Springer Nature
The registered company address is: 152 Beach Road, #21-01/04 Gateway East, Singapore 189721,
Singapore

# Preface

This book describes experiences of growing up gay/lesbian in the cities of Bombay[1] and Pune in India, in the late 1980s and 1990s. This is a retrospective study, wherein participants in their mid-thirties are describing their childhoods, adolescence, youth and growing-up years. So while I present this book to readers today, in times that are characterized by a lot of visibility to LGBTQ issues, it talks of a time defined by invisibility and silence and the resulting isolation of persons with same-sex sexuality. Readers may note that things have changed and yet have not. There are many more cities and small towns in the country today that are holding their very first LGBTQ Pride Marches, for instance; and yet the distress of a child who has to wear a particular type of school uniform based on the gender assigned to them at birth, remains the same and so does the police harassment of a *hijra,*[2] or familial violence faced by a lesbian woman. In fact, one could argue that today, much more than ever before, we are living in times of *intolerance of difference* and hate. There is much more surveillance on how we live, what we eat, what we read, and who we love and live with.

This book is a result of my decade-long engagement through research, therapeutic practice and activism in the broad area of LGBTQ rights; and more specifically with the question of the ways in which *difference* from naturalized heterosexuality affects individual life experiences across the life span. I explore experiences of growing up gay from two primary locations—as a mental health professional/activist and as a queer feminist activist. As a mental health professional/activist, I have witnessed the medicalization and pathologization of non-normative sexualities and gender expressions within psychological and

---

[1] In the 1980s and most part of the 1990s, Mumbai was still called Bombay. It was in 1995, after the Shiv Sena (a regional political party) formed a coalition government in the State of Maharashtra, that Bombay was renamed Mumbai after the Hindu goddess Mumbadevi. For several years thereafter and even now, people continue to use Bombay and Mumbai interchangeably.

[2] A transfeminine person, who is part of a close-knit community with distinct socio-cultural, religious practices that has traditionally been home to people of non-normative gender expressions in the Indian sub-continent.

psychiatric literature and practice. While there is increasing emphasis on gay affirmative literature, there still exist large gaps in understanding the lived experience of persons who transgress norms of gender and sexuality, and whatever is available as literature on affirmative practice is far from being mainstreamed or incorporated in the education and training of mental health professionals. As a queer feminist activist, I am witness to, and participate in, conversations around strategy-building and campaigns for assertion of queer rights; these assertions primarily represent adult queer persons. However, here too, non-heteronormative childhood/adolescence and its struggles with institutional forms of heteronormativity seem absent. This book is an attempt to give voice to the silences that I have encountered within the mental health literature as well as queer literature in India.

With respect to the representation of gay and lesbian lives in research and academic literature in India, I suggest that there is a near-absence of language, image, and discourse around childhoods that do not conform to the gender binary or the idea of naturalized heterosexuality; and yet there is a simultaneous public health discourse of 'risk and vulnerability' to HIV and other sexually transmitted illnesses that are linked, in the popular imagination, to gay and bisexual men, men who have sex with men (MSM) and transgender women. Reports of lesbian suicides, depression, suicides/self-harm among transgender persons, and substance abuse among LGBTQ youth, are a few other mental health concerns that are documented in literature in India. Thus, from no representation within certain discourses such as child rights/child welfare schemes of the state, and a proportionately higher representation within health/mental health literature as pathological-vulnerable-victim, to popular imagery of resilience and pride within LGBTQ campaigns, I suggest in this book that the lived realities of young gay and lesbian individuals are likely to be somewhere in between: in the experience of living, negotiating, passing, and asserting.

Using a life course and a critical psychosocial perspective to understand experiences of growing up gay has enabled me to: (a) understand the internal/psychic world of a gay/lesbian child and young person, while being attentive to ways in which childhoods and growing up years are constructed through naturalized heterosexuality and therefore the negotiations that the gay child has to undertake to navigate their way through the growing-up years; and (b) study growing up gay in the context of a historical time and space. For instance, what was it like growing up in 1990s Bombay/Pune? How visible were LGBTQ lives then? A critical approach in this book also means asking questions of representation of LGBTQ lives in disciplines and fields of enquiry—such as childhood studies, developmental psychology/life span studies, family studies—in India and uncovering heteronormative biases in their conceptions of childhoods, adolescence, and families.

In the writing of this book, particularly Chaps. 3–6, I have retained several first person narrative accounts of the study participants; in fact, narratives appear in two forms in this book. One form of the narratives is as prelude to each of the chapters from three to six. These narratives, while written in the form of a first-person account, are not gathered from one particular study participant. They are at times reflective of common/ shared experiences of study participants; at times they reflect things shared in conversations among friends, or at a meeting of our collective; and, at times, they are based on my own personal/ life experiences. The second form of narratives presented through chapters Three, Four, Five and Six are excerpts from interviews with individual participants.

I hope that the insights from this book would serve as a mirror to young queer persons and help them and their loved ones make better sense of the struggles and joys of growing up gay. These may also be useful for students and practitioners of mental health sciences, childhood studies, teachers and mentors to young people, to develop more empathy for diverse experiences and provide better support, services, and solidarity for all.

Mumbai, India                                                                                          Ketki Ranade
December 2017

# Acknowledgements

This book has been an exercise of *finding a voice*, a first person voice of experience—of myself and those of my participants. I am immensely grateful to all my study participants for lending their voices to this endeavor, and for sharing some of the most intimate, as well as mundane, aspects of their lives and growing-up years with me.

There are many people and institutions that have supported and helped to strengthen this work.

I would like to thank everyone involved with the Health and Population Innovations Fellowship Program, Population Council, India, and specifically Dr. Shireen Jejeebhoy and Prof. Pertti Pelto, my mentors during this fellowship during the years 2006–2009. It was during this fellowship that I first started working on the psychosocial aspects of growing up gay. Yogita Hastak and Sudeep Jacob Joseph for being the best research associates that one could ask for; Yogita, thanks for the tireless transcribing of interviews and for your deep empathy with all the study participants. Thanks to the Bapu Trust for Research on Mind and Discourse, Pune for housing the fellowship.

I owe a special thanks to organizations working on LGBT rights in Mumbai and Pune that supported my field work for this study. Samabhavana Society and Samapathik Trust, in Pune, and Humsafar Trust, in Mumbai, provided me immense support during the initial phases of collecting data.

I would like to thank Prof. Shubhada Maitra, my Ph.D. supervisor and friend; Prof. U. Vindhya and Prof. Nandini Manjrekar, my doctoral advisory committee members, and Prof. Surinder Jaswal, Deputy Director (Research), Tata Institute of Social Sciences (TISS), Mumbai for their inputs and encouragement throughout my doctoral work.

My colleagues at TISS, Prof. Ashabanu Soletti, Brinelle D'Souza, Dr. Smitha Nair, for your encouragement and for accommodating my writing schedules in the last one year.

Thanks to Shinjini Chatterjee and Priya Vyas, Springer India, for all your support and patience in the publishing process.

Dr. Asha Achuthan, I cannot thank you enough for your tireless and constructive engagement with my ideas throughout the writing of this manuscript, for your feedback and innumerable editorial suggestions every step of the way.

LABIA, Bombay as a space and the people who make this space, have over the years come to mean much more than being the initial contact point for meeting potential study participants. You all have become a significant part of my political and academic thinking and writing. Huge thanks and hugs to all friends and comrades at LABIA as well as several other queer groups across the country; I have learned immensely from all of you, and it is our shared learnings, experiences and dreams that have provided vision and support to this work.

My therapist, doctor, and go-to person, Dr. Neha Pande; words cannot express my gratitude towards you. It is your mirroring that has helped me become the person I am today.

Finally, I would like to thank my partners, friends, and families of choice; the many people who have nurtured me over the years and shown me the many meanings of the terms *growing up* and *home*.

# Contents

# About the Author

**Ketki Ranade, Ph.D.** is currently Assistant Professor at the Center for Health and Mental Health, School of Social Work, Tata Institute of Social Sciences, Mumbai. Ketki has worked for over a decade as a mental health service provider, trainer, researcher and activist and has developed mental health service programs in low income urban settlements and institutions in Pune, Maharashtra. Ketki has conducted research and published in areas such as medicalization of homosexuality, gay affirmative counselling, familial responses to gay and lesbian family members, and sexual rights of persons with psychosocial disability. Their areas of teaching include mental health policy, legislations and advocacy, clinical social work, interdisciplinary perspectives in mental health and qualitative research methodology. They have been a research fellow under the Health and Population Innovations Fellowship Programme (2006–09), Population Council, India. They were a member of the Expert Committee on Transgender Issues formed by the Ministry of Social Justice and Empowerment, Government of India in 2013. Ketki is also member of LABIA, a queer feminist LBT collective in Bombay. Ketki uses the gender pronoun 'they'.

# Abbreviations

| | |
|---|---|
| ABVA | AIDS Bhedbhav Virodhi Andolan |
| AIDS | Acquired Immune Deficiency Syndrome |
| APA | American Psychiatric Association |
| APsyA | American Psychological Association |
| CSA | Child Sexual Abuse |
| DSM | Diagnostic and Statistical Manual |
| HIV | Human Immunodeficiency Virus |
| ICD | International Classification of Diseases |
| IJP | Indian Journal of Psychiatry |
| IPC | Indian Penal Code |
| LBT | Lesbian, bisexual women and trans persons |
| LG | Lesbian and Gay |
| LGB | Lesbian, Gay, Bisexual |
| LGBTQ | Lesbian, Gay, Bisexual, Transgender, Queer |
| MHPs | Mental Health Professionals |
| MSJE | Ministry of Social Justice and Empowerment |
| MSM | Men who have sex with Men |
| NACO | National AIDS Control Organization |
| NALSA | National Legal Services Authority |
| NGO | Non-governmental organization |
| NHRC | National Human Rights Commission |
| PAGFB | Person Assigned Gender Female at Birth |
| PUCL | People's Union for Civil Liberties |
| TG | Transgender |
| WHO | World Health Organization |

# Chapter 1
# Growing Up Gay: Interrogating Disciplinary Frames

This book explores experiences of growing up—through childhood, adolescence, and young adulthood—of lesbian and gay individuals within their homes, schools, neighbourhoods, and among friends; their journeys of finding themselves and their communities while living in a heterosexually constructed society. It offers a glimpse into the lives of young children who often grow up feeling 'different' from their siblings, peers, and friends, and with constant messages about correct ways of being from parents, teachers, friends and counsellors/doctors. It describes unique challenges to growing up gay, alongside the complex processes involved in the decision of 'coming out'. These are with reference to the specific socio-cultural-relational contexts of the participants. The book further discusses the experience of meeting others like oneself, forming intimate, romantic relationships, bonds of friendship, finding political solidarity, constructing families of choice, and locating the meanings of these in one's own identity-development processes.

The book is based on an exploratory, qualitative study with young gay and lesbian persons in two cities of India, Bombay and Pune, and employs a life course perspective to explore the growing-up journeys of these young persons. The book includes layered narratives of the study participants along with an analysis of these growing-up experiences from a critical psychosocial perspective that is attentive to the subjectivities and the individual processes of making sense of an emerging non-normative sexuality within a socio-cultural-political context of homonegativity and gender binarism.

© Springer Nature Singapore Pte Ltd. 2018
K. Ranade, *Growing Up Gay in Urban India*,
https://doi.org/10.1007/978-981-10-8366-2_1

## 1.1  Looking for the Gay Subject in Childhood/s and 'Growing-Up' Literature

In attempting to understand 'growing-up' experiences of gay[1] individuals in urban India, I would like to begin by contextualizing this work within the broad literature on human growth and development, growing-up and childhood studies. Existing work on the lives of persons with non-normative sexualities, specifically gay men and lesbian women in India, is focused on adults and their rights and concerns. Most of this work does not reflect on the growing-up years of gay and lesbian persons as a subject of study (though descriptions of the growing-up years do form a part of first person narratives and anthologies of gay persons). In this chapter, I primarily suggest that sexuality and its emergence are not a one-time phenomenon of adult or even adolescent life, but instead a process. While this process has been studied in-depth and commented upon by several scholars of life span studies, often this commentary is about the development of normative sexuality. With this narrative being the dominant one, it gets naturalized and universalized, in turn invisibilizing the growing-up stories of individuals with non-normative sexualities. While I am aware that sexual non-normativity itself is a diverse phenomenon, in this book, I will focus only on growing-up experiences of young gay and lesbian individuals.

### *Perspectives on Growing-Up and Childhood Studies*

Childhood studies is one possible place to begin the exploration of research and literature on 'growing-up' years. Despite being an interdisciplinary field, childhood studies has been traditionally dominated by the discipline of developmental psychology and its theories of child development.

Developmental psychology is a branch of psychology that is concerned with studying childhood development and focusing on human growth across the lifespan. Developmental psychology divides the human life span into a series of age-graded segments, each segment characterized by physical, cognitive, emotional, and social development. Most texts of developmental psychology follow a chronological format from birth—or even inception—to death, with specified age limits for each period/stage, and certain milestones to be achieved in each of these stages. The origins of this discipline, in the post-war years, reveal that developmental psychology has primarily been concerned with the establishment of norms

---

[1]I use the term 'gay' in this book mostly to mean both men and women with same-sex sexual attraction, identity, and orientation. Thus, in most instances in the book, the term 'gay' is used to refer to both gay men and lesbian women, except in intances where I use the term 'gay men' specifically to refer to men. For further discussion on identities and terminology, please refer to Sect. 1.4 of this chapter: 'Gay', 'Lesbian', 'Queer'—contextualizing sexual identity labels.

of growth and development. It has done so through developing technologies of measurement of mental/psychological/cognitive abilities and has, thus, produced a classification of age-related abilities. Over the years, developmental psychology has produced life stages such as 'childhood' (which may be further divided into study of 'early' and 'late childhood' or 'infancy', with 'toddlerhood' predating 'childhood'), 'adolescence', 'adulthood' and so on, with a series of developmental tasks prescribed for each of these stages. It is primarily concerned with the statistical development of norms for each life stage and prescribing the same for the life span.

A critique of developmental psychology has arisen within childhood studies, and some of the main critical positions are concerned with the universality assumed by developmental psychology in understanding human growth and development, as well as the linearity accorded to these experiences. In addition, developmental psychology is seen as playing a role of regulation and legislation of what is 'normal'; departure from or delays to which, would be seen as pathological, and requiring intervention. Children and mothers have been traditionally the primary unit of inquiry in this branch of psychology, and examples of the regulation mentioned above would be related to norms of adequate mothering and nurturance, with implications for mothers in terms of amount of time spent with children, taking up paid work outside of home, day care for children, and what Burman (2007) refers to as responsibility for the 'moral performance of the next generation' (79). By introducing ideas of physical and psychological maturation, and by claiming universality of development experiences across the life span, developmental psychology has 'naturalized' human development and, by extension, anything which falls outside the standardized norm is deemed 'unnatural'. Cultural and contextual influences, including cultural and class variations in life expectancy, different perspectives on childhood, ageing, variations in family structures, and child rearing practices, are often ignored or treated as peripheral issues within this discipline (Burman 2007).

In addition to developmental psychology, one of the well-known contexts in which sociology has traditionally engaged with the study of childhood is that of socialization theory. Parsons and Bales (1956) describe the child as a being that needs to be moulded in order to be able to participate in society. This moulding/socialization of the child occurs in three stages. The first stage is referred to as 'primary socialization', where the child's personality is shaped by the family, and the values and attitudes that are imparted by parents to the children. The second stage is that of 'secondary socialization'. In this stage, the individual, usually a teenager or young adult, begins to become aware of societal expectations and what constitutes acceptable and unacceptable behaviour. The third or the 'tertiary' stage is when the individual as an adult is integrated into the larger society. Parsons states that the socialization of children and stabilization of adult personalities is the main function of the modern family. It is the family that serves as the primary link for the child to the external world. Apart from the family, there are other, secondary, agents of socialization such as the school, the neighbourhood, and peers that play a significant role in shaping childhood and adolescence.

A critical stance towards the traditional frameworks used to study childhood/s, within child development, developmental psychology, sociology, family studies, has emerged since the 1980s and '90s, under the broad head of a 'new' sociology of childhood (Tisdall and Punch 2012). The Piagetian idea of child development, with its fixation on universal, standardized and inevitable developmental stages, justifying adult supremacy (James et al. 1998, 18), and Parson's notion of adults as mature, rational and competent, whereas children viewed as "less than fully human, unfinished or incomplete" (Jenks 1996, 10), have been severely critiqued by these approaches. In fact, the idea of childhood, viewed in relation to the category 'adult', wherein childhood is seen as a temporary phase that will eventually end in adulthood, is fundamentally critiqued by thinkers within the sociology of childhood. Qvortrup (1994) explains this by describing the social construct of 'human becomings' rather than 'human beings' used in relation to children, which would explain the sparse attention given to studies of childhood within mainstream sociological research. One more conceptualization of childhood in this context is to think of children as dependants and needing protection; this views children as deserving of additional rights and protection and, at the same time also places restrictions on the enjoyment of certain rights and expects the exercise of certain obligations (Boyden and Hudson 1985). It is some of these conceptions of childhood/s, promoted within the traditional academic disciplines as well as in public opinion, that makes the 'rethinking of childhood/s' a difficult proposition. Mayall (2000) suggests that a major barrier in rethinking childhood/s, is the 'pleasing and reassuring' image of childhood that western psychology proposes. It is a conception of childhood as being innocent/uncorrupted by the realities of adult living and politics. Mayall states, 'Just as women have been assigned to the private and the domestic, we are taught to think of children as growing up there too, in a happy domain which enables them to develop, unmolested by the stresses of public life' (Mayall 2000, 246). In addition to the idea of being innocent and pure, there is also the conception of children as being unstable, unreliable, and incompetent; not having yet achieved 'adult maturity'. This image of the child as immature, incompetent, dependent and passive is common in Western as well as Indian notions of childhood (Bisht 2008). Thus, one of the challenges in rethinking our notions of childhood/s is the adult dilemma of choosing between the autonomy, or agency, of the child, and protectionism that predominates the adult conception of childhood/s.

Yet another dimension to be considered in the discussion on the conception of childhood/s in various disciplines is that the child is thought of as an individual, as a member of a family, rather than as part of a social group. Thus the development of the child is thought of as an individual/intra psychic or interpersonal (dyadic, often referring to the mother-child dyad) process alone, unconnected to the social structure. Mayall (2000) refers to this as the individualization and familialization of childhood. Familism, Chaudhary (2004) argues, is a significant reality of Indian families, wherein the child is presumed to 'belong to' the parents and is assumed to be mirroring the parental social identities. Then there is also the scholarization of childhood, where the assumption is that the proper activity or rather 'duty' of every child is to be a pupil and being engaged in any other activity, especially paid labour is unacceptable. Qvortrup (in Corsaro 2005) suggests that childhood can be thought of as a structural form, moving beyond individualistic, adult oriented, time bound perspectives. Qvortrup asserts that childhood may be a temporary period for children, but is a permanent structural category in society. Childhood is exposed to the same societal forces as adulthood and children are to be viewed as social agents, who contribute to the reproduction of childhood and society, through negotiations with adults and the creative production of cultures.

Tisdall and Punch (2012) state that newer approaches to childhood studies, that have been critical of the traditional models of child development, have set up a counter-paradigm in childhood studies; these include a few principles or what the authors refer to as 'mantras' in childhood studies: "childhood being socially constructed, recognition and focusing on children and young people's agency, and the valuing of children and young people's voices, experiences and/or participation" (Tisdall and Punch 2012, 8). This implies that childhood/s is/are to be viewed, not as a universalist category, but as being constructed socially and, therefore, as being variant and diverse. The focus thus has to move away from studying of norms and instead shift to change, transitions, relationships, contexts, and cultural variations that are neither stable nor static. It is then necessary to be cautious about notions such as the 'global child', in favour of a 'childhood in context'.

Children's participation and agency is another construct that has been focussed on within childhood studies. The traditional view of children as passive recipients and dependants, such as in the process of socialization, is questioned here. "Socialization is not seen as merely involving adaptation and internalization, but is viewed as a process of appropriation, reinvention, and reproduction" (Corsaro 2011, 20); as a collective and communal activity wherein children negotiate, share, and create cultures with adults and each other. This process has been termed by Corsaro (2005) as Interpretive Reproduction. Symbolic cultures in children's lives, such as children's media (cartoon, films), children's literature (fairy tales), mythical figures and legends (Santa Claus, The Tooth Fairy), are examples of how children engage with adults in co-creating culture.

Linked with the idea of children's participation is the notion of agency. Researchers working on childhood and young people remind us that the idea of agency is a complicated one. Children and young people, with their specific generational position and inter- and intra-generational relationships, have several opportunities for as well as constraints to act. Robson et al. (in Tisdall and Punch 2012, 14) describe "a continuum of agency, which varies depending on opportunistic and constrained contexts, created and expected identities, positions of power/lessness, life course stage, and state of emotions and wellbeing". Klocker (2007) suggests a notion of thick and thin agency that can be helpful in understanding this continuum of constrained agency of children and young people (85). In the context of this emphasis on children's participation and agency, Bluebond-Langner and Korbin (2007) ask a crucial question, about vulnerability. Vulnerability may be in the context of structural restraints, or may include deprivation, which is interpersonal in nature, or may even be a lack of adequate internal/intrapsychic resources, or it could be the result of an interplay of all these.

Laying out some of the conceptions of childhood/s, as reflected within the dominant disciplines/fields involved in the study of childhood/s and critical perspectives on the same, I seek to apply some of these ideas to my study of growing up gay; ideas relating to children's participation, agency in negotiating with normative/dominant prescriptions of a 'good' child, are explored in detail in Chap. 3, along with a discussion of vulnerability and difference from the dominant.

## Queering Childhood Development Studies

In this section, I attempt to bring a queer perspective to formulations within developmental psychology about childhood, adolescence, and life span development. First and foremost, the life stage models within developmental psychology are based on assumptions of compulsory heterosexuality/heteronormativity and the gender binary. Compulsory heterosexuality refers to the assumption that development 'naturally' proceeds in a heterosexual direction. It also refers to the pervasive assumption in society that all individuals are heterosexual. Thus, for instance, descriptions of adolescence as a lifecycle stage in textbooks of developmental psychology are full of details such as developing interest in the opposite sex, finding information about sexual intercourse, contraception use, unwanted pregnancy, and so on (Hurlock 1981). Experiences of internal processes of adolescents who may not 'fit' into the above description, and who may have non-heterosexual fantasies, attractions, crushes, or who may have no sexual attractions at all, are missing in the literature of 'normal' growth and development.[2] Similarly, all life cycle development research describes experiences of the stereotypical 'man' and 'woman'; any person and experiences falling outside of these gender binaries and their life trajectories are neglected. In fact, a substantial amount of research within psychology, about what can be broadly termed as 'sex difference' research, has viewed gender as a fixed, stable, singular identity, and framed within the dominant discourse of heteronormativity. This conception of inherent differences between the sexes is based on the two-sex model, wherein it is assumed that only two biological sexes exist and that these occupy positions on two opposite poles of masculinity and femininity, with respect to various psychological traits and abilities including cognitive abilities, verbal and non-verbal communication, aggression, leadership, moral reasoning, and so on.[3] Mainstream approaches to the development of gender, in children and adults, continue to function as key routes to legitimizing the binary

---

[2]Since the 1970s, in Euro-American contexts, there have been efforts at studying LGBT identity development and ways in which sexual orientation intersects with developmental experiences. However, these studies are often carried out by special interest groups and are treated as separate topics of research, while the mainstream narrative of developmental research continues to be dominated by heterosexism and gender binarism.

[3]Work in the area of androgyny and gender schema theory, pioneered by Sandra Bem in the 1980s, would be an exception to this research trend in psychology.

gendered categories. Thus, theories of child development and the development of gender, within the framework of developmental psychology, close down any possibilities of "emergence of new forms of sexed/gendered subjectivities" (Burman 2007, 8) that goes beyond the heteronormative script.

The majority of literature in Developmental Psychology comes from the American and European contexts and it is from these contexts that claims, regarding the universal nature of lifespan development, are often made (Burman 2007). For instance, while describing 'family', the literature often refers to nuclear households with family members that consist of a married couple with children, living together. Cultural variations in these, such as joint family structures, and the role of the extended family, neighbourhoods, and community, are not taken into consideration. Families outside of the heterosexual unit may not even find mention and, thus, experiences of children growing up in households comprising of same-sex parents, friends, or ex-lovers, seen as family/ies of choice, are not reflected in this mainstream literature. Universalist assumptions about child development do not work at multiple levels; they certainly do not apply to children who do not fit into the gender binary, or to children and young people with same-sex sexual desires, but they may equally not be true for any child whose context would be different from that of a child growing up in a western, white, nuclear household.

Cross-cultural psychology, cultural psychology, and indigenous psychologies are some of the schools of thought that have influenced developmental psychology and have argued in favour of contextually shaped and culturally constituted (as opposed to universal) experiences of development. There has been a tradition of scholarly work in these areas in the Indian context. For instance, Saraswathi (1999) suggests that the stage of adolescence, particularly for young girls in India (as well as for boys, particularly from the lower socio-economic strata), may not be a distinct phase, and can be viewed more in the context of a child-adult continuity of expectations and life experiences. Girl children, for instance, receive extensive training in their natal homes in becoming good wives and mothers, and their life experiences at the parental home, such as primary responsibility for sibling care, exposes them early to the role of motherhood. Similarly, for boys, the need to earn before they learn reduces the possibility of experiencing a stage such as the play stage of late childhood. Saraswathi (1999), therefore, states that "adolescence is the invention of a technological, industrial society that is marked by a discontinuity between childhood and adulthood" (214). However, even these scholars, who have inquired into the role of culture and context in shaping development, have limited their inquiry to growing-up experiences of young boys and girls, and men and women, with normative sexual and gender expressions.

Yet another concern with mainstream childhood development theories, from a queer perspective, is the idea of 'linearity' and 'time' that underlies these theories of development. Most models of growth and development tend to focus on stages of development that follow a linear track through the life span and are marked by developmental tasks and milestones that are to be achieved at 'appropriate' times. How does this idea of linearity and age-appropriate time, work in the context and life narratives of queer persons, who may follow a less rigid/normative, even an imaginative, life schedule? In her book, *Queer Time and Place*, Halberstam (2005) describes the notion of queer time as existing outside of the institutions of heterosexuality, family, marriage, and reproduction. She states: "Queer subcultures produce alternative temporalities by allowing their participants to believe that their futures can be imagined according to logics that lie outside of those paradigmatic markers of life experience-namely, birth, marriage, reproduction, and death" (Halberstam 2005, 2). So, if one were to think of queer time in the context of life span development then it would be a way of being that does not follow a strict pattern, or script, or have milestones of birth, education/job, marriage, reproduction, that are often associated with heterosexual growing up and life cycle stages. Queer time and, consequently, space would allow for reinterpretation of the ideas of *settling down, forming a family, becoming a responsible member of one's family, extended family and community,* tasks typically associated with becoming an adult.

Harvey (1990) states that, since we experience 'time' as some form of natural progression, we fail to realize or notice its construction. In fact, all time cycles, such as those described in life span studies, related to time of marriage, scheduling of (respectable/within heterosexual marriage) reproduction, are seen as naturalized and thus internalized. Harvey further asserts that different forms of time management, such as leisure, inertia, recreation, work, and family/domesticity, are adjusted to the schedule of normativity. However, some queer lives may follow a less normative life schedule, at times in response to the heterosexually constructed world around them. For instance, the process of a gay or lesbian young person knowing their sexuality, finding the language to talk about it, beginning to talk about it openly etc., would be a different process, in its complexity as well as the time taken for it, as compared to a heterosexual young person knowing about their sexuality. Thus, some queer persons, due to the normative structure of heterosexuality and gender binarism, would have a different life schedule compared to their heterosexual counterparts. However, there would be others who would follow a more imaginative life schedule as a result of challenging hetero-patriarchal structures of marriage, monogamy, biological family, and so on. This departure from norms, and creation of homosexual relationships as a subversion and resistance to social normalization [as described by Kingston (2009) in his article 'Subversive Friendships: Foucault on Homosexuality and Social Experimentation'], simply cannot be understood or measured in terms of normative developmental tasks or age-appropriate time.

The socialization processes such as that of Parsons, described above, tend to follow a reproductive model, wherein the existing social hierarchies and inequalities (Bourdieu and Passeron 1977) are reproduced through the institution of the family and other secondary sources of socialization such as school and neighbourhoods. For instance, social hierarchies of women as subordinate to men, and children to adults, are reproduced within the family. Applied to the context of lives of gay and lesbian persons, socialization primarily serves the function of making the gay or lesbian child aware of the normative script and the ways in which they differ from the same, fairly early in life. In addition, the primary and secondary sources of socialization play the role of 'correction' of deviance in the gay or lesbian child, whose desires and experiences do not fit the standard/heterosexual script. I discuss this idea extensively through examples of lived experiences of young gay and lesbian children within their homes, schools and among their peers, in Chap. 3 of this book.

Throughout the book, I bring out the multiple ways in which lesbian and gay individuals—children, adolescents, and young people—actively participate and negotiate with their socialization influences. They actively look for language, images, role models, and spaces that are affirmative of their sexuality and differ- ence. They also actively cope with, and work through, negative and pathologizing messages and make active choices about disclosure and non-disclosure about themselves. Thus, the traditional notion of 'moulding children' through socializa- tion influences is challenged at several junctures in this book. Also, while high- lighting agency and participation, I have discussed limits placed on individual agency by structures of power. I talk about vulnerability and dealing with difference at several places, particularly in discussing unique developmental challenges and sexual minority stress in Chap. 3.

Childhood studies researchers, are critical of traditional approaches to child development and are in favour of a socio-cultural contextual study of childhood/s, acknowledging the role of children in co-creating experience. However, even these theorists have seldom discussed experiences of gender non-conforming children, or children and adolescents with same-sex desires. In fact, partly because sexuality is seen as emerging during adolescence, there is very little work that has been done on childhoods of gay or lesbian persons. This book is an attempt to start this process of inquiry into gay childhoods and growing-up experiences.

## 1.2  Finding the Gay Subject in Psychological and Psychiatric Literature

Psychological, as well as sociological, literature on childhood seems to be almost silent on sexual and gender expressions of children and adolescents who do not fit the norm of the heterosexual gender binary. However, the same disciplines, par- ticularly the mental health sciences, have historically engaged extensively with non-normative sexualities and genders as 'deviant', 'abnormal' and 'unnatural'; that is to say, in ways that pathologize these sexualities and genders. In this section, I will explore this history of pathologization of homosexuality and the processes that led to its depathologization. I will then discuss the emerging area of study within psychology that focuses on LGBTQ lives, which has moved away from a language of deviance or pathology, and which, now, often employs a new lens of minority stress, vulnerability, risk to illness, and distress, as well as the need for affirmative practice.

## History of Medicalization of Homosexuality[4]

In the second half of the nineteenth century, homosexuality, which until then had been a theme only of religious and moral discourses, became a subject of enquiry in science and medicine. This led to a large body of work wherein sexologists, psychiatrists, and psychologists classified and created a range of sexual perversions and abnormalities in contrast to the 'within-marriage heterosexuality'. Thus, a range of 'perverted' sexualities were labelled and described in order to be able to define the 'normal' form of sexuality (Weeks 1981). Historically, the term 'homosexual' was coined and officially used much before the term 'heterosexual', to define that which was abnormal before describing the normal and the normative (Katz 1990). Krafft-Ebing (1922) was one of the first physicians to popularize the use of the term 'homosexuality', along with several other case studies of deviant sexual practices, in his work *Psychopathia Sexualis*, which viewed human sexual behaviour as a collection of terrible diseases. Beiber (1962), after a study of 100 homosexuals and 100 heterosexuals, concluded that the homosexual orientation was a result of a pathogenic family with a domineering mother and a detached or absent father. There were other psychoanalytical thinkers who attributed homosexuality to negative familial experiences or developmental issues. While Sigmund Freud himself did not view homosexuality as an illness and, in fact, considered all human beings to be born bisexual, he did describe homosexuality to be "a variation of the sexual function, produced by a certain arrest of sexual development" (Freud 1935). Other bio-medical theories, such as chromosomal abnormality or an excesses of hormones, have been proposed over time to explain the causation of homosexuality. Henry (1941), a psychiatrist, and his Committee for the Study of Sex Variants, scrutinized the bodies of homosexuals in an effort to document the sex-atypicality of their genitals and secondary sexual characteristics. Homosexual brains and nervous systems were also assumed to have some cross-gendered characteristics. LeVay (1991) argued that an area of the hypothalamus of homosexual men was closer in size to that of women than of heterosexual men. Some of the treatment methods that have been historically used to 'treat' homosexuals have included lobotomy, hypothalamotomy, implantation of testicular tissue of heterosexual men into homosexual men, induced seizures, electric shock, and behavioural methods such as masturbatory reconditioning, aversion therapy, and so on (Haldeman 1994; Silverstein 1991, 1996).

The influence of this thinking is reflected in homosexuality being classified as a form of mental illness in the first Diagnostic and Statistical Manual (DSM) of the American Psychiatric Association (APA) (1952). In the first edition of the DSM in 1952, homosexuality was classified under 'sociopathic personality disturbance'. This was later changed and, in DSM-II, which was published in 1968, it was classified under the category 'sexual deviance'.

---

[4]Parts of this section have been published before in Ranade and Chakravarty (2016).

In early 1970s America, several social movements that had 'equality and dignity for all' as their political goal—including the Civil Rights movement, the Feminist movements and later the Gay Liberation Movements—made a significant impact in challenging the medical view of homosexuality. Also, certain research studies—such as the seminal study by Hooker (1957), where she demonstrated that homosexual men are as well-adjusted as heterosexual men, and the Kinsey reports (1948, 1953), which demonstrated that being attracted to or being sexually active towards persons of the same-sex was not uncommon for adult American men and women—helped to build an argument in favour of declassification of homosexuality as a form of mental illness. In addition, advocacy by gay rights activists, which included 'sit-ins'—or what were popularly known as 'Zaps'—of annual psychiatry conferences and meetings, finally led to a referendum within the APA on declassifying homosexuality as a form of mental illness. In this referendum, 58% voted in favour of declassification and the APA released the following statement on homosexuality in 1973:

> Whereas homosexuality per se implies no impairment in judgement, stability, reliability, or general social or vocational capabilities, therefore, be it resolved that the American Psychiatric Association deplores all public and private discrimination against homosexuals in such areas as employment, housing, public accommodation, and licensing, and declares that no burden of proof shall be placed upon homosexuals greater than that imposed on any other persons. Further, the American Psychiatric Association supports and urges the enactment of civil rights legislation at the local, state, and federal level that would offer homosexual citizens the same protections now guaranteed to others on the basis of race, creed, color, etc. Further, the American Psychiatric Association supports and urges repeal of all discriminatory legislation singling out homosexual acts by consenting adults in private. [Robert Spitzer, Chair, APA 1973]

While homosexuality as a diagnosis ceased to exist in the DSM, a new variant—first in the form of Sexual Orientation Disturbance, and later Ego Dystonic Homosexuality—entered the DSM. It was only in the revised 3rd edition of the DSM in 1987 that homosexuality was entirely deleted from the list of mental disorders (APA 1987). Other classification systems of mental illnesses followed suit; the International Classification of Diseases (ICD) by the World Health Organization (WHO) removed homosexuality from its classification in 1992 (WHO 1992). It is thus important to note that there has been a long history of pathologization of homosexuality in the Euro-American context, and that the shift towards a position of depathologization within the mental health sciences is fairly recent.

In the Indian context, while most mental health practice continues to be guided by Euro-American models of mental health training and practice, the same does not seem to hold true when it comes to homosexuality. Mental Health Professionals (MHPs) in India have, at different points of time in history (after APA's declassification of homosexuality in 1973), conducted various kinds of reparative, conversion treatments with their homosexual clients. For instance, the Indian Journal of Psychiatry carried articles in the years 1978, 1982, and 1983 about the use of electrical aversion and other techniques of behaviour therapy for 'cure' and 'change' of homosexual orientation (Pradhan et al. 1982; Mehta and Deshpande 1983;

Sakthivel et al. 1978). Similar practices have been documented in other, more recent, studies about the use of masturbatory reconditioning, aversion therapy including mild electric shock, as well as hormonal treatments (Narrain and Bhan 2005; Ranade 2015; Kalra 2012). These methods have been internationally criticized, both on grounds of scientific efficacy as well as ethics (Serovich et al. 2008). In fact, the Yogyakarta Principles (2007) (Principles on the application of international human rights law in relation to sexual orientation and gender identity) describe any form of treatment aimed to cure/change sexual orientation as medical abuse. In 2001,[5] responding to a complaint by a gay rights activist on behalf of a boy who had been administered aversion therapy and non-prescription drugs to 'cure' his homosexuality, the National Human Rights Commission (NHRC) had cited the Indian Penal Code (IPC), Section 377 (which criminalizes homosexuality), and refused to address the violation. Despite this history, there has been a lack of concerted dialogue among mental health professional bodies in India about the scientific position of Indian mental health professionals vis-à-vis homosexuality. Do MHPs in India accept the international position with respect to sexual diversity and affirmative practice with Lesbian Gay Bisexual Transgender Queer (LGBTQ) groups adopted by several international bodies such as the APA, WHO, and others? Studies indicate that there have been large gaps and silences about homosexuality among mental health professionals in India. Parekh's study (2003) focussed on the extent to which sexual minority concerns are represented in mainstream research publications of MHPs in India. This study reveals that, among 829 papers, published between 1974 and 2000 in the Indian Journal of Clinical Psychology (an official publication of the Indian Association of Clinical Psychologists), there were only two papers on the subject of homosexuality. Similarly, there were only four research papers related to homosexuality published in the Indian Journal of Psychiatry between the years 1982 and 1995; all these papers were case studies of homosexual patients and their treatment outcomes. This situation however appears to be changing. More recently Narrain and Chandra (2015) edited a volume titled *Nothing to Fix–Medicalization of Sexual Orientation and Gender Identity*, which contains articles by mental health professionals and gender-sexuality activists in India on a range of issues including the journey of a mental health professional in understanding sexual orientation, social origins of internalized homonegativity/'ego-dystonicity', and guidelines for counselling LGBTQ individuals and their family members.

The 2009 Delhi High Court Judgment decriminalizing homosexuality was a major boost for the LGBTQ rights movements in India. Soon after this, a couple of papers appeared in the *Indian Journal of Psychiatry* (*IJP*), the official publication of the Indian Psychiatric Society, discussing the need for depathologization of homosexuality in clinical practice (Kalra et al. 2010). In 2012, in an editorial, the *IJP* clarified its position vis-à-vis homosexuality, stating that it is a normal variant

---

[5]Shaleen Rakesh v/s NHRC, 2001, Available at: http://lawandotherthings.com/2009/07/naz-foundation-and-nhrc/. Last accessed on 15th July 2017.

of human sexuality and underscored the need for more research on LGBTQ lives in India (Rao and Jacob 2012). Thus, like the situation in America that led to the removal of homosexuality from the list of mental disorders, in India too, the change in legal status of homosexuals, and a dynamic LGBTQ rights movement, has had a significant impact on attitudes of Indian MHPs. There have been more voices within the mental health fraternity who have been speaking in support of the cause of LGBTQ rights. In fact, a group of MHPs signed a petition addressed to the Supreme Court[6] of the country in the context of an appeal against the Delhi High Court Judgment of 2009, by various right-wing groups, seeking to reinstate Section 377 (section that criminalizes homosexuality) of the Indian Penal Code (IPC). The MHPs stated in their petition that it was their medical opinion that homosexuality is not a form of mental illness and that, on the contrary, a law like Section 377 causes tremendous psychological stress and trauma to homosexual persons.

In December 2013, the Supreme Court of India, in response to a challenge to the 2009 judgment of the Delhi High Court, upheld Section 377 of the IPC and, in effect, (re)criminalized homosexuality. Interestingly, the *IJP* in January 2014 published a letter to the editor titled, '*A fresh look at homosexuality*', where the author, while stating his sympathies with the gay rights cause, also expresses his reservation in accepting homosexuality as a 'normal' sexual variant, and argues in favour of the position of viewing homosexuality as a deviance. Verghese (2014) in his letter states,

> A normal variant cannot be considered completely normal. It is, in fact, an aberration in the psychosexual development, caused by genetic and psychosocial factors for which the person is not responsible. There are research findings, which suggest that there are structural differences in the brains of people with homosexual orientation… Every biological function has a physiological goal and purpose. Sexual activity has two goals. One is procreation to safeguard the continuation of the species. The second one is the experience of pleasure, which in fact, is to facilitate the sexual activity and to strengthen the bond between husband and wife.
>
> Homosexuality negates one of the goals of sexual activity procreation. Homosexuality has therefore, to be considered as an aberration in the psychosexual development caused by genetic and psychosocial factors…. (pp. 209–210)

In the context of this letter, I again wish to draw attention to what I have earlier referred (in the American context) as the relationship between law and medicine; both these, as tools of social control and regulation, work in tandem to maintain normative ideologies and define what is permissible, acceptable, normal conduct. It is amply clear, not only from the situation in India but the world over, that homosexuality has been one of those controversial issues that has been dealt with and, on occasion, resolved, not merely through what we consider 'scientific

---

[6]The mental health professionals petition to the Supreme Court is available at - http://orinam.net/377/wp-content/uploads/2014/04/CurativePetition_MentalHealth.pdf.

knowledge' and 'fact', but through the reconsideration of social/religious/moral attitudes and the opinions of medical/mental health professionals.

## LGB Psychology: Newer Trends and Directions

De-pathologization of homosexuality and shifts in scientific understanding, from the deviance model to a more inclusive of diversity model, has impacted knowledge creation, research, education, and practice within the mental health sciences of psychology and psychiatry. Some of the early reflections of this impact can be seen in the work of psychologists who proposed models of gay and lesbian identity development. These stage models of development of sexual identity can be seen as early efforts to make visible a development process that was hitherto completely invisible. This work can possibly be seen also as research attempting to shift the question of LGB sexual identity formation from a pathological etiology—Why did this happen? What caused this deviance?—to a 'how': a description of the experience of development of same-sex sexuality.

There were several models of gay identity development, or what were referred to as 'coming out models', that were proposed by LGB psychologists, mostly from America in the 1970s and 80s. One of the most popular among these was the one proposed by Cass (1979). Cass described a six-stage model of gay identity development. The stages include:

(a) Identity confusion: In this stage people attracted to members of their own sex begin to become consciously aware that information about homosexuality directly or indirectly applies to them. They then begin to experience discordance between these feelings and the heterosexual identity they had assumed to be true for themselves. This causes anxiety and or confusion and people, while living with these uncomfortable feelings, may privately label their thoughts, feelings and fantasies as possibly gay, while maintaining a public image of heterosexuality.

(b) Identity comparison: During this stage, people may begin to accept the possibility that they may not be heterosexual after all. This admission to oneself, that they may be gay or lesbian, reduces confusion to some extent; however, it makes them feel alienated from others. There is an increased sense of 'not belonging' to society at large and specific sub groups such as family and peers. Accepting the possibility of being gay leads many to realize that all the guidelines for behaviour, ideals, and expectations for the future, that accompany a heterosexual identity, are no longer relevant in their lives. This loss of a heterosexual blue print for life can cause considerable grief for some.

(c) Identity tolerance: People may learn to tolerate rather than fully accept their gay or lesbian self-image. As their feelings of alienation from others increase, they seek out gay and lesbian communities to reduce their isolation. People perceive an increased discrepancy between the way they see themselves and the way others perceive them (heterosexual social image).

(d) Identity acceptance: More and more validating and 'normalizing' contact with other lesbians and gay men, helps people to increasingly accept oneself. While passing as heterosexual becomes a habit by this stage, some selective self-disclosures may occur at this stage. There may also be only limited contact with heterosexuals and this reduces feelings of alienation.

(e) Identity pride—There is a strong sense of incongruence felt between the positive ways in which gay and lesbian individuals have come to accept themselves and society's devaluation of their identities. Thus they now not only accept but prefer their new identities over a heterosexual self-image and often an 'us' v/s 'them' dichotomy may be created. While the internal conflicts may be minimized by this stage, conflicts with a homophobic and heterosexist world outside may increase. People may be drawn towards rights based activism and engage more actively along these lines with the lesbian and gay community.

(f) Identity synthesis: The 'homosexual v/s heterosexual' dichotomy is relinquished and feelings of anger at the society reduce. Perceived social support and trust, rather than sexual orientation, become important criteria and people may place more trust in sensitive and supportive heterosexuals. Public and private aspects of the self become increasingly integrated into an identity that includes sexual orientation along with other dimensions of self.

Cass states that individuals may not necessarily pass through each and every stage of this model in a linear fashion. Moreover, identity development process may be foreclosed at any stage due to traumatic experiences or other life events.

Troiden's model (1984) is one more such model that views LG development as mediated by both external factors (heterocentrism and sexual prejudice) and internal factors (such as one's internalized homophobia and character strengths). More spiral than linear, Troiden's model suggests that individuals move back and forth between stages, and that not all individuals will experience all stages or sub-stages. Coleman (1981–1982) proposed another model consisting of five stages: pre-coming out, coming out, exploration, first relationships, and integration. Grace (1992) describes stages of emergence, acknowledgement, finding community, first relationships, and self-definition and reintegration. D'Augelli (1994) provided a life span approach to sexual orientation identity development and emphasized six developmental tasks. These include: exiting heterosexual identity, developing a personal gay identity status, developing a gay social identity, becoming a gay offspring, developing a gay intimacy status, and entering a gay community.

All these models of gay identity development perceive development to be linear, invariant, universal, inevitable, and predictable across individuals who share some real or hypothesized commonalities (Savin-Williams 2001). Whether these models truly reflect experiences of young gay and lesbian individuals is questionable. Critiques have pointed out that most identity development models have evolved from clinical and anecdotal data (Gruskin, in Hunter 2007, 61) and have had small samples and weak research designs (Evans and Levine 1990). In addition, most of these models are proposed in the western context and are often based on white, gay men's experiences and hence have been criticized for their ethnocentric assumptions. In fact, most of these models understate the importance of the social context within which the LG identity development occurs. While some of these models do refer to the idea of identity foreclosure and, in describing this, discuss the role of traumatic life events, these traumatic events, especially in the context of homonegativity, prejudice, and targeted violence, are not really explored; nor are the role of individual resilience, community solidarities, and activism for change discussed. Finally, these models minimize the tremendous variation in experience of LG individuals that is mediated by 'context' of social class, ethnicity, age, gender and other background factors (Kaufman and Johnson 2004).

Apart from work on LGB identity development models by individual researchers, the American Psychological Association founded the APsyA Division 44: Society for the Psychological Study of Lesbian and Gay Issues, in 1985, to engage with research, clinical practice, advocacy, training and education on issues related to minority sexual orientation, gender identity, and gender non-conformity. One of the seminal works of this Division was the creation of Guidelines for Psychotherapy with Gay and Lesbian Clients (APA 2000) that was a result of studies carried out with mental health professionals in America, and then in Europe with psychologists, to understand their current practices, including biased as well as exemplary practices (Garnets et al. 1991; Milton and Coyle 1998). In addition to these Affirmative Therapy Guidelines, APsyA Division 44 has also attempted to respond to the wide range of controversies and questions related to 'Sexual Orientation Change Efforts' and a range of conversion/reparative treatment practices to help clients change their sexual orientation. One of the results of these concerted efforts is the 'Manual on Appropriate Response to Sexual Orientation' (APA 2009). Similar efforts have been undertaken in U.K. by the British Psychological Society, which has developed a guidelines document titled 'Guidelines and Literature Review for psychologists working therapeutically with Sexual and Gender Minority Clients' (Shaw et al. 2012). In the Indian context, too, attempts have been made to document affirmative practices with LGB clients (Ranade and Chakravarty 2013a, b, 2016). However, since there is no taskforce or special interest group of mental health professionals in India working on these issues, these do not have the scope or the mandate necessary to influence mental health practice, education, or policy.

Another strand in the newer trends in mental health research with LGB identity is that of exploring the vulnerability and risk of LGB persons to various health and mental health problems. This kind of research mostly employs a public health approach to highlight the nature of stressors, stigma, and violence in the lives of LGB persons that puts them at a higher risk (compared to their heterosexual counterparts) for sexual health problems such as sexually transmitted diseases, including HIV, and for mental health problems such as depression, suicide, and substance abuse. There have been a range of epidemiological studies that suggest elevated rates of depression and mood disorders (Bostwick et al. 2010), anxiety disorders (Cochran et al. 2003), post-traumatic stress disorder (PTSD)

(Hatzenbuehler et al. 2009), alcohol use and abuse (Burgard et al. 2005), and suicide ideation and attempts, as well as psychiatric comorbidity (Haas et al. 2010) among LGBT adults. Research with LGBT youth suggests that they face a greater number of stressful events, and have access to less social support, than their heterosexual peers (Safren and Heimberg 1999). In the Indian context too, a study conducted with 150 Men who have Sex with Men (MSM), in Mumbai city, indicated that 45% reported current suicidal ideation, 29% screened in for current major depression, and 24% for some anxiety disorder (Sivasubramanian et al. 2011). There have been a few other reports that have documented suicides among LBT persons. A study with 50 queer persons, who had been assigned female gender at birth (and many of whom identified as gender non-binary or transgender), indicates that as many as 20 respondents of the 50 had attempted suicide at least once, and some more than once; seven others had seriously contemplated suicide in response to the violence and lack of support in their lives (Shah 2015). *Humjinsi*, a resource book on queer rights in India, documented over 30 cases of lesbian couples committing suicide in a period of five years (Fernandez 1999). According to Deepa (2005), a lesbian-rights activist documenting cases of lesbian suicides in Kerala, most women committing suicide are from Dalit, *adivasi*, and working class communities, and have therefore been subjected to multiple discriminations. In terms of sexual health risk, specifically HIV risk, MSM and *Hijras* are considered to be core high-risk groups for HIV infection in India (NACO 2007). As per a report of UNDP (2010), the overall adult HIV prevalence is 0.36%, and that among Men who have sex with Men (MSM) in India the rate is estimated to be 7.4%, and among *hijras/transwomen* it is even higher (17.5–41%). More recent figures from NACO suggest the national prevalence of HIV to be 0.26%; among MSM it is 4.3% (NACO 2015).

It is important to note here that the research trends I describe above, within LGB psychology and public health, while indicative of the de-pathologization of same-sex sexuality, can also be seen as a re-engagement or a re-entry of the homosexual into the clinic; albeit this time not as a deviant in the manner that deviance was understood previously, but as a group that is 'at risk' for morbidity as well as mortality. The implications of this have been multiple, and the construction of the sexually non-normative subject within health sciences has been undergoing a lot of changes. For instance, in the initial years of the HIV epidemic, gay men and MSM, were seen as carriers of the epidemic. Their lifestyle (read 'sexually promiscuous') was seen as leading to the deadly disease. Similarly, substance abuse, suicide risk and its higher prevalence among the LGBT community, has been attributed to the 'lifestyles' of these specific groups. However, these links between a community and its health/illness status have also undergone shifts with discussion on mediating factors, risk factors such as violence, discrimination, lack of social entitlements, and so on. One may then ask the question: Is there any change in the re-engagement of mental health sciences with homosexuality, and, if yes, what? One response to this is the change in the framework that defines this re-engagement/re-entry. The framework being used now is a psycho-social one, wherein psychological disturbance is sought to be viewed from and within a social lens. Thus pathology/disease is not located within the individual but is viewed as

occurring at the intersection of the individual psyche, the interpersonal and relational realm, as well as the social context, and hence intervention, too, is seen as
necessary at all these levels. If we were to look at the gay affirmative practice
guidelines mentioned above, all of these, irrespective of whether they were
developed by the American Psychological Association or the British Psychological
Society or with Indian mental health professionals/counsellors, emphasize the need
to focus on the impact of stigma on the mental health of gay persons, the role of
unique stressors in the lives of gay persons, the challenges faced by gay clients as a
result of being a minority, and understanding the intersection of LGB identity with
other minority identities and marginalized locations. Similarly, if one were to look
at the state/policy response to the HIV epidemic in India, it emphasizes as much
upon creating an enabling environment for MSM, gay men, *hijra*s and transgender
women, through decriminalization of homosexuality and welfare measures for
empowerment of the community, as upon clinical management of disease.

In order to dwell on this perspective further, I will first discuss sexual minority
stress, as proposed by Meyer (1995).

## Sexual Minority Stress: Prejudice and Discrimination as Social Stressors

Meyer (1995) uses the term 'sexual minority stress' to refer to the psychological
distress that is a result of the stigma, discrimination, violence experienced by sexual
minority individuals as a result of their sexuality. Minority stressors are conceptualized by Meyer as *internalized homophobia*, that refers to the 'gay person's
directing negative societal attitudes towards the self, leading to a devaluation of the
self and resultant internal conflicts and poor self-regard' (Meyer and Dean 1998,
161), *stigma* that relates to expectations of rejection and discrimination, and actual
*experiences of discrimination* and violence (Meyer 1995). A few defining features
of minority stress are: (a) it is *unique* and hence 'additive' to the general stressors
that everyone experiences and, in that sense, requires a response over and above the
one required to cope with other life stressors; (b) it is *chronic*, implying it is related
to relatively stable underlying social and cultural structures; and (c) it is *socially
based* and stems from social processes, institutions, and structures that are beyond
the individual (Meyer 2007). While focusing on the impact of gay-related prejudice,
stigma, and discrimination on the well-being and mental health of sexual minorities,
this model of minority stress does not suggest a singular notion of identity based on
sexual orientation, but includes multiple axes of identities that may further
marginalize or privilege an individual. In this sense, while describing the process of
minority stress, Meyer acknowledges the intersectionality of identities.
A distal-proximal distinction is useful to understand the processes of sexual
minority stress. Lazarus and Folkman (1984) described social structures as 'distal
concepts whose effects on an individual depend on how they are manifested in the

immediate context of thought, feeling and action—the proximal social experiences of a person's life' (321).

Garnets et al. (1990) suggest that prejudice events and experiences of victimization take away a person's sense of security and invulnerability. Allport (1954) describes vigilance as one of the traits that targets of prejudice develop. Some studies point to the extra energy that is expended examining reasons for one's sexuality and figuring out one's sexual identity while living and growing up in a heterosexist world, maintaining multiple identities, stress involved in the process of coming out (publicly identifying as LGBT), familial issues and a general lack of social support as some of the unique stressors related to a gay or lesbian identity (Miller and Major 2000). Smart and Wegner (2000) describe the cognitive burden involved in hiding and living in secrecy. In the Indian context, some of the gay-related stressors that have been documented include: pressure for heterosexual marriage and forced marriages; pressure to seek help/cure from doctors to change sexual orientation; and violence from natal family (Ranade 2015; Fernandez and Gomathy 2003; Ghosh et al. 2011; Shah 2015).

In the two sections above—'Looking for the gay subject in childhood/s and growing-up literature' and 'Finding the gay subject in psychological and psychiatric literature'—I have provided an overview of representation (or absence of the same) of same-sex sexuality within various disciplines and fields of study that are concerned with childhood, growth, development, well-being, and mental health. In the next two sections, I will discuss material related to development of self and identity, specifically sexual identities and their meanings in the contemporary socio-cultural context of urban India. In a study on growing up gay, this discussion on the nature of self, the emergence of self, and influences on the growing selfhood and identity, is necessary to lay out the multiple perspectives that have informed this work.

## 1.3  Identity Literature—Understanding the Intrapsychic, Symbolic, Dialogic and Collective Self

An increasing sense of identity… is experienced preconsciously as a sense of psychosocial well-being. Its most obvious concomitants are a feeling of being at home with one's body, a sense of 'knowing where one is going', and an inner assuredness of anticipated recognition from those who count. (Erikson 1959, 118)

This is the description, in Erikson's words, of achieving a sense of identity or developing a satisfactory psychosocial 'self-definition'. Erikson describes this identity formation as one of the major tasks of adolescence and by this identity formation, he does not mean generating a new selfhood all at once during adulthood, but instead synthesizing the various elements accumulated throughout growing-up years into an enduring sense of selfhood that maintains continuity and sameness. Identity formation is not a onetime task; instead, it is a lifelong project with a changing, dynamic self or psychosocial identity (Paranjpe 2000). This notion of identity or the Eriksonian self is made up of the body, the psyche, and the ethos (social, cultural context), and identities are seen as being situated in these three orders in which individuals live at all times. Hence, identity formation is not just about being integrated from within (oneself) but also being integrated into a social order of one's community. As stated in the quote above, identity formation is as much about a sense of well-being and comfort with one's body, mind, and one's future, as it is about recognition from significant others.

In this book, I use several of the ideas proposed by Erikson in the process of growing up and identity formation. For instance, from Chaps. 3–5, I discuss a continuity of experiences—those of childhood, experiences within family, school, college, friends, lovers, meeting others like oneself/LG community. All these experiences of the past and present, combined with hopes for the future, are synthesized into a person's sense of themselves. Here, I describe one aspect of this self: the gay self that grows up along with other aspects of the self. This growing up is a process and not a one-time event of coming out to oneself or others. This process is about the continuity in the range of experiences, some more banal and everyday, such as hiding one's sexual/romantic interests from the world, and some extraordinary, such as the first kiss/reciprocation of same-sex attraction, that are part of the journey that a gay or lesbian individual makes in the development of a sexual identity. I also discuss the role of the body-psyche in knowing about oneself, knowing about being different and making sense of this within the socio-cultural context that is heterosexually constructed and is modelled on the gender binary. I critically discuss, particularly in Chap. 4, identity formation as being more than just integration within oneself but instead as a negotiation with one's surroundings for recognition and validation.

Another Ericksonian idea that is centrally explored in this book is that of 'psychosocial reciprocity', which suggests that an identity can be found only in interaction with significant others. I discuss the challenges that a gay/lesbian child faces in the absence of this reciprocity within their own homes, families, in school, among their friends. In Chap. 3, I discuss some developmental challenges that are unique to growing up gay: absence of role models, and positive experiences of mirroring, coupled with images and language which is hostile and abusive can be a major challenge in the development of a gay/lesbian identity. It is important to mention that Erikson underlines the significance of ideology in helping young people chalk out their path from the present to the future and providing a perspective on life, world, and one's place in it. So in addition to psychosocial reciprocity, ideology is also an important pillar that supports identity development. Paranjpe (2000) explains this as follows, 'ideologies as shared beliefs and values provide a valuable support for budding identities in a number of different ways. While individuals derive a sense of belongingness, solidarity, and collective security by identifying themselves with the group's ideology, the groups in turn harness the individual's capacities in the service of collective goals. Ideologies also offer perspectives on a collective future...' (145). In Chap. 5, I discuss the role of meeting community i.e. meeting others like oneself, and a sense of belongingness that this experience produces for young LG persons. I also discuss another meaning of meeting community, that of finding a shared political language/ideology for social change and action. This kind of collectivization around a socio-political ideology can be an important source of strength and guidance in navigating a present and future that departs from the known familial/social heterosexual scripts.

I use several concepts from Erickson's identity development theory, particularly the developmental stage 'Identity versus identity confusion', which, as described by the linear identity development model, coincides with the life cycle stage of adolescence. I want to underline two things here—that when one is growing up at odds with social mores, the 'normative/expected' developmental experiences of psychosocial reciprocity and mirroring from significant others may occur much later in the life of a gay/lesbian individual. Secondly, as mentioned above, while discussing 'queer time', most gay lives may not follow a linear, normative life schedule, and hence may not attain expected developmental goals as per the heterosexually determined time-table for growth and development.

In addition to the psychosocial identity development theory, I also use *internalization theories of identity development*, the idea of the *contextual or relational self*, as well as the concept of *collective identities* in this book.

Internalization theories are based on a central insight of symbolic interactionism: we internalize how others see/perceive us. This is also reflected in Mead's (1934) work that defines the self as constituting of 'I' and 'Me'. Here 'I' is the subject, the dynamic, novel, spontaneous part of the self, and 'Me' is the object, the perspective a person takes towards themselves when taking on the role of the other. Rosenberg (1979) builds further on this with the idea of 'self-concept'. Self-concept is defined as the totality of a person's thoughts and feelings towards themselves as an object of reflection. This self-concept is further thought to be consisting of self-referring dispositions, physical characteristics, and identity with four major sources of characterization—personal/individual identity, role-based identity, category-based identity, and group membership based identity. Two of the internalization theories that I mention here and discuss later, especially in Chap. 4, are Burke's (1991) Identity Control Theory and Stryker's (1980) Identity Theory. Burke views identity as a set of meanings applied to the self in a social role; these meaning-sets act as a standard/reference to understand who one is in a given situation (identity standard) and what are the expectations in order to maintain that identity in the eyes of the self and others (reflected appraisals). Thus, an identity, according to Burke and Reitzes (1991, 840) "is a continuously operating, self-adjusting, feedback loop; individuals continually adjust behaviour to keep their reflected appraisals congruent with their identity standard".

Research on socially constructed identities has focused on a singular dimension of identity, such as identity based on gender, ethnicity, or sexual orientation. Stryker's identity theory (1980) conceptualizes a multifaceted self, composed of multiple identities arranged hierarchically in an identity salience structure. Salience is based on two dimensions of one's commitment to the identity: interactional (extensiveness of interactions in a social network through a particular identity), and affective (extent of emotional investment in relationships premised on the identity). Deaux (1993) conceptualizes identity as both defined internally by self and externally by others. This implies that there is a personal self, consisting of personal attributes and then there are multiple social identities that exist within a social context. Deaux suggests that it is the ongoing negotiations and relationships between one's personal and social identities that contribute to the experience of multiple identities. Jones and McEwen (2000) in their research with women college students found that, at the centre of multiple identities, is a core sense of self. This core was frequently described by participants as their 'inner identity' as contrasted with an 'outside identity' or the facts of their identity which could be named by others. Both these models of multiple identities acknowledge that construction of self and identities is an ongoing process and that multiple contextual factors determine the importance attached to each dimension of identity. Jones and McEwen (2000) suggest that salience of identity dimensions is rooted in internal awareness and external scrutiny (for instance, race for black women). They also state that the experience of difference from others shaped identity, and salience was lowest when it came to privileged (which often includes sameness as others) dimensions of identity (for instance, sexual orientation for heterosexual women). Thus, both difference and privilege mediate the relative salience of different dimensions of identity. In Chap. 4, I discuss the complex processes by which individuals decide to disclose or not disclose their sexual identities, and ways in which they live and talk about their gay self. Here, I use several of the ideas described above about identity salience and multiple identities.

Another conceptualization of the self that I use is that of the 'contextualized self' with a more permeable boundary that is socially constituted. Here, the self is viewed as dialogical and is enacted in a social space. Thus, the self is viewed as having a social origin or is seen as socially embedded, as well as being primarily 'relational' in nature (Gergen 1994). Misra (2010) suggests that the Indian view of self maintains a self—other continuity, has tolerance for dissonance, and emphasizes self-control and mind training. Miller et al. (1990) state, "an Indian child is encouraged to develop an adult self, which is more responsive to family and community demands and responsibilities and more dependent on family status, prosperity and approval. Indians thus develop a more 'familial self.'" (122). Sociologists—such as Das (1979) in her paper, 'Reflections on the Social Construction of Adulthood'—suggest that the adult self is constructed through social norms, duties, and responsibilities associated with one's gender, age, ordinal position in one's natal family (eldest, youngest among siblings), and is communicated and monitored through immediate family as well as *biradari* (community). Dube (1988), while discussing construction of gender among Hindu girls in Patrilineal India, also suggests the significance of family structure and the wider kinship context in the process of self/identity development. It is these larger social processes that provide the organizing principles for hierarchies of social groups, individual position in the social group, formation of family and household, norms regarding marriage, inheritance, resource allocation, and so on. Individual identity in such a collectivist culture[7] will have to be seen as located within this context and often expressed as an interdependent self. The interdependent self is more tacit, embodied, encouraged by cultural practices and public meanings, and reflects culture bound designs of human life (Markus and Kitayama 1998). Cross cultural research within psychology, such as a study by Dhawan et al. (1995), states that Indian participants, compared to their American counterparts, made a large number of references to social identities. They described themselves more in terms of role, group, caste, class, and gender. Another study by Tripathi (2005) suggests that people in India use categories of family, country, language, and occupation in order of salience. This is to suggest that in the Indian context, individualism is often subordinated to 'familialism'. Roland (1991) states that Indians include family members within their sense of selfhood, and 'we-ness' over 'I-ness' constitutes the core of selfhood. Thus, an indigenous perspective on self that includes interdependence and relational dimensions as well as expression of self in terms of social identities of kinship, family and caste, becomes centrally relevant in the discussion of self and identity in the Indian context (Kakar 1978). Some of this discussion forms the backdrop to Chap. 4, where I explore meanings of sexual identity development and the process of coming out.

Yet another dimension of identity—collective identity—has, at its centre, the idea of self-categorization: identifying the self as a member of a particular social grouping. Other aspects include evaluation (positive or negative attitude a person has towards the social grouping), importance, attachment, interdependence, behavioural involvement, and so on (Ashmore et al. 2004). A sense of 'we-ness' or connection to other members of the group as well as to the category itself is an essential component of collective identity. An important aspect dealt with in collective identity literature is about the identity serving as the base for group mobilization and joint action. All of these aspects of collective identity will be examined in the analysis chapter on role of LGBTQ community/ies in the lives of queer people.

## Perspectives on Sexual Identity and Sexuality

Sexuality, articulated as 'identity' and seen as a dimension of personhood, and an attribute of the self, can be traced to the emergence of the 'homosexual' and a range of other 'deviant/pervert' sexualities produced by the bio-medical discourse of the

---

[7]This is not to suggest a dichotomy of individualist versus collectivist or western versus eastern culture. In a globalized world such a compartmentalization would not be possible and there are degrees of individuation and individualization in all cultures. Moreover, as suggested by Sinha and Tripathi (2003), 'individualist' and 'collectivist' can be thought of as orientations that co-exist within individuals and cultures, that find expression in diverse contexts. In this chapter, and later in the book, I do cite research from the Indian context that supports the idea of a socially/familially embedded self, as one of the analytical lenses to discuss findings of my study.

19th century in the Euro-American context (Weeks 1981). Interestingly, the term 'homosexual' was coined and officially used much before the term 'heterosexual' came into existence. This was part of the process of describing that which was abnormal and deviant, in order to describe and establish the 'normal' and the normative (Katz 1990). There are varying perspectives on what forms, shapes and causes a person's sexuality.

Biological determinism that is the idea that all of human behaviour is governed solely by an individual's genes, or some aspect of physiology, has had a strong influence in our understanding of sex, gender, and sexuality (Spanier 1995). Viewed from this perspective, sex is understood in the framework of a binary of 'man' and 'woman' with associated chromosomal and sexual characteristics. Embedded in the idea of the gender binary is the notion of heterosexuality—sexual attraction between the opposite sexes. Since sex is seen as inborn, and sexual attraction attributed to biology, both the idea of gender binary and heterosexuality are posited as 'being natural', universal, and therefore normal. In the context of homosexuality too, gay rights activists have seen an opportunity in biological determinism. The argument is that if homosexuality is seen as inborn then it could not only be seen as natural/normal—and therefore acceptable—but also any efforts to 'change/cure' homosexuality can be questioned by asserting the innate, inborn, '*as god intended it to be*' (unhampered by humans), nature of homosexuality. In fact, 'homosexuals' have often actively engaged in scientific studies and experiments in the hope of locating scientifically authentic biological proof of homosexuality that would increase their social acceptability (Biswas 2007). Biswas, in her essay, 'The Lesbian Standpoint' (2007, 265) states, "'Homosexuals' have lent their bodies, minds and beings to the scientific gaze in the hope of securing a self-knowledge that would give them the security of an identity, a difference, and a justification for assimilation into the mainstream". Thus, on the one hand, while gay rights activists would like to use the biological causation argument to argue that homosexuality is inborn, natural, and unwarranting of change, on the other hand, the very same biological cause can be argued to be a biological developmental error, in need of correction. Achuthan et al. (2007) therefore suggests that there exists a vexed relationship between LGBT activists and science/medicine, with the LGBT activist seeing science as an ally at times to legitimize homosexuality, while medical knowledge rooted in biological determinism continues to produce the homosexual as the 'pathological subject'.

Social constructionism, a perspective that views reality and knowledge as constructed by individuals and groups and not as universal givens, is another influential strand in understanding sexuality. Social constructionists state that there is nothing natural about heterosexuality or homosexuality and that several social processes interact in complex ways to construct normative notions of sexuality. Rubin (1984), in her essay, '*Thinking Sex: Notes for a Radical Theory of the Politics of Sexuality*' discusses the political nature of sexuality and builds a compelling argument for social construction of normative sexuality. One of the propositions that Rubin (1984) discusses is that of Sexual Essentialism. Sexual essentialism refers to the idea that sex is a natural, biological force that exists prior to social life and that shapes institutions. Sex is thus viewed as unchanging, asocial, and transhistorical. This idea of sexual essentialism has been reproduced in disciplines of psychiatry, medicine, and psychology, which have been some of the dominating disciplines in sex research. These disciplines view sex as a property of individuals that resides within individual hormones and psyches without historical and social determinants. This proposition of a biological/psychic origin of sexuality, that is uninfluenced by the social milieu and remains static across centuries, implies that sexuality is universal and our ideas of 'acceptable', 'normal' sexuality are frozen in time. However, if we look at the history of sexuality, we witness that, across different historical contexts and at the same time period in different communities, ideas of normative sex differ widely. Walkowitz argues that the "'interplay of social forces such as ideology, fear, political agitation, legal reform, and medical practice can change the structure of sexual behaviour and alter its consequences" (In Rubin 1984, 149).

Rubin (1984) uses the term 'charmed circle' to refer to the socially constructed notion of the most accepted, pure, blessed and healthy form of sexuality between adults i.e. monogamous, heterosexual sex, within wedlock, for procreation based on the Victorian notion of 'pure, forever, romantic love'. Social institutions such as religion, science, family, law and state, education, and media play a crucial role in upholding the socially constructed ideals of the pure, moral, right kind of sexuality. The charmed circle then becomes the reference point for producing a range of sexualities, choices, and behaviours that fall outside of the charmed circle and that can be judged as inappropriate, bad, sinful, unhealthy, abnormal, unnatural, and damned. Thus, according to the social constructionists, homosexuality is socially created—not biologically—in opposition to the 'natural' and 'virtuous' 'within-marriage, heterosexuality'.

Marriage and family thus become important institutions for regulation and control of sexuality. Marriage is viewed within psychology as a '*relationship*' and, within developmental psychology as a '*milestone*' that young adults must reach at an age-appropriate time. On the other hand, marriage/family is seen, within sociology as an institution, with legal, quasi-legal underpinnings and religious, moral, and social prescriptions. This institution is seen as playing a significant role in maintaining the hegemony of heterosexuality, as well as the marginality of homosexuality and all other forms of sexual and gender expressions that fall outside the gender binary of man and woman. Marriage as relationship would imply that the rules and norms that govern it come from *within* the couple/family system (an intrapsychic and interpersonal dimension), whereas marriage as institution implies that the rules and norms of 'normality', 'appropriateness' come from outside (social and institutional dimension) (Morgan 1985). Morgan (1985) goes further from marriage as institution to describe the 'medicalization of marriage'. He states that, in modern societies, there is an increased professionalization around marriage. There has been development of specialized theories and knowledge base about marriage and relationships, wherein 'marital problems' are treated as a class of problems, which can be delineated from other kinds of problems, wherein cure and solutions are prescribed by trained professionals. There exists a clear shift from marriage guidance, which was often led by priests, ministers, and was focused on repairing the marriage, to marriage counselling carried out by the 'experts', doctors, and therapists and with a non-directive focus. The definition of marriage is restricted to adult, heterosexual, legal relationships, and the primary model of family is that of a nuclear one. Both marriage and family are assumed to be universal. Sexuality is seen as an important component within the marital relationship and is restricted to heterosexual, peno-vaginal sex leading to orgasms. Absence or problems with the same is seen as cause of marital and family dysfunction which is often then treated at the clinic/marriage counselling centre. Within this conception and practice of the clinic, the homosexual, bisexual, asexual, poly sexual, are labelled as perverts and prescribed different forms of treatments.

In the Indian context, marriage is seen as compulsory and as an essential gateway to adulthood and respect within the family as well as the extended clan and community. As mentioned earlier, in the Indian context, the self of an individual is constituted, mediated, and lived through a matrix of social duties, responsibilities that are determined by the institution of family and kinship and that operate within the larger matrix of religion, caste, *gotra*, region, and so on. Sexuality is thus prescribed to have a life within this context; through marriage, procreation, and reproduction of the familial/kinship norms.

It is also necessary to underline the role played by the State in legitimizing the institution of marriage and defining what constitutes family, marriage, parenthood. Legislation is an important tool used to decide the validity of marriage, inheritance of property, and control of sexuality. It has been argued by Morgan (1985) that, depending on the nature of the State, control on sexuality would differ; a conservative, traditional State, for instance, would lay heavy emphasis on keeping the family intact and have high moral taboos around sexuality and therefore stricter legislations that make access to contraception, abortions, and divorce difficult. A conservative, capitalist State would encourage families to consume more, spend less on welfare, and view the family as a more desirable substitute for the state in matters of care for the elderly, children, the disabled, the sick and so on.

It may be argued that, in modern capitalist societies with free markets and state support of liberal policies, sexual expression is actively encouraged and supported by large commercial interests, media and advertising. In fact, stimulation of consumption and commercial leisure activity is an important feature of modern capitalism and the eroticization of the everyday, and sexual symbolism, are a significant part of this consumption drive. One may then ask the question: Do modern capitalist societies promote sexual liberation? Marcuse (1964) refers to this as pseudo-liberation, where a state of hypersexuality is created through artificiality and commercial manipulation of desire, with no challenge to any of the existing structures of repression. Marcuse has used the term 'repressive desublimation' here to argue that repression has appeared in another guise, not reduced, or abolished. The idea of 'Pink Money', referring to the purchasing power of the gay community, would be a good example of this pseudo-acceptance and integration by the capitalist market economy, viewing LGBT people as a significant consumer group with disposable income, and designing products that target LGBT individuals and couples. It can be argued that the increased tolerance and even visibility to LGBT lives in mainstream media and popular culture that one sees in the developing countries, is part of this market-driven plan to find newer target audiences and this does not mean any 'real' shifts away from the heterosexism and patriarchy that underlie institutions of marriage, family, kinship and the state.

## 1.4 Contemporary LGBTQ Assertions in India

For over a decade now, especially after the judgment of the Delhi High Court in 2009 decriminalizing homosexuality, there has been a lot of visibility within mainstream media and popular culture (at least in urban India) to issues faced by the LGBTQ community. There have been many more books written about queer lives, many more interviews of queer activists published in newspapers and magazines, many more films made about our lived realities, many more online and street-based campaigns and pride marches that talk about LGBTQ rights. In fact, the Supreme Court judgment on Section 377 in December 2013, that re-criminalized homosexuality, received strong resistance not just from the queer community in India and around the world, but also from straight allies and liberal-minded activists and intellectuals across the globe. Similarly, the NALSA judgment of the Supreme Court on rights of transgender persons in 2014, and several state level policy documents and bills on transgender rights, which followed the same, are milestones in the vibrant movement for LGBTQ rights in India.

### *'Gay', 'Lesbian', 'Queer'—Contextualizing Sexual Identity Labels*

LGBTQ movement/s in India use 'sexual identity' (as well as gender identity), and denial and violation of human rights due to the same, as the primary anchor of collectivization and action. In other words, sexuality is seen as a recognizable/ identifiable attribute of the self, an identity that, due to its 'difference' from dominant heterosexuality, can become the source of discrimination and violence. In this book, when I use gay, lesbian or queer, I use these as identity labels to mark experiences of individuals with same-sex sexual desires. However, as pointed out earlier, sexuality may not always form a part of the social identity of a person; social identities in India are often created and lived through a range of other prescriptions related to one's position in the family and community, one's age, birth order in the family, caste, class, religion, gender location, and so on. It is therefore necessary to note that for several persons, sexual attraction, desire, preference, fantasy, behaviour, orientation and sexual identity may not always have a congruent, coherent, and linear progression. One may thus have the social identity of the eldest son of the family, good provider for one's wife and children, care giver to elderly parents, advisor to younger siblings and their spouses and children, and also be a man who has sex with men (MSM), and this aspect of his sexuality may not be seen by him/others as part of his other social identities. The point I wish to emphasize here is that there is a lot of diversity in sexual expressions, identities, and varied dimensions, such as that of language, social class, caste, region that determine sexual subjectivities. So, while I discuss growing-up experiences of those who self-identify as gay or lesbian, there have also been those who do not identify with these labels, and their experiences are not explored in this book.

Another dimension to the discussion about naming/articulating sexual identities is that of invisibility and absence of affirmative language to refer to non-normative sexualities. The language used to talk about normative sexuality often tends to be structured around relationships, roles, and milestones that exist within the heteronormative script. For instance, terms such as husband, wife, spouse, imply a conjugal/sexual relationship; roles of parenting and milestones such as reproductive events are other markers of sexuality for which there exist a range of terms, expressions that are not only socially acceptable and easily available but are affirmative and celebratory. Language that does exist to talk about non-normative sexualities and gender expressions may often be derogatory, implying a deficit/lack of masculinity/femininity. As suggested by Shah (2015), individuals and groups who do not find their identities and expression represented in language, create new words/language, reclaim/re-appropriate terms of abuse as also borrow from other languages to speak about themselves. The acronym LGBT (lesbian, gay, bisexual, transgender) would be an example of this borrowing, which has now become part of organizing, activism, and campaigns, as well as part of the media and public vocabulary in India to talk about non-normative genders and sexualities. The Q that often gets added to the acronym LGBT represents 'Queer', and has been part of the re-appropriation of the language of oppression and abuse that has been historically used in the Euro-American context to refer to homosexuals in a derogatory way. A parallel in the Indian context is possibly the term *hijra*, which has been often used as a derogatory term to refer to a person assigned male gender at birth and who is seen as a *lesser man/impotent*; however the name/label *hijra* is claimed with pride by many who see themselves as belonging to a third gender, outside of the male-female binary.

It is necessary to note that identity labels and names are constituted by and performed within a cultural as well as legal, political and policy environment. Thus, the borrowed language of LGBTQ that I refer to above is also framed within the context of the legal campaign against Section 377, HIV/AIDS epidemic and the policies, services and international funding associated with the same. The Supreme Court judgment on transgender rights (NALSA 2014) as well as the Expert Committee Report on Transgender Concerns (MSJE 2014) is an example of the way in which international human rights language pertaining to gender expression and identity has been used along with local, socio-cultural/religious expressions such as *hijra*s, *shiv-shakti*s, *jogappa*s, which may not be 'individual gender identity labels'.

In this book, I use the terms gay, lesbian, and, at times, queer. I use 'gay' to refer to persons assigned male gender at birth (and many of them see themselves as men) who desire and are attracted to men. I also use the term 'gay' sometimes as an umbrella term to refer to persons with same-sex desires/identity/orientation. This is because, in the course of my field work and in conversations with queer friends, I have seen many persons assigned female at birth (many of whom see themselves as women) who desire women, use the term 'gay' for themselves instead of lesbian. This is partly due to the negative connotations associated with the word 'lesbian' that many people grow up with and hence prefer 'gay' as a generic term for same-sex sexuality. However, I do retain and use the term 'lesbian' to refer to women who love/desire women; many of the participants in my study used this as an identity label for themselves as well. Finally, I use the term 'queer' in this book to talk about people who use it as a political stance; an ideology more than as an identity term. Several of the participants used 'queer' to refer to a way of being and doing activism; a political perspective that involved challenging structures that perpetuate inequalities and exclusion. These include but are not restricted to hetero-patriarchy and homo-negativity. As Narrain and Bhan (2005) state, queer resistance and struggle is not about an 'assimilationist' agenda of tolerance and acceptance. It is, instead, an objection to all hierarchies and power structures that oppress.

While I discuss same-sex sexuality and sexual identities in this book, I wish to underline that gender and sexuality are intimately interconnected. In fact, it is the binary way of thinking about gender in terms of man and woman that is at the foundation of the binary idea of sexuality in terms of homosexual and heterosexual. Several of the life narratives that I discuss in this book include elements of gender non-conformity alongside same-sex sexual identity development. I also wish to point out that just as identity categories and labels exist within a socio-cultural space, there is also a dimension of time, a historical temporality, to these. As Shah (2015) point out, the category label 'lesbian' has been used to refer to all persons assigned gender female at birth (PAGFB), who are attracted to women, irrespective of whether these PAGFB see themselves as women or not. There has also been the description of the butch (masculine) lesbian person and, more recently, gender non-binary, gender queer, or trans person. I mention this range of descriptions and, at times, overlapping category/labels, to suggest that identity categories are pro-duced (rather than discovered)[8] within the context of the existing discourse. So, when I first started interviewing research participants in the cities of Mumbai and Pune in 2008, many referred to themselves as lesbian and at times gay. The lan-guage of queer and trans/gender queer entered our vocabularies a bit later and several of my participants, who previously identified with the identity label lesbian, preferred later on to talk about themselves as queer, gender queer, non-binary, using language and labels that were a better fit to their experience of their gender and sexuality.

---

[8]In conversation with Asha Achuthan, May 2017 about sexual identities in post-colonial India.

## *LGBTQ Organizing in India—A Brief Historical Account*

Writing about the history of LGBTQ movement/s in India reveals certain events and forces that have played a significant role in the collectivization as well as visibility of the queer community in India. Emergence of the HIV/AIDS epidemic, and an increasing recognition of diverse sexual practices within and outside heterosexual marriage that included sex between men, is an important milestone that over two decades led to more organizing and visibilizing of LGBT issues in India. In the initial years of the epidemic, the National AIDS Control Organization (NACO) was established under the Ministry of Health and Family Welfare in 1986. Influenced by international aid agencies and global dialogue on HIV/AIDS, NACO eventually, in its National Aids Control Program II (1999–2006) began to consider women in sex work, MSM as well as gay men, as 'bridge populations' (Ramasubban 2008). Thus, though seen as 'sexual deviants' and 'carriers of fatal infection' (to the heterosexual population), there was at least articulation in a state document about the existence of gay men and MSM in India. HIV/AIDS activists as well as gay activists played a crucial role over the years in shifting this position of the NACO. NACO now runs separate target intervention programmes for MSM, and transgender (TG) persons including *kothi*s and *hijra*s. Services under this program include not merely health services but also empowerment-based interventions. The National program encourages MSM and TGs to form their own local community-based organizations to carry out HIV/AIDS related work. This has led to the growth of several organizations led by TG or MSM persons, advocating HIV prevention as well as a broader agenda of sexual health and human rights. In fact, from the pathologizing of MSM, gay men, and TG as 'bridge populations', the current National HIV/AIDS policy emphasizes collectivization, affirmative action and creating an enabling socio-legal and political environment for MSM, TG groups (NACO 2007).

International and national attention to the HIV epidemic from civil society organizations as well as the state machinery created a platform that lead to widespread collectivization among *hijra*s, *kothi*s and men who have sex with men (MSM) across the country. The policy, program, and research initiatives, as well as the funds that came into the country for fighting the epidemic, have played a vital role in highlighting issues of sexual and gender minorities, sensitizing the health infrastructure and empowerment of the hijra/*kothi*/transgender and MSM community. In fact, the first recorded protest talking about LGBT rights in India was organized by AIDS Bhedbhav Virodhi Andolan (ABVA), and took place in 1992 against police harassment of gay men (Narrain and Bhan 2005). Later in 1994, Kiran Bedi, the then Inspector General of Prisons (Tihar, Delhi) refused access to condoms to the male inmates of Tihar jail, citing Section 377 and stating that allowing access to condoms would be like promoting homosexuality; and, instead of condoms, the inmates needed counselling to avoid such unnatural sexual acts. It was then that the ABVA moved court through a civil writ petition to strike down Section 377 and ensure access to safe sex to all prisoners. I will discuss the campaign against Section 377 as a milestone in LGBTQ organizing in India later in this section.

Apart from the public health language of the HIV discourse, another quarter from where issues of lesbian women were being articulated was from the autonomous women's movements in India. While the women's rights movements in India predominantly organized around the issue of violence in women's lives and in doing so talked about women in heterosexual marriages, conversations about same-sex relationships, women's desires did take place in smaller groups. In fact as early as 1987, when newspapers reported that two women constables from Bhopal had married each other and as a result had lost their jobs, several women's groups had protested and written letters asking for the women to be reinstated. In 1990, during the National Conference of Women's Movement in Calicut, for the first time women's sexuality was discussed and there was a separate session to talk about 'single women'. In 1994, at the Tirupati conference of the autonomous Women's Movement, a lesbian group proposed that there be a separate session and in 1997, at the Ranchi conference, such a session was organized by Stree Sangam and Saheli (groups working with lesbian women in Bombay and Delhi) (Biswas 2011). Thus, women's groups, particularly queer feminist groups, had begun talking about violence against lesbian, bisexual women within their natal and marital homes, lesbian suicides, women running away from home with their women partners, and so on. One of the most visible articulations of this was seen during the protest demonstrations in the wake of the violence and controversy surrounding the release of the film *Fire* (a Hindi language film depicting a same sex relationship between two middle class Hindu women) (CALERI 1999). However, this solidarity within women's movements has not been without its challenges and hesitation. As Shah (2005) notes, while violence against lesbian and bisexual women was condemned, homonegative attitudes and comments, refusal to allow a group working on lesbian women's rights to carry their banner at a Women's March, are examples of the struggles and constant negotiations.

It is interesting to note that, while the history of the HIV-related organizing of gay men, MSM, *hijras, kothis* and trans women dates back to the late 1980s and early 1990s, and a comparable time line exists for lesbian organizing in India (mostly autonomous, a mix of funded and unfunded/voluntary through the decade of 1990s and early 2000s), the two have been parallel histories with very few meeting points, possibly due to the differences in perspective and politics. However, one of the major common agenda on which almost all groups across the country have come together in India is that of decriminalization of homosexuality by reading down of the Section 377 of the IPC. The impetus for this campaign on decriminalization came from arrests of workers working on HIV/AIDS education and prevention with Bharosa Trust, Lucknow under Section 377 on the charge that they were promoting homosexuality. In parallel, reports of police harassment of *hijras*, MSM, and gay men, as well as violence against lesbian women documented by the People's Union for Civil Liberties (PUCL-K 2001) were published. Around this time in 2001, Naz Foundation, an NGO working on HIV/AIDS, filed a petition challenging Section 377. A group of individuals, NGOs, and groups working on women's rights, sexuality rights, and child rights, later came together under the umbrella called Voices Against Section 377 and joined in as petitioners in the Naz petition. The campaign against Section 377, that has now spanned over a decade and a half and has seen the decriminalization of homosexuality in 2009 and the re-criminalization in 2013, has been referred to as a significant platform that brought together groups, collectives, NGOs and individuals representing rights of LGBT, *hijras, kothis*, from across the country. Some other developments in the context of the campaign against 377 is that it was for the 377 case that for the first time parents of LGBT individuals (mostly middle-class, well-respected, heterosexual citizens and in some instances, senior citizens) came together to file a petition in support of their children's rights. Similarly, mental health professionals across the country filed responses in the court stating that homosexuality is a normal variant in the spectrum of human sexuality, and condemning the use of medical treatment for cure of homosexuality.

The present vibrant and visible state of the queer movement/s in India needs to be viewed within the above-mentioned historical context as well as the more recent Supreme Court Judgment on transgender rights, followed by the Central and several state governments' efforts to formulate legislation and policy on transgender rights.

Finally, after having laid out detailed perspectives on non-normative sexualities, identities, and their representations within mental health sciences and childhood studies, I conclude this introductory chapter with a few questions that I take up for consideration in this book. In the current context of research, academic writing and activism in India with respect to non-normative genders and sexualities, is there space to talk about the 'Gay Child'? Is there a need to do so? What are the particularities of growing up gay in heterosexually constructed contexts of family, educational institutions, neighbourhoods, communities, popular culture, policy and legal frameworks? How, and in what ways, do these specific experiences of growing up gay inform our understanding of child and youth development, family studies, health and risk? Do these experiences that do not follow a heterosexual schedule of growing up teach us something about our methodologies to study human development? Does the study of difference and marginality have to always be a study of distress and isolation? In the following chapters, I attempt to respond to some of these.

# References

Achuthan, A., Biswas, R., & Dhar, A. K. (2007). *Lesbian standpoint*. Kolkata: Sanhati. Available at: https://www.researchgate.net/profile/Anup_Dhar/publication/268745355_Lesbian_Standpoint/links/5474d2120cf29afed60fc1e0/Lesbian-Standpoint.pdf, last accessed on 1st April, 2018.

Allport, G. W. (1954). *The nature of prejudice*. Reading, MA: Addison-Wesley.

American Psychiatric Association (APA). (1952). *Diagnostic and statistical manual of mental disorders*. Washington: APA.

American Psychiatric Association (APA). (1973). *Homosexuality and sexual orientation disturbance: Proposed change in DSM-II. Position statement*. Washington: APA.

American Psychiatric Association (APA). (1987). *Diagnostic and statistical manual of mental health disorders (DSM-III-R)*. Washington: APA.

American Psychiatric Association (APA). (2000). Guidelines for psychotherapy with lesbian and gay clients. *American Psychologist, 55*(12), 1440–1451.

American Psychological Association Task Force. (2009). *Appropriate therapeutic response to sexual orientation.* Washington, DC: APA. Retrieved July 15, 2017, from https://www.apa.org/pi/lgbt/resources/therapeutic-response.pdf.

Ashmore, R. D., Deaux, K., & McLaughlin-Volpe, T. (2004). An organizing framework for collective identity: Articulation and significance of multidimensionality. *Psychological Bulletin, 130*(1), 80–114.

Beiber, I. (1962). Homosexuality: A psychoanalytic study. In R. Bayer (1981) *Homosexuality and American psychiatry: The politics of diagnosis.* New York: Basic Books.

Bisht, R. (2008). Who is a child? The adults' perspective within adult-child relationship in India. *Interpersona, 2*(2), 151.

Biswas, R. (2007). The lesbian standpoint. In B. Bose & S. Bhattacharyya (Eds.), *The phobic and the erotic: The politics of sexualities in contemporary India.* Calcutta, London: Seagull Books.

Biswas, R. (2011). Of love, marriage and kinship: Queering the family. In S. Sen, R. Biswas, & N. Dhawan (Eds.), *Intimate others: Marriage and sexualities in India.* Kolkata: Stree.

Bluebond-Langner, M., & Korbin, J. (2007). Challenges and opportunities in the anthropology of childhoods: An introduction to "children, childhoods, and childhood studies". *American Anthropologist, 109*(2), 241–246.

Bostwick, W. B., Boyd, C. J., Hughes, T. L., & McCabe, S. E. (2010). Dimensions of sexual orientation and the prevalence of mood and anxiety disorders in the United States. *American Journal of Public Health, 100*(3), 468–475.

Bourdieu, P., & Passeron, J. C. (1977). *Reproduction in education, society, and culture.* Beverly Hills, CA: Sage.

Boyden, J., & Hudson, A. (1985). *Children: Rights and responsibilities* (No. 69). Minority Rights Group.

Burgard, S. A., Cochran, S. D., & Mays, V. M. (2005). Alcohol and tobacco use patterns among heterosexually and homosexually experienced California women. *Drug and Alcohol Dependence, 77*(1), 61–70.

Burke, P. J. (1991). Identity processes and social stress. *American Sociological Review, 56,* 836–849.

Burke, P. J., & Reitzes, D. C. (1991). An identity theory approach to commitment. *Social Psychology Quarterly, 54,* 239–251.

Burman, E. (2007). *Deconstructing developmental psychology.* NY: Routledge.

CALERI (Campaign for Lesbian Rights). (1999). A citizen's report—Khamosh! Emergency Jari Hai. Lesbian Emergence, New Delhi.

Cass, V. C. (1979). Homosexual identity formation: A theoretical model. *Journal of Homosexuality, 4*(3), 219–235.

Chaudhary, N. (2004). *Listening to culture: Constructing reality from everyday talk.* New Delhi: Thousand Oaks.

Cochran, S. D., Sullivan, J. G., & Mays, V. M. (2003). Prevalence of mental disorders, psychological distress, and mental health services use among lesbian, gay, and bisexual adults in the united states. *Journal of Consulting and Clinical Psychology, 71*(1), 53.

Coleman, E. (1981–1982). Developmental stages of the coming out process. *Journal of Homo-sexuality, 7*(2/3), 31–43.

Corsaro, W. A. (2005). *Sociology of childhood* (2nd ed.). California: Sage.

D'Augelli, A. R. (1994). Identity development and sexual orientation: Toward a model of lesbian, gay, and bisexual development. In E. J. Trickett, R. J. Watts, & D. Birman (Eds.), *Human diversity: Perspectives on people in context* (pp. 312–333). San Francisco: Jossey-Bass.

Das, V. (1979). Reflections on the social construction of adulthood. In S. Kakar (Ed.), *Identity and adulthood.* USA: Oxford University Press.

Deaux, K. (1993). Reconstructing social identity. *Personality and Social Psychology Bulletin, 19,* 4–12.

Deepa, V. N. (2005). Queering Kerala: Reflections on Sahayatrika. In A. Narrain & G. Bhan (Eds.), *Because i have a voice. Queer politics in India* (pp. 175–196). Delhi: Yoda.

Dhawan, N., Roseman, I. J., Naidu, R. K., Thapa, K., & Rettek, S. I. (1995). Self-concepts across two cultures—India and the United States. *Journal of Cross-Cultural Psychology, 26*(6), 606–621.

Dube, L. (1988). On the construction of gender: Hindu girls in patrilineal India. *Economic and Political Weekly*, WS11–WS19.

Erikson, E. H. (1959). Identity and the life cycle. *Psychological Issues, 1* (1). New York: International University Press.

Evans, N., & Levine, H. (1990). Perspectives on sexual orientation. *New Directions for Student Services, 51*, 49–58.

Fernandez, B. (1999). *Humjinsi: A resource book for lesbian, gay and bisexual rights in India.* New Delhi: India Centre for Human Rights and Law.

Fernandez, B. & Gomathy, N. B. (2003). *The nature of violence faced by lesbian women in India.* Mumbai: Research Centre on Violence Against Women, Tata Institute of Social Sciences. Retrieved July 15, 2017, from https://www.tiss.edu/uploads/files/8The_Nature_of_violence_faced_by_Lesbian_women_in_India.pdf.

Freud, S. (1935). *Letter to a mother of a homosexual man.* Retrieved July 15, 2017, from http://www.lettersofnote.com/2009/10/homosexuality-is-nothing-to-be-ashamed.html.

Garnets, L., Hancock, K., Cochran, S., Goodchilds, J., & Peplau, L. (1991). Issues in psychotherapy with lesbians and gay men: A survey of psychologists. *American Psychologist, 46*, 964–972.

Garnets, L. D., Herek, G. M., & Levy, B. (1990). Violence and victimization of lesbians and gay men: Mental health consequences. *Journal of Interpersonal Violence, 5*, 366–383.

Gergen, K. J. (1994). *Realities and relationships: Soundings in social construction.* Cambridge, MA: Harvard University Press.

Ghosh, S., Bandyopadhyay, B. S., & Biswas, R. (2011). *Vio-Map: Documenting and mapping violence and rights violation taking place in the lives of sexually marginalized women to chart out effective advocacy strategies.* Kolkata: SAPPHO for Equality.

Grace, J. (1992). Affirming gay and lesbian adulthood. In N. J. Woodman (Ed.), *Lesbian and gay lifestyles: A guide for counselling and education* (pp. 33–47). New York: Irvington.

Gruskin, E. P. (2007). Treating lesbian and bisexual women: Challenges and strategies for health professionals. In S. Hunter (Ed.), *Coming out and disclosures: LGBT persons across the life span.* NY: The Haworth Press Inc.

Haas, A. P., Eliason, M., Mays, V. M., Mathy, R. M., Cochran, S. D., D'Augelli, A. R., Silverman, M. M., Fisher, P. W., Hughes, T., Rosario, M., & Russell, S. T. (2010). Suicide and suicide risk in lesbian, gay, bisexual, and transgender populations: Review and recommendations. *Journal of homosexuality, 58*(1), 10–51.

Halberstam, J. (2005). *In a queer time and place: Transgender bodies, subcultural lives.* NY: NYU Press.

Haldeman, D. C. (1994). The practice and ethics of sexual orientation conversion therapy. *Journal of Consulting and Clinical Psychology, 62*(2), 221.

Harvey, D. (1990). The condition of postmodernity: An enquiry into the conditions of cultural change.

Hatzenbuehler, M. L., Keyes, K. M., & Hasin, D. S. (2009). State-level policies and psychiatric morbidity in lesbian, gay, and bisexual populations. *American Journal of Public Health, 99*(12), 2275–2281.

Henry, G. W. (1941). Sex variants. A study of homosexual patterns. *Southern Medical Journal, 34*(8), 897.

Hooker, E. (1957). The adjustment of the male overt homosexual. *Journal of Projective Techniques, 21*(1), 18–31.

Hurlock, E. (1981). *Developmental psychology—A life span approach* (5th ed.). Delhi: Tata McGraw Hill.

James, A., Jenks, C., & Prout, A. (1998). *Theorizing childhood.* Cambridge: Polity Press.

Jenks, C. (1996). *Childhood.* Abingdon: Routledge.

Jones, S. R., & McEwen, M. K. (2000). A conceptual model of multiple dimensions of identity. *Journal of College Student Development, 41*(4), 405–414.

Kakar, S. (1978). *The inner world: A psycho-analytic study of childhood and society in India.* India: Oxford University Press.

Kalra, G. (2012). Pathologising alternate sexuality: Shifting psychiatric practices and a need for ethical norms and reforms. *Indian Journal of Medical Ethics, 9*(4).

Kalra, G., Gupta, S., & Bhugra, D. (2010). Sexual variation in India: A view from the west. *Indian Journal of Psychiatry, 52*(Suppl. 1), S264.

Katz, J. N. (1990). The invention of heterosexuality. *Socialist Review, 20*(1).

Kaufman, J. M., & Johnson, C. (2004). Stigmatized individuals and the process of identity. *The Sociological Quarterly, 45*(4), 807–833.

Kingston, M. (2009). Subversive friendships: Foucault on homosexuality and social experimentation. *Foucault Studies, 7,* 7–17.

Kinsey, A. C., (Ed.) (1953). *Sexual behavior in the human female.* Bloomington: Indiana University Press.

Kinsey, A. C., Pomeroy, W. B. & Martin, C. E. (1948). *Sexual behavior in the human male.* Philadelphia: Saunders.

Klocker, N. (2007). An example of thin agency: Child domestic workers in Tanzania. In R. Panelli, S. Punch, & E. Robson (Eds.), *Global perspectives on rural childhood and youth: Young rural lives* (pp. 81–148). London: Routledge.

Krafft-Ebing, R. (1922). *Psychopathia sexualis.* Brooklyn: Physicians and Surgeons Book Co.

Lazarus, R. S., & Folkman, S. (1984). *Stress, appraisal, and coping.* New York: Springer.

LeVay, S. (1991). A difference in hypothalamic structure between heterosexual and homosexual men. *Science, 253*(5023), 1034.

Marcuse, H. (1964). *One-dimensional man: Studies in the ideology of advanced industrial society.* Retrieved July 15, 2017, from http://www.marcuse.org/herbert/pubs/64onedim/odmcontents.html.

Markus, H. R., & Kitayama, S. (1998). The cultural psychology of personality. *Journal of Cross-Cultural Psychology, 29*(1), 63–87.

Mayall, B. (2000). The sociology of childhood in relation to children's rights. *The International Journal of Children's Rights, 8*(3), 243–259.

Mead, G. H. (1934). *Mind, self, and society from the standpoint of a social behaviorist.* Chicago: University of Chicago Press.

Mehta, M., & Deshpande, S. N. (1983). Homosexuality. A Study of treatment and outcome. *Indian Journal of Psychiatry, 25*(3), 235.

Meyer, I. H. (1995). Minority stress and mental health in gay men. *Journal of Health and Social Behavior,* 38–56.

Meyer, I. H. (2007). Prejudice and discrimination as social stressors. In I. H. Meyer, & M. E. Northridge (Eds.), *The health of sexual minorities: Public health perspectives on lesbian, gay, bisexual, and transgender populations* (pp. 242–267). Berlin: Springer.

Meyer, I. H., & Dean, L. (1998). Internalized homophobia, intimacy, and sexual behavior among gay and bisexual men. In G. M. Herek (Ed.), *Stigma and sexual orientation: Understanding prejudice against lesbians, gay men, and bisexuals* (pp. 160–186). Thousand Oaks, CA: Sage.

Miller, J. G., Bersoff, D. M., & Harwood, R. L. (1990). Perceptions of social responsibilities in India and in the United States: Moral imperatives or personal decisions? *Journal of Personality and Social Psychology, 58*(1), 33.

Miller, C. T., & Major, B. (2000). Coping with stigma and prejudice. In T. F. Heatherton, R. E. Kleck, M. R. Hebl, & J. G. Hull (Eds.), *The social psychology of stigma* (pp. 243–272). New York: Guilford Press.

Milton, M., & Coyle, A. (1998). Psychotherapy with lesbian and gay clients. *The Psychologist, 11,* 73–76.

Ministry of Social Justice and Empowerment. (2014). *Report of the expert committee report on issues relating to transgender persons.* Retrieved July 15, 2017, from http://socialjustice.nic.in/writereaddata/UploadFile/Binder2.pdf.

Misra, G. (2010). The cultural construction of self and emotion. *Personality, Human Development, and Culture: International Perspectives on Psychological Science, 2,* 95.

Morgan, D. H. J. (1985). *The family, politics and social theory.* London: Routledge & Kegan Paul.

NACO. (2007). Targeted interventions under NACP III, operational guidelines, Vol. I, high risk groups. Retrieved July 15, 2017, from http://iapsm.org/pdf/Guidelines/nacp-hiv-aids-stds/Guidelines%20for%20Targeted%20Interventions%20Under%20NACP%20III%202007.pdf.

NACO. (2015). *Annual report, 2015–16*. Retrieved July 15, 2017, from http://naco.gov.in/sites/default/files/Annual%20Report%202015-16_NACO.pdf.

NALSA v/s Union of India. (2014). Supreme Court judgement on transgender rights. Retrieved July 15, 2017, from http://judis.nic.in/supremecourt/imgs1.aspx?filename=41411.

Narrain, A., & Bhan, G. (2005). *Because I have a voice—Queer politics in India*. New Delhi: Yoda Press.

Narrain, A., & Chandra, V. (2015). *Nothing to fix: Medicalization of sexual orientation and gender identity*. New Delhi: Sage.

Paranjpe, A. C. (2000). *Self and identity in modern psychology and Indian thought*. New York: Kluwer Academic Publishers.

Parekh, S. (2003). Homosexuality in India: The light at the end of the tunnel. *Journal of Gay & Lesbian Psychotherapy, 7*(1–2), 145–163.

Parsons, T., & Bales, R. F. (1956). *Family: Socialization and interaction process*. London: Routledge & Kegan Paul.

Pradhan, P. V., Ayyar, K. S., & Bagadia, V. N. (1982). Homosexuality: Treatment by behaviour modification. *Indian Journal of Psychiatry, 24*, 80–83.

PUCL-K (People's Union for Civil Liberties—Karnataka). (2001). *Human rights violations against sexuality minorities in India: A PUCL-K fact finding report about Bangalore*. Bengaluru: People's Union for Civil Liberties-Karnataka.

Qvortrup, J. (1994). Childhood matters: An introduction. In J. Qvortrup, M. Bardy, G. Sgritta, & H. Wintersberger (Eds.), *Childhood matters. Social theory, practice and politics* (pp. 1–24). European Centre, Vienna. Aldershot: Avebury.

Qvortrup, J. (2005). The structure of childhood and children's interpretive reproductions. In W. A. Corsaro (Eds.), *Sociology of childhood* (2nd ed., p. 30). California: Sage.

Ramasubban, R. (2008). Political intersections between HIV/AIDS, sexuality and human rights: A history of resistance to the anti-sodomy law in India. *Global Public Health, 3*(S2), 22–38.

Ranade, K. (2015). Medical response to male same-sex sexuality in western India: An exploration of "conversion treatments" for homosexuality. In A. Narrain & V. Chandran (Eds.), *Nothing to fix: Medicalization of sexual orientation and gender identities* (pp. 90–123). Delhi: Sage Yoda Press.

Ranade, K., & Chakravarty, S. (2013a). Conceptualising gay affirmative counselling practice in India—Building on local experiences of counselling with sexual minority clients. *Indian Journal of Social Work, 74*(2), 235–252.

Ranade, K., & Chakravarty, S. (2013b). *Gay affirmative counselling practice resource and training manual*. A Saksham Publication, TISS. Retrieved July 15, 2017, from http://www.academia.edu/22507988/Gay-Affirmative_Counselling_Practice_Resource_and_Training_Manual.

Ranade, K., & Chakravarty, S. (2016). "Coming out" of the comfort zone: Challenging heteronormativity through affirmative counselling practice with lesbian and gay clients. In P. Bhola & A. Raguram (Eds.), *Ethical issues in counselling and psychotherapy practice: Walking the line* (pp. 141–154). Singapore: Springer.

Rao, T. S., & Jacob, K. S. (2012). Homosexuality and India. *Indian Journal of Psychiatry, 54*, 1–3.

Roland, A. (1991). *In search of self in India and Japan: Toward a cross-cultural psychology*. Princeton: Princeton University Press.

Rosenberg, M. (1979). *Conceiving the self*. New York: Basic Books.

Rubin, G. S. (1984). Thinking sex: Notes for a radical theory of the politics of sexuality. In C. S. Vance (Ed.), *Pleasure and danger: Exploring female sexuality*. UK: Routledge & Kegan Paul Books.

Safren, S. A., & Heimberg R. G. (1999). Depression, hopelessness, suicidality and related factors in sexual minority and heterosexual adolescents. *Journal of Consulting and Clinical Psychology, 62*(2), 261–269.

Sakthivel, L. M., Rangasamy, K., & Jayaraman, T. N. (1978). Treatment of homosexuality by anticipatory avoidance conditioning technique. *Indian Journal of Psychiatry, 21*, 146–148.

Saraswathi, T. S. (1999). Adult-child continuity in India: is adolescence a myth or an emerging reality? In T. S. Saraswathi (Ed.), *Culture, socialization and human development: Theory, research and applications in India.* New Delhi: Sage.

Savin-Williams, R. C. (2001). *Mom, dad, i'm gay: How families negotiate coming out.* Washington, DC: American Psychological Association.

Serovich, J. M., Craft, S. M., Toviessi, P., Gangamma, R., McDowell, T., & Grafsky, E. L. (2008). A systematic review of the research base on sexual reorientation therapies. *Journal of Marital and Family Therapy, 34*(2), 227–238.

Shah, C. (2005). The roads that E/merged: Feminist activism and queer understanding. In A. Narrain, & G. Bhan (Eds.), *Because I have a voice. Queer politics in India* (pp. 143–154). Delhi: Yoda.

Shah, C., R. Merchant, S. Mahajan, & S. Nevatia. (2015). *No outlaws in the gender galaxy.* Zubaan.

Shaw, E., Butler, C. A., Langdridge, D., Gibson, S., Barker, M., Lenihan, P., et al. (2012). Guidelines and literature review for psychologists working therapeutically with sexual and gender minority clients. British Psychological Society.

Silverstein, C. (1991). Psychological and medical treatments of homosexuality. In J. C. Gonsiorek & J. D, Weinrich (Eds.), *Homosexuality: Research implications for public policy* (pp. 101–114). Newbury Park, CA: Sage.

Silverstein, C. (1996). History of treatment. In R. P. Cabaj & T. S. Stein (Eds.), *Textbook of homosexuality and mental health* (pp. 3–16). Washington, DC: American Psychiatric Press.

Sinha, D., & Tripathi, R. C. (2003). Individualism in a collectivist culture: A case of coexistence of opposites. In T. S. Saraswathi (Ed.), *Crosscultural perspectives in human development.* New Delhi: Sage.

Sivasubramanian, M., Mimiaga, M. J., Mayer, K. H., Anand, V. R., Johnson, C. V., Prabhugate, P., & Safren, S. A. (2011). Suicidality, clinical depression, and anxiety disorders are highly prevalent in men who have sex with men in Mumbai, India: Findings from a community-recruited sample. *Psychology, health & medicine, 16*(4), 450–462.

Smart, L., & Wegner, D. M. (2000). The hidden costs of stigma. In T. F. Heatherton, R. E. Kleck, M. R. Hebl, & J. G. Hull (Eds.), *The social psychology of stigma* (pp. 220–242). New York: Guilford Press.

Spanier, B. (1995). Biological determinism and homosexuality. *NWSA, 7*(1), 54–71.

Stryker, S. (1980). *Symbolic interactionism: A social structural version.* Menlo Park, CA: Benjamin Cummings.

Tisdall, E. K. M., & Punch, S. (2012). Not so "new"? Looking critically at childhood studies. *Children's Geographies, 10*(3), 249–264.

Tripathi, R. C. (2005). Hindu social identities and imagined past: The faceoff between ram temple and martyred Mosque at Ayodhya. *Psychological Studies—University Of Calicut, 50*(2/3), 102.

Troiden, R. R. (1984). Self, self concept, identity and homosexual identity: Constructs in need of definition and differentiation. *Journal of Homosexuality, 10,* 97–109.

UNDP. (2010). *Hijras/transgender women in India: HIV, human rights and social exclusion, issue brief.* Retrieved July 15, 2017, from http://www.undp.org/content/dam/india/docs/hijras_transgender_in_india_hiv_human_rights_and_social_exclusion.pdf.

Verghese, A. (2014). A fresh look at homosexuality. *Indian Journal of Psychiatry, 56,* 209–210.

Weeks, J. (1981). Inverts, perverts, and Mary-Annes: Make prostitution and the regulation of homosexuality in England in the nineteenth and early twentieth centuries. *Journal of Homosexuality, 6*(1–2), 113–134.

World Health Organization (WHO). (1992). *ICD-10 classification of mental and behavioural disorders.* Geneva: WHO.

Yogyakarta Principles. (2007). Yogyakarta principles on the application of international human rights law in relation to sexual orientation and gender identity. Retrieved July 15, 2017, from http://www.yogyakartaprinciples.org/principle-18/.

# Chapter 2
# Researching Same-Sex Sexuality

In this chapter, as I explicate the methodology used in the current study, I begin by discussing trends in research studies conducted on homosexual/LGBT issues, especially within the Indian context, and describe the methodological frameworks used in these studies. Every kind of research inquiry is situated/contextual—these are contexts of theory, practice, beliefs, values, professional training, disciplinary parameters, and personal experience. I take an example of two kinds of studies, under the broad stream of medicalization of homosexuality, to discuss this issue further. I then discuss in detail the life course theory as informing the methodology of this study and also a critical psychosocial approach that has shaped the conceptualization and analysis of this work. Following this I discuss my own location in carrying out this study and give a brief description of the research questions that the study sought to answer. I also discuss the context of the research participants and the site/cities where interviews were conducted and process of the same. I conclude this chapter by discussing issues related to research ethics.

## 2.1 Studies on Lesbian, Gay Lives, and Identity Development: How Have These Been Done?

Sexual orientation as an identity category emerged from the medical model of homosexuality in the late 1800s. Since then several descriptions of the 'pervert', 'inert' homosexual, and the biological and psychological differences between homosexual and heterosexual males appear in medical literature, along with several experiments on treating of the homosexual (See Bieber 1962; Haldeman 1994; Silverstein 1991, 1996). The Kinsey study and subsequent reports in 1948 and 1953 were a major departure from the studies that viewed homosexuality as a perversion. Kinsey merely studied sexual behaviours of men and women using a survey method with 10,000 men and women and concluded that about 37% of post-pubertal men

© Springer Nature Singapore Pte Ltd. 2018
K. Ranade, *Growing Up Gay in Urban India*,
https://doi.org/10.1007/978-981-10-8366-2_2

and 20% of post-pubertal women had same-sex sexual experiences, and that 13% of men and 7% of women had had more same-sex sexual experiences than cross-sex ones. Later, with declassification of homosexuality from the list of mental illnesses in the DSM, studies focused on lesbian, gay models of identity development (see Cass 1979; Troiden 1979), lesbian, gay health and mental health (see Remafedi 1987; D'Augelli and Hershberger 1993; Garnets et al. 1990) have been conducted, mostly within the disciplines of psychology, psychiatry, and public health, and have mostly come from the American context and are more often based on the experiences of white, American gay men.

In the Indian context, academic research on LGBT lives (covering gay, bisexual men and trans women) has been initiated in the context of HIV/AIDS and is strongly influenced by positivist, quantitative research paradigms shaped within the public health epidemiological research tradition. Most of this is behavioural research and is motivated by public health concepts of disease prevention and developing evidence-based interventions. Monitoring and evaluation of research that is aimed at developing effective programs and making policy recommendations for the health and well-being of MSM, gay, bisexual men and trans women is common (see Thomas et al. 2009; Humsafar Trust 2002; Dandona et al. 2005; Joint United Nations Program 2010). There exists some research that focuses on mental health, specifically depression and suicide among MSM, gay men, and the context of stigma, HIV, negative life events, and violence (see Chakrapani et al. 2014; Sivasubramanian et al. 2011; Tomori et al. 2016). These studies, too, have employed quantitative methodologies to answer questions of risk and vulnerability to mental health problems.

There has also been research focused on the socio-historical context of same-sex desire in India (see Vanita and Kidwai 2000). There are ethnographic studies focusing on sub-cultures, language, rituals of local identities such as the *hijras*, *arvanis*, *kothis* (see Nanda 1994; Reddy 2006; Mahalingam 2003). Very little research that discusses lives of lesbian, bisexual women exists, and most of this research has been exploratory and has often employed qualitative research methods to study lived experiences of violence, stigma, and discrimination associated with being lesbian/bisexual, queer (see Fernandez and Gomathy 2003; Ghosh et al. 2011; CREA 2012; Biswas et al. 2016). Similarly research, with persons whose gender identity and expressions do not fall within the binary of men and women, as well as research with trans masculine persons, is only beginning to emerge (Shah et al. 2015; Biswas et al. 2016). In addition, there is a lot of documentation, by NGOs and human rights groups, that includes narratives of LGBTQ lived realities. There are also biographical accounts and anthologies of gay men, lesbian women, as well as trans persons. Thus, there are a range of academic, NGO reports, research studies, and fiction and non-fiction writing, depicting lives of LGBTQ persons in India.

In the context of the methodology of research in the area of sexual orientation, Hammack (2005) suggests that there has been a philosophical schism in sexual orientation research, with divergent—rather, discordant—conceptualizations of sexual orientation. These include two main strands that dominate research in this area: essentialism and constructionism. For an essentialist, sexuality is an intrinsic, internal, characteristic of an individual that transcends history, culture, and society. So, sexual orientation is seen as a universal, ahistorical, context-free, trait of an individual. On the other hand, for the constructivist, sexual orientations are 'products of particular historical and cultural understandings rather than being universal and immutable categories of human experience' (Bohan 1996, xvi; cited in Hammack 2005, 270). Thus sexual orientation is seen as a system developed by human beings to make sense of sexual desire and this system is responsive to and constituted by socio-political, cultural, and historical contexts. This intellectual division of perspectives seems irreconcilable and, as Hammack (2005) suggests, 'the validity of each philosophical approach does not rest on empirical discovery, as data can substantiate both positions' (274). In other words, there exists data that supports both a biological-essentialist position of origin of sexual orientation as well as a social constructivist one. Thus, it is possible to collect data to support either or both of the positions. This situation points to several serious methodological problems of ontology as well as epistemology. Some of these are: comparability of research findings, fragmentation of knowledge, as well as one of the issues that I wish to raise and discuss here further—the political nature of research itself. In order to discuss, the situated/contextual and political nature of research and the endeavour of knowledge building, especially with a subject such as homosexuality, I would like to cite examples of two kinds of research studies that would fall under the broad stream of medicalization of homosexuality.

Historically, medical science, particularly psychiatry and allied mental health sciences, such as psychology, have viewed homosexuality as an abnormality and a perversion. This view has led to several assumptions about homosexuality that have guided medical research on the subject. One of these assumptions is that there are properties intrinsic to homosexuals that make homosexuality a pathological condition. This assumption is often seen to be underlying research studies aimed at looking for differences between the 'normal' heterosexual and the 'pervert' homosexual. Studies comparing brain structures of homosexuals and heterosexuals, genital and hormonal make-up, personality structures and other psychological traits, are examples of studies motivated by the belief in a basic (read biological/structural and psychological) 'difference' between the normal and the ab-normal (see Krafft-Ebing 1922; Mantegazza 1932; Kolodny et al. 1971; Freud 1955). A related belief is that homosexuality is caused by faulty learning or is a result of arrested development. Studies looking for a 'cause' for homosexuality, studying childhoods of adult homosexuals and looking for traumatic early sexual experiences, inadequate parenting, cold and distant fathers and over-involved, enmeshed mothers, that led to the child becoming homosexual are examples of studies (see Bieber 1962; Freud 1955) situated within the belief that adult homosexuality is a result of unresolved traumatic childhoods. The other side of this includes studies that are located within the belief that homosexuality is as normal as heterosexuality. Some studies, such as the one conducted by Hooker (1957), assert that homosexuality is a normal form of sexuality. In her study, Hooker administered three projective tests to 30 homosexual men and 30 heterosexual men and asked experts (who were unaware of the sexual orientation of the subjects taking the test) to evaluate the results; these experts were unable spot any differences between responses of homosexuals and heterosexuals. Studies such as these were used to advocate declassification of homosexuality from the list of mental disorders in the DSM (Bayer 1981). This idea, that political and ideological positions affect conceptualization and results of research studies, is reflected also in the review of studies related to conversion/reparative treatments for homosexuality. Haldeman (1994) reviews a range of research studies aimed at conversion of homosexuality and raises several methodological questions that highlight the fact that the researchers are influenced by their belief that homosexuality is a pathology that needs cure. Some of the studies reviewed by Haldeman use different psychological and even religion-based methods to cure homosexuality and claim a moderate to high success rate of these methods in curing homosexuality. Haldeman's review of these studies points to several methodological limitations that compromise the claims of cure made by these studies. These include lack of clear and inclusive definitions of sexual orientation—unless that which will be changed is clearly defined, what has changed cannot be measured. Often sexual orientation is narrowly defined in these studies as only sexual behaviours and that too without clarity on frequency, persistence, duration; as a result individuals with predominantly homosexual behaviours or fantasies are clubbed with bisexuals, as also individuals having occasional same-sex behaviours and dominantly heterosexual fantasies, and so on. Outcomes in these studies have often included subjective impressions of the therapists (who are highly motivated and invested in seeing their treatment methods work) and self-report of participants (highly susceptible to social demands). Criteria to measure success are often unclear: does success mean abstaining from homosexual behaviours and staying celibate? Does it include expansion of sexual repertoire to include heterosexual behaviours, while same-sex behaviours continue? Does it mean fulfilling of social obligations such as marriage or having a child, does it include complete substitution of homosexual acts and fantasies with heterosexual ones? Often these studies have been conducted with clinical samples and follow-up data after termination of treatment are unavailable.

In the examples of studies that I cite here, all the studies were conceptualized within a positivist paradigm and collected data using quantitative measurements. However, even with their claims of neutrality, lack of bias and objectivity, these studies were motivated in certain core beliefs—those which considered homosexuality to be unnatural, pathological, and sinful, and those that considered homosexuality to be a normal, natural aspect of human sexuality. Thus the claim of positivist research to objective, universal (acontextual) evidence needs to be questioned in favour of a more situated and subjective knowledge that is shaped by psychic forces and interpersonal contexts as much as by socio-political, cultural context.

The idea of evidence gathering to arrive at an 'objective truth'—detached, impersonal, observable knowledge that exists independently/separately of us—has been challenged within the qualitative paradigms of research. These emphasize subjectivity, experience, narrative of the researched about their lived experiences and their meaning making processes and, most importantly, 'context' in the process of knowing. The situated nature of the researcher, the researched, and therefore, the knowledge that is viewed as co-created by them, is at the essence of qualitative research frameworks (Neuman 2002; Harding 1987). Also, reflexivity of the researcher regarding their own context, location, and motivation for the study is a feature of some kinds of qualitative studies (Alvesson and Sköldberg 2009). This study too is conceptualized and situated within my own location as a queer feminist activist and a mental health professional/activist. I will be discussing this more extensively in a later section on researcher location.

## 2.2   The Life Course Theory and Critical Psychosocial Approach in the Study of Growing Up Gay/Lesbian

Growth and development of human behaviour has been studied with two main approaches, prior to the development of the life course approach/theory. One is primarily the approach followed by developmental psychology: studying individual lives using a longitudinal/temporal framework, and by understanding different life cycle stages throughout the life span of an individual. The second is the social exchange approach that was used to study the effects of social structures on individual lives (Giele and Elder 1998). Life course theory, more commonly termed the life course perspective, however, uses a multidisciplinary paradigm for the study of people's lives, structural contexts, and social change (Elder et al. 2003). Life course theory adopts a social constructionist perspective to the study of human lives. It does not view life course as something that is 'there', a flow of personal experience through time that needs to be studied; instead it views life course as an interactional achievement, a social form that people themselves interpretively produce and use to *make sense* of their everyday lives (Holstein and Gubrium 2000).

Life course theory has four distinct principles: (i) time and place, (ii) life-span development, (iii) agency, and (iv) linked lives. The principle of time and place, which implies a socio-historical dimension to events, is significant in the context of sexuality studies as notions of 'normative', 'moral', 'appropriate/acceptable' forms of sexual behaviors and identities are produced and are responsive to context, time, and place. Cohler and Hammack (2007) state that questions of development and normality cannot be considered independently of time and space. In fact, societal transformations fundamentally alter the life course of gay and lesbian individuals. Hence, historical time and context, and the prevalent discourse of sexuality, morality, and normality, become inevitable in the study of gay, lesbian life experiences. In the present study, for instance, most participants were growing up in the 1980s and 1990s. This time period and space with its political, economic, and social features, is significant in shaping the experiences of participants as they were growing up and discovering their sexuality. For instance, the 1980s and early 1990s was a time of pre-liberalization or rather beginning of liberalization reforms in

India, when there was no internet yet, there were no mobile phones/smart phones, no social media; there were primarily two national television channels; private broadcasters and cable television only began to appear in the 1990s in the urban centres of India. This was also the time when HIV/AIDS work had just begun in the country. The sexual and reproductive health rights discourse, which has largely informed discussions on sexuality and rights within civil society organizations, governmental and non-governmental organizations, and academia, had not yet been heard of. In this sense, the idea of sexual rights had not yet been articulated in state policy. It was in this historical context that most of the study participants were growing up and making sense of their sexuality. I will further discuss this time frame of the 1980s and 1990s, specifically in the context of the cities of Bombay and Pune, where I conducted the study, in a later section.

The emphasis on historical time and context in life course perspective has also developed in response to recognition of generation and cohort effect (Elder 1975). Hammack (2005) states that, in an attempt to account for historical time in the development experiences of gay men and lesbian women in America, life course theorists have identified cohorts such as pre-war (World War II), post-war, post-stonewall, AIDS, post-AIDS and so on. Hammack (2005, 276) states: "Pre-War gay life was characterized by massive secrecy, furtive sex, and the inevitability of marriage and reproduction. The post-war urban culture, increasingly populated by hordes of soldiers who had engaged in homosexual behaviour, witnessed the birth of urban gay communities, with more gay men choosing to live a nonheterosexual lifestyle... The Stonewall Inn riots of 1969 provided significant maturation and momentum to the Gay Civil Rights Movement..." In the Indian context too, certain milestones (as discussed in Chap. 1) such as the decriminalization of homosexuality in 2009, re-criminalization in 2013, or HIV-AIDS work from the 1990s and national attention to the situation of gay men, MSM, *hijra*s, and trans women in this context, could be seen as forming a similar time and space context to understand growing-up experiences of gay/lesbian individuals. Being a gay teenager in India in the decade of 2000, or the current decade from 2010 onwards, would be distinctly different from growing up in the 1980s and 1990s.

Another aspect of 'time', as referred to in life course theory, is that of the temporal pattern of events and timing of life transitions. The timing of life transitions, has long-term impacts, through effects on subsequent transitions. In the context of this study, for several participants, a sense of being different predated the emergence of sexuality and puberty and, thus, many of them experienced a sense of isolation, a sense of 'not fitting in' and therefore, alienation, from an early age. This implies that LG children, who were gender transgressive from early childhood, much before the emergence of their sexuality, possibly faced greater challenges in growing up. The life course perspective also recognizes continuity and linkages between different life stages, such as childhood and adolescent experiences, and the impact of these on later experiences in adulthood. This is one of the core ideas of this book, that the gender transgressions of childhood, and corrective responses that these receive, are fundamentally connected, in an affective, cognitive, and experiential manner, with sexual explorations and making sense of the same during adolescence, and later decisions of disclosure/non-disclosure, as well as self-categorization as a queer person, and development of collective identities. Furthermore, as discussed in chapter one, the idea of life transitions, life stages, developmental milestones, and the timing of the same, have largely been conceptualized within a heterosexual life framework, and these do not apply in a direct or a similar way in the non-normative life schedules of many queer persons.

The second principle of life course theory is that of life-span development, which includes studying the progressive series of changes and maturational processes that occur among humans throughout the life span and are influenced by both genetic endowments as well as environmental phenomena. The study of life span includes the study of different life stages such as childhood, adolescence, adulthood, each with its developmental tasks and milestones, and continuity throughout life span i.e. every new life experience is shaped and mediated by earlier experiences and attached meanings. Applying the life span development approach to studying 'growing-up' experiences of gay and lesbian persons implies that sexuality is viewed to be a significant context that affects the childhood, adolescence, and life course of an individual with same-sex desires. The underlying assumption is that being attracted to individuals of the same-sex can have an impact on all aspects of living across the lifespan. In the current research, this perspective is used to study the processes, milestones, and challenges faced by young gay and lesbian individuals in their childhood years, adolescence, and young adulthood, within families, schools/colleges, peer cultures, and work spaces. The life course perspective also draws on traditional theories of developmental psychology, which look at the events that typically occur in people's lives during different stages. The life course perspective however differs from these psychological theories in one very important way. Developmental psychology looks for universal, predictable events and pathways, but the life course perspective calls attention to how historical time, social location, and culture affect the individual experience of each life stage (Hutchison 2011). In this sense the life course perspective, 'acknowledges the dialectical process between internal and external, biology and culture, person and society' (Hammack 2005, 269)

Agency is based on the assumption that humans are not passive recipients of a predetermined life course but make decisions that determine the shape of their lives (Hitlin and Elder 2007). Life course theory assumes that reality is co-created through interactional and interpretative processes and practice; that individuals construct their own life course through choices and actions they take within opportunities and constraints placed on them by social structures. Thus, the nature of reality itself is such that it is discursively established by participants in the discourse (Holstein and Gubrium 2000). In studying the processes of 'growing up' gay or lesbian, I acknowledge that every individual participant has actively interpreted, impacted and engaged with their experiences of growing up years to develop a narrative of these years; of things happening within themselves as well as outside of them. The ways in which participants in this study have worked through invisibility, silences, and hostility around same-sex sexuality, to find affirmative spaces, and develop and consolidate their sexual identity, are examples of the individual agency of participants that I discuss throughout this book.

The core life course principle is of 'linked lives'; the perspective that lives are lived interdependently and reflect socio-historical influences (Marshall and Mueller 2003). This principle of linked lives implies both the influence of links/relationships between people as well as that between people and their communities and the wider world (Hutchison 2011). The development of a sense of identity as a sexual being is not a phenomenon that occurs in isolation; rather, it is mediated by several social linkages. It is social structures that dictate the norms of sexuality and gender and are constituted by practice of the same. Similarly, the practice of normative gender or sexuality expressed in, for instance, rules about marriage in a given society—Who marries whom? What is the gender, caste, class, age of the two parties entering into a marriage?—cannot float free, but are responsive to and constrained by the circumstances, which those social structures constitute (Connell 1987). Thus, personal life and collective social arrangements are linked in a fundamental and constitutive way and, hence, to study one without attention to the other would provide us with only a partial picture. Moreover, in the context of marginalized sexualities, the role of interconnectedness with others like oneself, and self-categorization in development and assertion of identity is vital.

In addition to a life course perspective that forms the methodological base for this study, I also use a critical psychosocial approach as an analytical framework that brings together the personal and the collective/social to understand growing up gay in a heterosexually constructed world. In describing a critical psychosocial approach to studying growing up gay, I rely substantially on the work of Frosh (2003) in the paper titled, 'Psychosocial Studies and Psychology: Is a Critical Approach Emerging?' Frosh argues in this paper that, while the term has been used extensively in social psychology and I suggest a similar usage in social work, 'psychosocial' is often used in a way that takes the 'individual' for granted, and seeks to understand ways in which this individual interacts with, interprets, and makes meaning of the 'social'. On the other hand, a similar essentialist description of the social or of the group may take place without attention to subjectivities. Thus while using psychosocial, the separateness, and dichotomy between the individual/psyche and the social is often maintained. Frosh suggests the need to examine psychosocial "as a seamless entity, as a space in which notions which are conventionally distinguished—'individual' and 'society', are instead thought of together, as intimately connected or possibly even the same thing" (2003, 3). The nature of the self/subject from a psychosocial perspective is then both as an agent and actor, and also subject of and subjected to external forces and social structures of class, caste, gender, religion, ethnicity, and so on. Frosh states, "The important point is that the subject is not a pre-given entity, nor something to be found through searching; it is rather a site, in which there are criss-crossing lines of force, and out of which that precious feature of human existence, subjectivity, emerges" (2003, 6). It is thus a challenge, while employing a psychosocial perspective, to be attentive to the social as constructing the personal and the subject not being independent of sociality, but without losing sight or rather holding onto the 'experience' of the personal.

One of the questions that arises then is that if a subject is always socially embedded and constructed then is there such a thing as a 'subject' that is more than the social conditions that produce it? In response, Frosh describes Judith Butler's formulation of the agential subject as, "… subjects are constructed by and in power… But this does not mean that subjects have no agency; rather, their agentic status is *what they are produced with*, and it enables them to take hold of power and use it…" (2003, 10).

In this book, the growing up gay person that I seek to understand and study is constituted and responsive to social and relational forces, while being an active, meaning making, negotiating, coping subject. This psychic narrative of growing up is simultaneously shaped by socio-cultural and personal, relational influences.

As mentioned earlier, 'psychosocial' is often used in literature to mean a study of social adjustment or a study of social influences on individual behaviours or a study of interpersonal relations (Frosh 2003). However, when I use the term psychosocial in this book, I use it to refer to a coming together of internal/intrapsychic processes and social forces that are in a constant dialogue, negotiation and process of shaping each other. It is in this sense that I employ a critical psychosocial perspective in this study.

## 2.3   Contexts of the Study

The current study is conceptualized within a qualitative research paradigm and is informed by a critical psychosocial approach and a life course framework. The study is exploratory in nature, since there is sparse literature on growing up experiences of gay and lesbian individuals in India. It seeks to explore experiences of growing up through childhood, adolescence, and young adulthood, of lesbian and gay youth within their social and institutional contexts of family, marriage, law, medicine, media, educational institutions, peers, and neighbourhoods.

While the study seeks to understand growing up experiences, it does so retrospectively by conducting in-depth interviews, wherein the study participants are asked to recall their experiences of childhood and their growing up years. This study has been conducted in the cities of Mumbai and Pune and participants were contacted using a snowball method. The process of the interview and seeking participants is described in a later section. Here, I only wish to note that the limitations or scope of knowledge as applied to qualitative, exploratory, retrospective studies—such as claiming partial and contextual knowledge and not claiming generalizability of knowledge, recall and recency effect in retrospective narrativization, and so on—apply to this study too.

## *Locating the Researcher*

Frank (1979) suggests that gathering life histories is a collaborative project involving the consciousness of the investigator as well as the research subject. In fact, in the qualitative research tradition, most researchers acknowledge the role of their own professional training and conceptual orientation, as also their personal skills and resources for understanding phenomena and experience (Honigmann et al. 1976). Others such as Devereux (1967) have suggested that eliminating the subjectivity of the researcher in behavioural and social sciences is neither desirable nor possible, and that even if one were to claim objectivity in the development of tools/methods of collecting data, at the interpretative stages, the researcher's perspective is bound to appear. Devereux (1967) suggests that, in order to maintain research rigor, it would be advisable to knowingly acknowledge and reflect on researcher subjectivity, instead of not being consciously aware of it.

A large part of my 'self' and 'identity' that I bring to this study is that of a mental health professional and activist. I have been trained both within the clinical paradigm/s of psychopathology/mental illness, counselling/psychotherapy as well as within the broader framework of social justice and rights and, specifically, advocating for rights of persons with psychosocial disabilities. I was able to put this training into practice during my work within a mental health advocacy and service organization in Pune. Thus, what I bring to this study is a critical lens to mental health knowledge and its practice/s, as well as experience of therapeutic work with persons in distress. My world view and practice as a therapist has been strongly influenced by ideas from attachment-based therapeutic work, self-psychology, and a developmental lens—seeing linkages between experiences of growing up years and adult emotional life and helping adult clients work through traumatic experiences of early life. Thus, in my practice with adult gay men, lesbian women, a few trans women, and persons with intersex variations, I have seen that childhood experiences of isolation and alienation from family and significant others form significant themes in our adult lives. Yet, we know so little about these growing up experiences in lives of individuals with non-normative sexual and gender expressions. Apart from counselling work with LGBT clients, I have worked as a trainer and researcher with gay men, MSM, and *kothis*, and bring these experiences too. I have been in long-term therapy myself with a psychiatrist-therapist trained in object-relations therapy. This fairly long journey of working through early conflicts, the angst of growing up as a queer person myself, and piecing together these multiple narratives of my personal, professional, and political life, are inseparable from the process of writing about growing up gay.

The other perspective I bring to this study is a more recently acquired queer feminist activist identity. I have been a member of a queer feminist collective in Bombay since 2011. This position has given me exposure to, and helped me to engage closely with, LGBTQ movement/s within the country and collective organizing for campaigns. Being a member of an LBT collective makes me an insider to some parts (groups and individuals with feminist political leanings) of the LGBTQ community in Bombay.

Finally, I have grown up in Bombay and lived and worked in Pune for over seven years. The primary reason for choosing these two cities as sites for gathering data is my familiarity with these cities, and with groups and NGOs working here.

This book is an outcome of a decade-long engagement with NGOs, collectives, and individuals from within the LGBTQ communities that I was involved with in varied capacities since 2005. Initially, I worked on LGBTQ mental health concerns as a counsellor and a trainer in Pune and later, under a research fellowship, conducted a study on mental health concerns of sexual minorities and their experiences of mental health services. I have tried to consolidate some of these learnings during my doctoral studies in the last five to six years, during which time I also became member of an LBT collective in Bombay.

## *Locating the Researched*

The study was carried out in the cities of Mumbai and Pune. Both these cities, particularly Mumbai (earlier Bombay), have had a long history of LGBTQ organizing. *Humjinsi*, a resource book on Lesbian, Gay and Bisexual Rights in India, lists a date line to document some of the major events/actions in the history of lesbian/gay organizing in India (Fernandez 1999). Some of the significant moments in this date line as pertaining to the city of Bombay include: staging of a Marathi Play, *Mitrachi Goshta* by Vijay Tendulkar in 1981 in Bombay and Thane focusing on the inner conflict of a woman who realizes she is lesbian; in February 1986, *Savy* magazine publishes a coming-out interview of Ashok Row Kavi, a first for the Indian media; in 1990, *Bombay Dost*, India's first gay and lesbian magazine makes a debut; in 1993, Udaan, a group of working class gay men is formed in Bombay; in 1994, the Humsafar Trust, India's first gay NGO, is registered in Bombay; in 1995, Stree Sangam, a lesbian and bisexual women's group is formed in Bombay and they start a zine, 'Scripts' in 1998 to talk about queer women's lives. In addition, since the mid-1990s in Bombay and early 2000s in Pune, several NGOs and community based organizations working with MSM, gay men, and transgender persons (TGs), have been established to carry out HIV related work. Apart from HIV/AIDS awareness, prevention, testing and treatment work, most of these organizations have been involved with running drop-in centres and support groups to create safe spaces for sexual minorities. They have also been involved with rights-based advocacy work to assert rights of sexual and gender minorities. Several autonomous groups that carry out advocacy, political/collective action as well as work to create safe spaces for socialization, partying, and meeting up with other gay and lesbian persons, have been coming up since 2000 in both cities; more so in Bombay. Some of these organize regular social events and parties for LGBT people to meet. There have been a series of queer-themed business ventures that have come up in Mumbai city including a queer-themed store and a publishing house. In addition, queer film festivals are an annual feature in Bombay and there have been several queer-themed film screenings in Pune too. The older queer-themed magazines such as *Bombay Dost*, started in 1990, and *Scripts*, started in 1998, have been running for years, and many new publications—including queer anthologies, and books on queer erotica—have appeared in the last couple of years.

While there are collectives and NGOs in Mumbai that focus on the lives and issues of lesbian, bisexual women and trans persons (LBT), there are no such organized collectives or groups in Pune for LBT persons. Olava (Organized Lesbian Alliance for Visibility and Action) was a group that was formed in Pune in the year 2000, which shut down later in two to three years (Dave 2012). However NGOs working with gay men, MSM, trans women, and *hijras*, do exist in Pune city and there also exist a few groups that organize social events, parties, and film festivals for LGBT persons.

Thus, there is a vibrant queer social and political life in both Mumbai and Pune. The presence of these queer spaces mentioned above in both the cities made it possible for me to access gay and lesbian participants for this study.

The average age of participants in this study was thirty-three years, and interviews were conducted with them in two phases, 2007–08, and 2011–13. Thus, most of the participants were growing up in the late 1980s and 1990s in the cities of Mumbai and Pune and, while the date line I mention above does indicate a few instances of LGBT organizing and visibility, my interview narratives do suggest a great deal of isolation and invisibility initially, until the participants got in touch with the queer communities in their cities through reading a newspaper article, an online chat, or through a helpline.

A total of forty participants were interviewed for the study, of these twenty-five self-identified as gay and fifteen self-identified as lesbian. A total of fifteen participants were from Pune and twenty-five were from Mumbai. The lower number of participants from Pune is due to fewer spaces to meet potential participants from the community (as compared to Mumbai) and limited weekend access, since I was living in Mumbai for part of the duration of the study. Also, in general, in both cities, meeting gay men was much easier as there were many more NGOs and groups working with them and this increased access. Access was also linked with my own location; during this time period, I was mostly engaged with NGOs working with gay men, MSM, and *kothis*, as a mental health professional and trainer. With respect to lesbian women, there were no groups in Pune that worked on issues of lesbian women (in 2007–08 and 2010, when I was interviewing participants in Pune), after the closure of OLAVA in 2002–03, and in Bombay, while there were groups, my access to these groups was limited at the time of conducting interviews. Hence, the lower numbers of lesbian women participants in this study.

As noted, the average age of the participants was thirty-three years, with the youngest participant being twenty-four years old and the oldest one being forty-five. A total of four participants had studied up to 12th Standard and twenty-three were graduates, while thirteen had completed some kind of postgraduate degree in subjects such as English literature, Social Work, Computer Science, Business Administration, Medicine, Law and so on. Eighteen of them were employed as professionals in various institutions such as banks, corporate businesses, hospitals, call centres, and teaching institutions. Interestingly, eleven of them were working in NGOs. All of these were NGOs working on LGBT rights, HIV, or women's empowerment. This higher number is partly because NGOs were a contact point for me to seek potential participants and partly because some of them said that their queer identity was central to who they saw themselves to be currently, and hence had chosen to work in the area of empowerment of women and LGBT persons.

Among the forty participants, nine were from a lower socio-economic strata (self-reported and as understood in terms of income, occupation, and type of housing), thirteen from the middle socio-economic strata, and eighteen from the upper socio-economic group (self-reported and as understood in terms of individual and family income, type of housing, ownership of assets). In case of two participants, their parents belonged to the lower socio-economic strata and they have moved upward on the socio-economic ladder and hence are counted as belonging to the middle socio-economic strata. However, they grew up in conditions of considerable deprivation. In terms of living arrangements, ten were living independently, twenty-four with family, and six were living with their partners. All six persons living with partners were lesbian women. Of these six, I had interviewed four; two couples and two others whose partners were not part of the study. Among the ten participants living independently, many had weekend or occasional living together arrangements with their partners. Of these ten participants, four were women and six were men. This implies that of the fifteen lesbian women who participated in the study, ten were living with partners or independently, and only five were living with family. Among these five, one participant was living with her daughters after separation from her husband, and another one, who was in a heterosexual marriage, was living with her husband and son. Only three of the lesbian participants were living with their natal families and of these two were not in remunerative employment at the time of the interview. That lesbian women need to separate from families or move out of family homes under the 'cited reasons' of education or job opportunities in order to be able to live out their lives is explored in greater detail in later chapters. Living independent of family is also an indicator of class and, while there were many gay men in the study who belonged to upper class backgrounds and were professionals with sound income, not many of them were living independently. This trend is discussed later in analysis and possible explanations are discussed.

Of the forty study participants, thirty-five were unmarried, while five were married at some point in their lives. Of these five, two were women and three were men. At the time of the interview, one man and one woman had divorced and separated respectively, while three others continued to be married. Among the forty participants, most grew up in the cities of Mumbai or Pune, except seven, who grew up elsewhere and were currently living in these cities for educational or occupational reasons. Of these seven participants, some grew up in various places in India: in Nasik; in a village in Vidharbha; in a small town in Rajasthan; moved between several cities such as Bangalore, Hyderabad, Delhi. Two participants grew up in other countries; one a Middle Eastern country and one an African country. There were three participants who were Muslim; one, both of whose parents were Muslim and two with one Muslim parent each. There were three participants who were Dalit and Buddhist, and three were Christians. All the others were Hindu.

Twenty-five participants were currently living in Mumbai and fifteen in Pune. A few grew up in places other than Mumbai and Pune. Growing up experiences for LG persons in Mumbai and Pune are comparable on several counts. Experiences within family and school settings, and in community environments such as the *chawls* in Mumbai and the *vadas* in Pune, were similar. Differences emerged primarily in terms of access to the LGBTQ community. Many of the participants from Pune, both men and women, talked about accessing community first, or, rather, primarily, in Mumbai. This was due to a more visible queer presence in Mumbai as compared to Pune.

## *The Interview*

> ... the guiding principle for [life histories] could be that all autobiographical memory is true: it is up to the interpreter to discover in which sense, where, and for what purpose.
>
> [Passerini 1989, pp. 197; quoted in Sangster 1994, pp. 5]

In this study, an interview guide was used, which served as a broad guideline to steer the conversation. Participants were encouraged to talk about their life experiences along a timeline, starting from some of their earliest childhood memories to the current time. The time line thus became a tool on which conversations about life events, transitions and life trajectories could be pegged. Participants were free to move back and forth on the timeline and for some the narratives began from the present time and went back into childhood and for some the conversation began at some point in the middle which the participant saw as a significant moment in their narrative. Some others started with their childhood and earliest memories. Thus, participants did a free-flow style of storytelling, which was recorded. Invariably, life stories included conversations about complex, multiple interjecting trajectories. These were explored using probing follow-up questions, while intermittently referring to the interview guide.

Since participants were asked to recollect events and experiences, and the meanings of the same, right from their childhood, the study can be said to be using a retrospective design, and limitations of such a design apply to this study too. Recollection of events, talking from memory, or what may be referred to as constructing a life narrative, in the present is bound to be mediated by current and other intermediate experiences, one's current world view/ideology, language, politics, and so on. In this sense, it would not be possible to observe or know with precision the exact event/s that occurred at a particular point of time in the life story, say for instance in class IV, in school, when the person was nine years old in the year 1985. However, the narrative about that event/s as constructed by the person would be accessible. Moreover, this narrative would not be seen as a single instance, but would be viewed in light of the person's overall life narrative, which in turn would be contextualized. Thus, the interview process in this study was not about evidence gathering or truth finding, but instead about close listening, curiosity, establishing a relationship with the participants, empathy, humour, and solidarity.

Interviews were undertaken in two phases, including a pilot phase; the first one in 2007–08 and the second over a period of almost two years, between 2011 and 2013. Due to the paucity of time, several interviews were conducted over a single sitting lasting for an average of two to three hours with breaks. Some were conducted over two sessions. Interviews were conducted in participants' homes, coffee shops, NGO drop-in centres, and even public gardens, in both cities. All the interviews were audio recorded after seeking consent from participants and were later transcribed. Data transcripts were read and re-read, and coding was done using a computer package (MAXQDA 11). Themes that emerged from the codes were used to carry out a thematic analysis of the data that is presented as four chapters in this book.

The snowball method that is widely used in qualitative research studies, particularly while researching stigmatized communities that may often be invisibilized/hidden due to fear of stigma and discrimination, and that are seen as difficult to reach (Heckathorn 1997), was used to contact potential participants. I spread the word around about the study among friends from within the queer community and on social networking sites and NGO spaces. After getting the first contacts through these multiple points, I conducted their interviews and that of those referred by them. To ensure diversity in the background of participants, I contacted NGOs, social/party spaces, and activist groups in both cities. Also, a few of my ex-clients, who had sought counselling services from me earlier from within the LG community in Pune, served as contact points. Some of the participants that were contacted through NGO spaces in Bombay city had been interviewed before for other kinds of research projects in the area of sexual health. However, most of the participants were being interviewed for a qualitative study with a life course perspective for the first time.

## *Use of Narrative Data*

In this book, narrative data has been used in two ways. One use is that of the first person narrative data that has been taken from the interviews with the study participants. As mentioned above, the process of using this data has been as follows: transcription of the entire interview as well as any follow-up interviews; coding and re-coding of transcripts as per emerging themes; coded segments or participant quotes illustrative of each theme collated together. Finally, in the writing of each theme, the original words of the participants have been retained to explain each theme emerging from the participant data. Each of these quotes has been further qualified with details of the participant/speaker such as age, gender, sexual identity, and location.

The second use of narrative data is the one in the prelude section of each of the following chapters. Chapters three, four, five and six start with a section titled 'Prelude'. The narratives that are used here are illustrative of the themes and the discussion that will be carried forward in the chapter. In this sense, these narratives are a prelude, an introduction in a first person narrative format, to what lies ahead in the chapter. These introductory narratives serve as a way to draw the reader into the lived experience of the participants without any interruptions or analysis. These narratives, while written in the form of a first person story, are not gathered from one particular study participant. They are, at times, reflective of common/shared experiences of study participants; at times, they refer to informal conversations with me as a co-activist, friend, or a chat among a group of friends; sharing at a support group meeting or meeting of a collective; my own personal experiences; and so on. As a result, these prelude narratives do not end with demographic details of a specific participant or their location.

## 2.4  Ethical Concerns in Doing Research with Sexual Minority Groups

Consent from the research participants was the starting point for the data collection phase of this study. Most participants read about the study or were told about the same by their friends from within the queer community. In the few instances where I contacted the staff of an NGO, participants heard about the study from them. Participation was entirely voluntary. In the case of two of the research participants, they had sought services from a counselling centre in Pune where I had worked earlier. They heard about the study and expressed interest in participating. Thus, while my colleagues and I had provided direct services to them at some point, it was ensured that they did not feel the pressure or burden to participate in the study. Moreover, they had stopped seeking services at this centre, at the time they decided to participate in the interview.

In addition to seeking consent, participants knew that there were no direct benefits they would receive by participating in the study. The intention of 'no harm' and yet the possibility of distress, on recounting some traumatic material from the growing-up years, was discussed with the participants. Participants were promised counselling referral services in case they needed it. They were also assured that I would negotiate fees for these services, if they were not in a position to pay for the same. Some of the participants were already plugged into support networks in the community and, in this sense, did have access to other safe spaces, apart from the clinical/therapeutic space.

While it is important to acknowledge that a study like this can evoke distressing memories, the interview process itself was constructed in a manner that ensured a safe, engaging, space for the research participants. There were disclosures about sexual abuse in childhood, worries about HIV status, suicide attempts, non-disclosure of same-sex desires to spouses, and discussion of several relation-ship stressors with me. Some of the participants, especially those who were isolated, made requests for being introduced to potential dating, sex partners. All of these issues were discussed over a period of time, where information resources such as e-lists of the LGBTQ community, books, films, party and social spaces for LGBTQ, were shared with the participants. Often, there were no follow-up actions that the participants expected, but just having a conversation, a few laughs, and answering a few questions pertaining to my own life, seemed to help. These conversations happened during interviews as well as later, over phone calls and sometimes e-mail. One of the participants did ask for and was provided a contact of a counsellor in Bombay. This participant shared that she wanted to seek counselling services for a while but was always apprehensive. However, after the interview, and after hearing about my work in the mental health sector, she felt a level of trust and confidence to seek professional help.

Given that the 'out' gay and lesbian communities in Mumbai and Pune are not too large and often the same people meet each other at a gay party, a book launch, a pride march, a protest meet, a dating site, confidentiality becomes a significant ethical concern. For instance, I would realize while conducting an interview or during data collection that, though I had contacted two persons through two unconnected sources/contact, people in the study knew each other or had dated each other at some point in the past. Thus, while the interview followed an informal conversational style, I ensured that I never divulged any details of my research participants to any of the other participants. However, while personal details were kept confidential, information about other resources, which is valuable and scarce in a heterosexist world, was shared freely (wherever relevant) with all participants. For instance, one of the participants had talked about shops where she could easily buy large size men's shirts, which she likes to use without facing too much of dis-comfort or awkward reactions from the staff. A similar issue came up with another participant, and this information about the shop with friendly staff was anony-mously shared with the person. Another example would be while talking about safe public spaces to hangout as a queer couple, participants discussed their experiences with various parks and restaurants, and this information was shared with other participants if conversations about safe public spaces came up during interviews. In addition to not divulging information about participants, all the identifying markers of all participants such as names, place/area of residence, affiliations with NGOs, groups, and so on are masked.

Self-disclosure and boundaries with study participants is another issue that I would like to discuss here. As a feminist researcher and practitioner, I firmly believe in acknowledging and working to reduce the power imbalance in a research as well as a therapeutic relationship. One of the ways to do this is to deconstruct the expert stance of the researcher and conduct the study as a collaborative process. Another related one would be to not hide one's real self and vulnerabilities behind an expert/researcher garb. I did struggle with the latter in a few instances. While a feminist orientation in therapeutic work and political engagement with mental health advocacy equipped me with the politics and self-reflexivity to deconstruct the expert position, my own struggles with my sexuality, relationships, non-engagement with queer political spaces till much later, made transparency and appropriate, rather, necessary self-disclosure (during the interview process) a challenge for me at times. As I discuss in chapter four, decision about disclosure or non-disclosure about one's sexuality is a complicated one. It has to do with elements of internalized homonegativity and internal conflict, as much as with absence of support networks, perception of threat, violence, and discrimination.

This study is an outcome of a decade-long engagement with LGBTQ communities that I first approached as an 'expert-outsider' and later as an insider, and this has meant a considerable shift in my stance. I therefore need to acknowledge that, based on my location today as a queer feminist activist and learnings that come thereof, I would have done some parts of this study differently, particularly with regard to participation of the study participants in the process of analysis and writing. In that sense, while this is a study within the qualitative framework and the interview narratives are a product of a collaborative process, the analysis and writing has been mostly done by me. In addition to my privileges of education, caste, class, religion, I have had the privilege of the researcher of analysing, interpreting, and representing the stories shared by my study participants, based on my understanding and the analytical lens that I employ. These questions of power imbalance in production of knowledge remain, though I have tried to be aware of the same, both in the process of the interview and in the analysis and writing of the life stories shared by the participants.

To summarize, using a life course and a critical psychosocial perspective, through in-depth interviews with forty self-identified gay and lesbian study participants from the cities of Mumbai and Pune, I describe, in the following chapters, experiences of childhood and adolescence of lesbian and gay individuals, their process of consolidating their sexual identities, decisions regarding disclosure of the same, their same-sex adult romantic relationships, and engagement with the queer community/s.

# References

Alvesson, M., & Sköldberg, K. (2009). *Reflexive methodology: New vistas for qualitative research*. Sage.

Bayer, R. (1981). *Homosexuality and American psychiatry: The politics of diagnosis*. New York: Basic Books.

Beiber, I. (1962). Homosexuality: A psychoanalytic study. (1981). In Bayer, R. (Ed.) *Homosexuality and American psychiatry: The politics of diagnosis* (p. 46). New York: Basic Books.

Biswas, R., Banerjea, N., Banerjee, R., & Sumitha, B. (2016). *Making liveable lives: Rethinking social exclusion*. Kolkata: Sappho for Equality.

Bohan, J. S. (1996). *Psychology and sexual orientation: Coming to terms*. New York: Routledge.

Cass, V. C. (1979). Homosexual identity formation: A theoretical model. *Journal of Homosexuality, 4*(3), 219–235.

Chakrapani, V., Shanmugam, M., Sivasubramanian, M., Samuel, M., Carmen, L., Newman, P. A., et al. (2014). Influence of sexual minority stigma and HIV-related stigma on mental health: Testing the minority stress model among men who have sex with men in India. In *7th IAS Conference on HIV Pathogenesis and Treatment*. Abstract no. WEPE545.

Cohler, B. J., & Hammack, P. L. (2007). The psychological world of the gay teenager: Social change, narrative, and "normality". *Journal of Youth and Adolescence, 36*(1), 47–59.

Connell, R. W. (1987). *Gender and power*. Cambridge: Polity Press with Blackwell Publishers.

CREA, (Creating Resources for Empowerment and Action). (2012). *Count me in! research report on violence against disabled, lesbian and sex-working women in Bangladesh, India and Nepal*. New Delhi: CREA Publications. Retrieved July 15, 2017, from http://www.creaworld.org/sites/default/files/TheCountMeIn%21ResearchReport.pdf.

Dandona, L., Dandona, R., Gutierrez, J. P., Kumar, G. A., McPherson, S., Bertozzi, S. M., & Asci FPP Study Team. (2005). Sex behaviour of men who have sex with men and risk of HIV in Andhra Pradesh, India. *Aids, 19*(6): 611–619.

D'Augelli, A. R., & Hershberger, S. L. (1993). Lesbian, gay, and bisexual youth in community settings: Personal challenges and mental health problems. *American Journal of Community Psychology, 21*(4), 421–448.

Dave, N. N. (2012). *Queer activism in India: A story in the anthropology of ethics*. Duke University Press.

Devereux, G. (1967). *From anxiety to method in the behavioral sciences* (Vol. 3). Walter de Gruyter GmbH & Co KG.

Elder, G. H. (1975). Age differentiation and the life course. *Annual Review of Sociology, 1*, 165–190.

Elder Jr, G. H., Johnson, M. K., & Crosnoe, R. (2003). *The emergence and development of life course theory*. US: Springer.

Fernandez, B. (1999). *Humjinsi: A resource book for lesbian, gay and bisexual rights in India*. New Delhi: India Centre for Human Rights and Law.

Fernandez, B., & Gomathy, N. B. (2003). *The nature of violence faced by lesbian women in India*. Mumbai: Research Centre on Violence Against Women, Tata Institute of Social Sciences. Retrieved July 15, 2017, from https://www.tiss.edu/uploads/files/8The_Nature_of_violence_faced_by_Lesbian_women_in_India.pdf.

Frank, G. (1979). Finding the common denominator: A phenomenological critique of life history method. *Ethos, 7*(1), 68–94.

Freud, S. 1955. From the history of an infantile neurosis. In *Standard edition* (Vol. 17, pp. 3–104). London: Hogarth Press.

Frosh, S. (2003). Psychosocial studies and psychology: Is a critical approach emerging? *Human Relations, 56*(12), 1545–1567.

Garnets, L. D., Herek, G. M., & Levy, B. (1990). Violence and victimization of lesbians and gay men: Mental health consequences. *Journal of Interpersonal Violence, 5*, 366–383.

Ghosh, S., Bandyopadhyay, B. S., & Biswas, R. (2011). *Vio-Map: Documenting and mapping violence and rights violation taking place in the lives of sexually marginalized women to chart out effective advocacy strategies*. Kolkata: SAPPHO for Equality.

Giele, J. Z., & Elder, G. H., Jr. (1998). Life course research: Development of a field. In J. Z. Giele & G. H. Elder Jr. (Eds.), *Methods of life course research: Qualitative and quantitative approaches* (pp. 5–27). CA: Sage.

Haldeman, D. C. (1994). The practice and ethics of sexual orientation conversion therapy. *Journal of Consulting and Clinical Psychology, 62*(2), 221.

Hammack, P. L. (2005). An integrative paradigm. *Human Development, 48*(5), 267.

Harding, S. (1987). Introduction: Is there a feminist method? In S. Harding (Ed.), *Feminism & methodology*. Bloomington/Milton Keynes.

Heckathorn, D. D. (1997). Respondent-driven sampling: A new approach to the study of hidden populations. *Social Problems, 44*(2), 174–199.

Hitlin, S., & Elder, G. H., Jr. (2007). Time, self, and the curiously abstract concept of agency. *Sociological Theory, 25*, 170–191.

Holstein, J. A., & Gubrium, J. F. (2000). *Constructing the life course*. New York: General Hall Inc.

Honigmann, J. J., Caulfield, M. D., Chilungu, S. W., Eches, R., Wald, P., Hellbom, A. B., et al. (1976). The personal approach in cultural anthropological research [and comments and reply]. *Current Anthropology, 17*(2), 243–261.

Hooker, E. (1957). The adjustment of the male overt homosexual. *Journal of Projective Techniques, 21*(1), 18–31.

Humsafar Trust. (2002). *A baseline study of knowledge, attitude, behavior and practices among men having sex with men at selected sites in Mumbai.* Mumbai: Humsafar Trust.

Hutchison, E. D. (2011). *Dimensions of human behavior: The changing life course.* CA: Sage.

Joint United Nations Program on HIV/AIDS. 2010. *India MSM country snapshots–country specific information on HIV, men who have sex with men (MSM) and transgender people (TG).*

Kinsey, A. C. (Ed.). (1953). *Sexual behavior in the human female.* Indiana University Press.

Kinsey, A. C., Pomeroy, W. B., & Martin, C. E. (1948). *Sexual behavior in the human male.*

Kolodny, R. C., Masters, W. H., Hendrix, J., & Toro, G. (1971). Plasma testosterone and semen analysis in male homosexuals. *New England Journal of Medicine, 285,* 1170–1178.

Krafft-Ebing, R. (1922). *Psychopathia sexualis.* Brooklyn: Physicians and Surgeons Book Co.

Mahalingam, R. (2003). Essentialism, culture, and beliefs about gender among the aravanis of Tamil Nadu, India. *Sex Roles, 49*(9), 489–496.

Mantegazza, P. (1932). *Sexual relations of mankind.* New York: Anthropological Press.

Marshall, V. W., & Mueller, M. M. (2003). Theoretical roots of the life-course perspective. In *Social dynamics of the life course* (pp. 3–32).

Nanda, S. (1994). *Hijras.* Wiley.

Neuman, L. W. (2002). *Social research methods: Qualitative and quantitative approaches* (7th ed.). Pearson Education Limited.

Passerini, L. (1989). Women's personal narratives: Myths, Experiences, And Emotions. In *Interpreting women's lives: Feminist theory and personal narratives* (pp. 189–197).

Reddy, G. (2006). *With respect to sex: Negotiating hijra identity in South India.* Yoda Press.

Remafedi, G. (1987). Adolescent homosexuality: Psychosocial and medical implications. *Pediatrics, 79*(3), 331–337.

Sangster, J. (1994). Telling our stories: Feminist debates and the use of oral history. *Women's History Review, 3*(1), 5–28.

Shah, C., Merchant, R., Mahajan, S., & Nevatia, S. (2015). *No outlaws in the gender galaxy.* Zubaan.

Silverstein, C. (1991). Psychological and medical treatments of homosexuality. In J. C. Gonsiorek & J. D. Weinrich (Eds.), *Homosexuality: Research implications for public policy* (pp. 101–114). Newbury Park, CA: Sage.

Silverstein, C. (1996). History of treatment. In R. P. Cabaj & T. S. Stein (Eds.), *Textbook of homosexuality and mental health* (pp. 3–16). Washington, DC: American Psychiatric Press.

Sivasubramanian, M., Mimiaga, M. J., Mayer, K. H., Anand, V. R., Johnson, C. V., Prabhugate, P., et al. (2011). Suicidality, clinical depression, and anxiety disorders are highly prevalent in men who have sex with men in Mumbai, India: Findings from a community-recruited sample. *Psychology, Health & Medicine, 16*(4), 450–462.

Thomas, B., Mimiaga, M. J., Menon, S., Chandrasekaran, V., Murugesan, P., Swaminathan, S., et al. (2009). Unseen and unheard: Predictors of sexual risk behavior and HIV infection among men who have sex with men in Chennai, India. *AIDS Education & Prevention, 21*(4), 372–383.

Tomori, C., McFall, A. M., Srikrishnan, A. K., Mehta, S. H., Solomon, S. S., Anand, S., et al. (2016). Diverse rates of depression among men who have sex with men (MSM) across India: Insights from a multi-site mixed method study. *AIDS and Behavior, 20*(2), 304–316.

Troiden, R. (1979). Becoming homosexual: A model of gay identity acquisition. *Psychiatry, 42,* 362–373.

Vanita, R., & Kidwai, S. (Eds.). (2000). *Same-sex love in India: Readings from literature and history.* New Delhi: Macmillan.

# Chapter 3
# Exploring Early Years: Childhood and Adolescence of Young Gay and Lesbian Persons

*Prelude*[1]

**experiences of childhood, gender, and sexuality**

*narrative one:*

*when people talk about childhood as this carefree time—best years of their life with no worries and lots of play and laughter—i am filled with a deep sense of disconnect with this image. when i think of childhood, i think of it as a scary time... when everyone thought it was ok for them to comment on all my ways of being, my gestures, way of walking, talking, clothes, how much and when is it ok for me to be upset and cry... as a young boy you have very little control on what can happen to you, you know.*

*so when i think of my childhood, i think of it as a time i never ever want to revisit again.*

*narrative two:*

*childhood was fine only ya: loving parents, adorable sister; i was the only son. they were chill with everything i liked doing. i wasn't great at studies but loved to play football and watch all the cookery shows with ma. i wanted to be a chef; they thought it was cute. the problem came later when i was to start college and said i want to do home science. what was cute at age eleven, wasn't so at age nineteen, i guess... then there were other pressures from friends to have a girlfriend.*

---

[1]The narratives in the prelude section are illustrative of the themes and discussion that will be carried forward in the chapter. These narratives, while written in the form of a first person story are not gathered from one particular study participant. They are at times reflective of common/shared experiences of study participants, at times they refer to informal conversations with me as a researcher, activist, friend or chat among group of friends; sharing at a support group meeting or meeting of a collective; my own personal experiences and so on. Read more in Chap. 2 about Use of Narratives in this book.

© Springer Nature Singapore Pte Ltd. 2018
K. Ranade, *Growing Up Gay in Urban India*,
https://doi.org/10.1007/978-981-10-8366-2_3

*narrative three:*

*it was during my summer break after finishing 8$^{th}$ Std. that my cousin, came to stay with us for a few months. he offered to teach me to swim and we started going to the pool together. it started out as he feeling me up and stroking my penis while he was teaching me to float in the pool and then led to more in the changing rooms and later at home, on the terrace… it was immensely pleasurable. i did not know that my body could give me so much joy. i was in love. we never really talked about it. what did this mean to him? to me? i did not even know the word gay then, i wonder whether he did either; he was only two years older than me. we would just seek each other out every time he visited us over the next couple of years. and then one day, after a few years, he came to visit during his semester break at engineering college and acted aloof at first. he then told me and other cousins that he had a girlfriend at college and showed us her picture from his wallet.*

*my heart broke. this was the first in a series of heartbreaks that came in the following years with men. men, who were unsure, confused; men, who desired me and wanted to be with me but also get married. then there were those who were terrified of the world finding out the truth about them and so always had a girlfriend as a cover.*

*about labels, i think they are limiting and cannot even begin to capture the essence of experience. some would argue that my first sexual experience with my cousin was sexual abuse as i was underage, but i don't think of it as abuse at all. it was a very pleasurable sexual initiation and what is under-age, legal age, appropriate age for sex anyway? consent for me is about how ready you feel to say yes… similarly, the men who i called confused or those who wanted girlfriends or wives to take care of the house and parents and cooking and cleaning; should i be using the label 'bisexual' for them or internalized homophobia or just accruing benefits of plain and simple patriarchy. i don't think any ONE of these labels would capture the meaning of their (our) realities…*

*narrative four:*

*school is this strange place for people like us ya. i have heard this from so many of my queer friends. it's a place that reinforces all kinds of normativities: what a girl should be like and what a boy should be like, and then who is a good child/good student, and then all the bullying that takes place of people who do not fit these rigid boxes of good girl and good boy, who by the way are good because they are not showing any interest in each other, but are also good because ultimately they are interested in each other, heterosexual, you know (laughs)…*

*despite this, school is also a place where people find their gay/queer self ya. my own experience but also of so many of my friends of falling in love, exchanging love notes, gifts, holding hands, carving out initials on forearm and school benches, jealousy between best friend and girlfriend—all this also happened in school for so many of us.*

*so while i struggled with the skirt and blouse uniform of my school and tried to hide under an oversized jacket saying, i was always feeling cold; imagine in Bombay, being cold 24 by 7 (laughs). it was also at school that i first had these massive crushes on my teachers and knew that i was attracted to women.*

*i remember having this huge crush on a math teacher. she was a trainee teacher. they used to always be super friendly, also when i think back now, i think they used to also be a bit nervous of facing the whole class. so with this teacher, i used to help out with the attendance, cleaning the board, fetch chalks and charts from the staff room—basically anything to be around her. she was of course completely unaware of what was going on inside my head and probably thought of me as this cute, helpful kid (laughs)*

*narrative five:*

*i think the idea of 'trishankhu'* (refers to a king in Hindu Mythology, who lived being suspended mid-air between heaven and earth) *best describes my early psychic life. it is this sense of belonging and un-belonging, togetherness and alienation, all at once that i constantly experienced. i will narrate an incident from the time when i was probably twelve or thirteen as an example.*

*there was this festival called 'bhondla' being celebrated in our chawl. this festival is celebrated by young girls and women, among hindu maharashtrians, usually during navratri. during the celebration, the women go around a 'rangoli' with the motif of an elephant at the centre, holding hands and singing traditional songs. these songs are mostly about relationships of married women with their in-laws and husbands and also about fertility of the soil and of the woman.*

*i remember that evening, everyone had started gathering in the courtyard for this ritual of songs and prayer and i was very uncomfortable in participating in this ritual. i guess, it was just this idea of celebrating marriage and banter between women about conjugal life and young girls jokingly being given life lessons by their mothers and grandmothers about how they should look, groom, behave, sit, walk and talk in order to be blessed with a good husband—all this just made me sick. so i was sitting at home trying to do some homework and hoping that i can avoid this whole thing. that's when my father insisted that i join my mother and elder sister in the 'bhondla' festivities. i tried going down and coming back up a couple of times, only to be yelled at by father for not going out and being with girls my age. after this, i remember spending that whole evening, hiding below the stair case of the first floor, the floor between the courtyard and my parents' house.*

*this is what i mean by 'trishankhu'—being in a limbo, not belonging, neither inside the home, nor outside it!*

In this chapter, I focus on early years of young lesbian and gay persons and dwell on experiences of childhood that predate the onset of puberty and emergence of sexuality. Childhood becomes an important period in the study of growing up as LG because many LG persons are aware of their same-sex sexual attractions even in the pre-puberty years (D'Augelli 1996). They may not have labelled it as 'gay' or may not even define this attraction in sexual terms until later. However, *a sense of difference* from their peers has been reported in several studies with LG individuals (Savin-Williams 1998). The sense of 'difference' from people around, including friends, family, school and almost every institution that the child comes in contact with, is often a hallmark of the experience of growing up for the LG child. Allport (1954) points out that, in contrast to other minorities such as ethnic or religious minorities, sexual minorities are minority even within their own homes and families. Most LG individuals grow up in heterosexual families and hence they are not imbued with a gay identity at birth. They must discover it on their own with no role models in the parents to help consolidate a minority identity. Often, they cannot count on parental support for protection from discrimination from the outside world (Allport 1954; Martin 1982). Thus, depending upon several factors in the environment, many LG individuals may come out to themselves during adolescence or early adulthood. However, there are also several LG individuals who, under the influence of heterosexual socialization, and experiences with the same and the opposite sex, may remain unaware of, or avoid using a label for, their same-sex sexual attraction and encounters, till late adulthood or mid-life (Jensen 1999); some may never identify with a label such as gay, lesbian, bisexual or queer, while continuing to have same-sex sexual/romantic/affective fantasies and relationships.

Most participants in this study too reported a sense of being different from their siblings and friends from early years; even as early as five and six years of age. For most participants, both gay and lesbian, this sense of difference in early years was markedly felt, expressed, and read by others in the form of gender non-conforming behaviours. Most gay men recalled being termed 'sissy' or effeminate, and several of the lesbian women participants were labelled in their childhood as 'tomboys'. Gender non-conformity was seen most starkly, for both gay men and lesbian women, in areas such as clothes, grooming, play, hobbies, and preference of opposite sex play mates. While areas of gender non-conformity were similar for boys and girls, the ways in which this non-conformity was expressed, and its consequences, differed with gender and age. Here, it is important to note that, while several studies have found a relationship between gender non-conformity in childhood and adult homosexuality, childhood gender non-conformity is not always and invariably linked to same-sex sexual orientation in adulthood (Green 1985; Bailey and Zucker 1995). Thus, there are many children who demonstrate traits and behaviour that do not fit in with the gender script associated with their assigned gender, who grow up to adopt a heterosexual sexual orientation. Similarly, there are children who fit in perfectly with the script of their assigned gender and perform 'gender appropriate' behaviours and who grow up to be gay/homosexual. In the present study, too, there were several participants who reported gender conformity in their dressing, mannerisms, and interests.

This chapter also dwells on experiences of the LG adolescent as a sexual and a social being. Adolescence is a time of experimentation and exploration for all young people. However, LG adolescents have an additional task of exiting from their heterosexual socialization, and the expectations that follow from it, and developing a new self (D'Augelli 1996; Mallon 1998). Ordinarily, some of the developmental tasks that individuals have to achieve during adolescence include starting the process of individuation from parents, socialising with peers, forming an identity, exploring intimate relationships and orienting themselves to the future (Coleman and Remafedi 1989). Unfortunately, the primary task for LG youth is entry into a stigmatized role and the major developmental task for them includes passage into that social identity. This process of self-identification and acceptance may be slow and long-drawn-out for some, and many gay, lesbian adolescents may make efforts to 'pass' as heterosexual as a way of dealing with the overwhelming feelings of fear of rejection and isolation from family and close ones. The challenges in the process of self-identification, as well as the unique developmental challenges that LG adolescents talked about in this study, are discussed towards the end of this chapter.

Finally, the process of growing up through childhood and adolescence takes place in a context, and is responsive to the same. The section on correction of gender non-conformity and sexual expression through the growing-up years, by parents/family, teachers/school, peers, doctors/counsellors, describes the response of the environment to the emerging self of the LG young person. These experiences of 'correction of same-sex sexuality' in turn impact the development and consolidation of LG identity. The correction responses recorded here occurred in specific interpersonal contexts of home, school or a doctor's clinic but are a reflection of the larger regulation and control processes that institutions of family, education, and medicine implement, to produce normal, productive, and reproductive, heterosexual men and women. Pyne (2014) refers to correction programs for gender non-conforming children as an 'ensemble of disciplinary techniques, drawing children, and their families, into an enclosure of dangerous power relations' (80). 'Power' is used here in Foucauldian terms to mean, 'power/knowledge', wherein—instead of being imposed through force—power is produced and exercised through discourse or 'scientific' knowledge. In other words, power is not used to directly exclude or punish gender non-conforming children, but instead used by 'experts', through technologies of assessments, tools of surveillance and interventions for children labelled as 'deviant', to fashion, shape, or mould their behaviours and make them 'normal' again. Rose and Miller (2010) elaborate on this notion of a self-reinforcing loop of power/knowledge with their concept of an *enclosure,* a 'bounded locale' in which expert authority is consolidated (286). In the context of gender non-conforming children, this 'expert authority' has meant the authority of child development professionals, psychiatrists, social workers, educationists, and so on. Foucault (1978) explores psychiatric power as one of the modern disciplinary powers historically executed within the asylums. However, this power, over the 19th century, gradually permeates into the family, where the family becomes the site, where the roots or origins of madness are to be detected. Philo (2011) states that it is in this context of childhood as signalling adult pathology, that psychia-trization and surveillance of childhoods becomes important. In the section on correction of gender non-conformity, I discuss, through the participant narratives, the multiple ways in which families, mental health professionals, and educationists collude with each other to produce the often shaming experience of correction of gender non-conformity in children.

## 3.1  Gender Non-conformity in Childhood: Clothes and Grooming

Retrospective studies with adults in western literature indicate that over three quarters of lesbian and gay persons reported a feeling of being different during their childhood and adolescence (Bell et al. 1981; Troiden 1979). In a study by Savin-Williams of gay youth between the ages fourteen to twenty-five, most of them remembered feeling different from other boys their age from their earliest childhood. Many of the boys attributed this difference to gender non-conformity or feminine appearance, behaviours, and interests. Childhood experiences of departing from family/peer norms in concrete ways such as atypical gender expression and sexual interest in individuals of the same-sex may be experienced by the child as not a 'good' dif-ference but a 'bad' one. This could cause feelings of being misunderstood, isolated, shamed, and be suppressed and internally repressed (Savin-Williams 2005).

In the current study, several gay men recalled being interested, as children, in wearing their sisters' or mothers' clothes, make-up, lipstick, and cosmetics. A few participants talked about draping their mothers' *dupatta* like a *saree* when they were alone at home; others talked about being interested in trying out all the cosmetics they could lay their hands on. One participant described his fascination for bright colours and big designs and prints on his shirts. He said that he had been most interested in wearing colourful shoes; yellow, pink, green. Another participant described the difference in the fitting of clothes for girl and boy clothes and said that he had liked to alter his shirts and clothes at the waist so as to get a snug fit. Some of the participants also described that they had been fascinated by, and would try to imitate, the mannerisms of the women around them such as aunts and mothers.

I learnt from my mother only how to wear the towel on the head after a bath…

[Akshay, 26 year old gay man says this about the time when he was 12 years old]

When girls buy their clothes, they do a little alteration so as to shape it up for themselves, right? One day, I also took my shirt and with a needle and thread was altering it by tightening it around the waist…

[Kumar, 30 year old gay man says this about the time when he was 10 years old]

I was really very fond of her cosmetics and my father used to tell me why I need so many cosmetics and I would say, I need them as my skin is dry (laughs)…

[Shashank, 38 year old gay man, when he was 8]

Several lesbian women reported keeping their hair short, wearing shirts and pants, avoiding jewellery and make-up. Some also discussed being uncomfortable going to a 'ladies parlour' and did not like waxing and other beauty treatments.

> I wanted my hair to be short. Also piercing my nose and all, I didn't like it, but that also was forced on me. And even rings and all, I didn't like them much, I can't remember if I wore them or not, I didn't like things like this, like gajra and all also. I liked to wear shirt pant but I was not allowed only... whatever girls could wear I wore, like skirts, midi, punjabi dress...
>
> [Sneha, 31 year old lesbian woman at age 11]

One of the participants compared her own growing-up experiences with that of her mother. She had heard stories about her mother being a *'late bloomer'* and having been a tomboy in her childhood and how that changed with puberty and how her mother had become beautiful and feminine as an adult woman. It was in this context that this participant spoke about her own growing up,

> When I hit 13 I wrote in my diary, nothing has happened to me. I have not blossomed into the swan, I am still the ugly duckling... because then I was like a boy, who would always have short hair, would be playing with the boys, would be on my bike, sporting some kind of a wound or the other. I was like this *mast insaan* (carefree person)...
>
> [Joanna, 40 year old lesbian woman says about her teenage years]

Discussing gender stereotypes associated with men and women, one of the participants who described himself as a 'neatness freak', someone who would take care of his skin, trim his hair neatly, be particular about his clothes, watch his weight, and whose sister was the exact opposite and would wear anything from the wardrobe, wear the same shoes for months on end, said the following:

> ... mom had this thing about introducing us to guests and she would introduce me as her daughter and my sister as her son...
>
> [Sahil, 25 year old gay man]

A lesbian woman participant talked about the stereotype of a woman's body and stated that not only would the fact of her wearing shirts and trousers, and playing with toys such as 'He-Man', draw attention, but also the fact that she was tall, was commented upon. This participant said that older members in their extended family would comment on how tall she was and how difficult it would be to find a groom for her. Another participant describes how she would fit into the stereotype of 'young men', who would be chivalrous around beautiful young women. She described her ways of relating to her women friends in their adolescence as follows,

> In my group they used to always call me the tomboy. I was always treated as the tomboy. If we went out in a taxi or something, I would be opening the door for them and that kind of stuff...
>
> [Claire, 41 year old lesbian woman says about her college years]

There are several facets to the experience of one's gender and expression of the same. These include the assignment of gender to a person at birth, based on their primary sexual characteristics, a person's sense of *felt gender* or gender orientation (what and how they see their gender to be), gender performance which occurs in an interpersonal and social space, and, finally, '*reading of*' a person's gender by others. The gender non-conformity among the participants of this study included all these facets.

One of the participants, who self-identifies as a lesbian, stated that she has often heard terms/words that imply manly, masculine, or tomboy being used by others to describe her. She said:

> ...that word that is there purshya (manly), my cousin sister would always use it on me, she still does. She says, 'tu purshya ahes' (you are manly)
>
> > [Sneha, 31 years, lesbian woman says about the time since she and her cousin were teenagers]

Almost all gay participants who were seen as effeminate in their childhood and growing-up years talked of different terms (often of abuse) used to describe their gender non-conformity. These included, '*chakka*', 'six', '*baylya*', 'sissy', and so on. One of the participants said:

> We say *randolya* for effeminate in Marwadi so my father used to keep saying are you randolya?
>
> > [Ashok, 32 year old gay man says about his childhood years]

Another participant stated:

> My sister used to call me *baylya* (effeminate) and this used to make me cry and then she would say, *kay mulin sarkha radtos*? (Why are you crying like a girl?)
>
> > [Dilip, 24 year old gay man says about his childhood]

A participant, who identifies as gay, talked about his mannerisms, his gait, and talk, being seen as effeminate by people around him. He said:

> My neighbours, whoever was there in my village, they often used to make fun of me saying, you are a guy and yet why do you talk like a girl? Why do you behave... walk like a girl?
>
> > [Amol, 34 year old gay man says about his high school years]

There were participants in this study who were completely gender-conforming and there were also those who stated that they were versatile in their gender expression, and their clothes or grooming and mannerisms could not be slotted in the gender binary of male and female. One of the participants stated that she likes to dress up in a feminine way in a certain context and at certain times, but she likes, and can carry off, shirts and pants and shoes and male attire too.

> When I was 16 to 20 years old, I was very much fem. I had really long hair. Then when I went to the US, one of my steady girlfriends didn't like me having make-up on and wanted me to try short hair and I am comfortable in both, so I cut it. Then again I grew it back, then again I cut it... so people cannot judge whether I am fem (feminine) or butch (masculine)...
>
> > [Leona, 33 year old lesbian woman, about her late teens]

## 3.2  Play, Playmates and Hobbies

Several of the participants spoke of an interest in games and hobbies that were typically associated with the opposite sex. Many gay men recalled playing games such as '*bhatukli*' or '*bhandi-kundi*' (kitchen games played by children, usually girls, with small utensils) in their childhood. Several of them talked about being interested in music, harmonium, drawing, chess, and so on. Cooking and helping out in the kitchen was reported by many participants. Interest in, and aptitude for, dance, including participating in dance competitions in school or performing at a public/social function, was quite popular among the gay men interviewed in this study.

One of the participants talked about his interest in cooking:

When I was in 5$^{th}$ Std. in school, there was this time when my mother was very ill for a while. It was at that time that I tried cooking and found it very relaxing and enjoyable. My sister was very bad at it but I was quite good. Then I started practicing regularly, especially making rotis...

[Mihir, 30 year old gay man, when he was in class 5 in school]

Two gay male participants talked about their inclination for dance from childhood, and how they saw themselves as playing the part of the woman/girl dancer. Interestingly, these performances were not undertaken in secrecy or in private, but were part of a public performance and the participants reported being appreciated for their talent. Here, it is important to note that, while effeminate behaviours for boys were generally reprimanded, the context of this gender performance was important. In both the quotes below, gender transgression was seen as ability/talent and took place within the context of a community event and an annual school gathering. Thus, the allowance for, or even celebration of gender transgression in this context is possible primarily because this transgression is viewed as part of performance and talent and certainly not personhood or an attribute of the self. The age of the participants is also important. As will be discussed later in the chapter, at a younger age, the pressure for gender conformity is lower, and these behaviours were even seen as 'cute', or habits that the boys will eventually grow out of.

...so I used to dance to Sridevi numbers...when there was something happening in the colony and they would put big speakers, then I used to go dance and since I danced well, everyone would move aside and I would be dancing in the center and everybody else would watch me. Those days there were films like Nagina and all that were on, so I used to do the nagin (snake) dance and I felt that I was only the ichadari nagin (human who can transform into a snake and vice versa) (laughs) and when my mom used to fight with me I used to tell her that mi tula dasen (I will sting you) (laughs)...

[Mansoor, 33 year old gay man, when he was 11 years old]

when we were in 5$^{th}$ std., we had some gathering happening and in that sir had set a dance in which we all had to be girls. At that time we had gotten so involved in the practice, we all had started speaking *aga-tuga* (using female pronoun for each other)... even sir used to tease us saying, *kuthe geli majhi heroine?* (Where is my heroine?)

[Dilip, 24 year old gay man, when he was in 5$^{th}$ Class in school]

Most of the lesbian women recalled being interested in sports and outdoor activities, such as football, cricket, climbing trees, riding bicycle and going on trips in the rain, playing pranks and so on.

> I used to play with my brother's *He-Man* (a cartoon character) and I hated dolls. I would either throw them or break their arms…
>
> [Mithun, 35 year old lesbian woman says this about herself when she was about 8 years old]

> My dad was the fun guy… we would go riding on bikes and go fly planes. He would teach me how to play gulli-danda, marbles; everything he taught me…
>
> [Joanna, 40 year old lesbian woman talks about her pre-teen years]

Several gay men talked about being most comfortable in the company of girls and doing things with them such as sitting together chatting, playing indoor games, eating together in school breaks, and so on. Many of them reported being uncomfortable in the company of boys who would play macho games or engage in physical exercise.

> My friendship used to be better with girls than with boys. I was not fitting in with the boys standards. With girls, I liked their company, they all used to call each other *aga* (female pronoun in Marathi) and I also started calling everyone around me *aga* only… *mazya sentence chi melody mulin sarkhi hoti* (the melody in my sentences was like girls)
>
> [Mansoor, 33 year old gay man about his early teenage years]

> I used to be mostly friends with girls but then after 6th Std., I started mingling little bit with the boys. I used to play some cricket or kabaddi with them but they would tease and taunt so much that later I stopped playing with them
>
> [Salil, 28 year old gay man]

A significant theme that many gay participants shared was that of dislike for traditionally masculine sports such as football, cricket, tennis, and the pressure they had to face from family members (usually fathers) as well as peers to play these games. Experiences of teasing, bullying, and taunts about disinterest in these 'boy/ outdoor' games, caused high levels of distress for many of the gay participants.

One of the participants, whose grandfather, father, and uncles, have been professional cricket players talked about the difficult time he had in avoiding this game. He said:

> I was pushed towards it and I hated it that much more… I didn't like the game. I found it was too boring, I didn't understand the rules and I certainly didn't want to play it. Frankly I was scared… you see a ball coming towards you at that speed, I would duck for cover, I found it very scary. So that was another thing, when I ducked for cover my father would say, 'stop being a girl'!
>
> [Avinash, 28 year old gay man says this about the time between 8/9 years to 16/17 years]

> … and the tennis session would be like for an hour and every 10 minutes I used to check my watch and think I will get to go in another 40 minutes, in another 30 minutes and things like that…
>
> [Amit, 33 year old gay man talks about the time when he was in 8th Std.]

Many of the lesbian participants too discussed about their comfort in playing with boys and some stated that they disliked doing girly things while growing up. One of the participants talked about how suffocated she felt with all the girly stuff. While noting that they had many male friends, some participants also pointed out that, around the time of puberty, their interactions with boys underwent a shift and they started spending more time with girls. While these participants did not state that this shift was enforced upon them by family members or other authority figures, they stated that there was a strong expectation of gender segregation between boys and girls post-puberty, which impacted their interactions with their male peers.

One of the participants, who would play football and go cycling with her brother and his mates said:

Till about the 7th or 8th Std., I did that. Then after that, things changed... I think socialization happened (laughs) so I stopped playing with the boys and started taking walks with my best friend, and we started doing more girly things like sitting around in groups and talking... It happens almost automatically...after some time, even the boys stop wanting to play with you... you know with someone, who is probably developing breasts...

[Pradnya, 33 year old lesbian woman talks about her teen years]

The suggestion in the above narrative, of '*things changing*' with puberty, implying increased prescription of gender normative behaviours as well as increased surveillance of girls after they have attained puberty, is linked with the emergence of sexuality, it's control, and the expectation and preparation for heterosexual marriage and motherhood. At this time, norms around appropriate gender roles and sexuality become much more explicit and clear; gender segregation being one such norm referred to in the above quote.

The limited research that does exist, mostly in the western context, on gender non-conformity in children, indicates that gender non-conformity in boys is much more devalued and pressures to conformity are much higher on 'sissy boys' than on 'tomboy' girls (Martin 1990). Several explanations for this are proposed, including the status differential hypothesis, or the social status model that suggests that differences in social status between male and female gender roles influence the way men and women are viewed when they violate gender-based norms (Feinman 1981, 1984; Rosenkrantz et al. 1968). Since a higher level of social status and prestige is associated with the male gender role, men departing from the highly valued and socially sanctioned masculine gender norms are seen as losing status, and are perceived more negatively than a gender non-conforming woman moving into a highly valued male role (Feinman 1981). However, this does not necessarily translate as 'tomboy' girls being rewarded for their gender transgressions. In fact, the control over girls and regulation of their behaviours increases with puberty, as discussed earlier. Another explanation for the differential evaluation of cross-sex behaviours in boys and girls is the belief that '*girls grow out of it*' and learn gender-appropriate behaviours with puberty, but that boys with gender non-conformity in childhood are more likely to become gay as adults. Herek (1994) and McCreary (1994) proposed a Sexual Orientation Model to explain why gender role transgressions in men are less tolerated than that in women. Sirin et al. (2004)

state, 'The basis for this model comes from prior research showing that feminine-typed gender role characteristics in men, as opposed to masculine-typed gender role characteristics in women, increased the likelihood of men, but not women, being perceived as homosexual' (120).

Finally, among the gay men and the lesbian women who participated in this study, there were also participants who adhered closely to their assigned gender script. So, there were gay men who enjoyed sports such as football, and there were lesbian women who wore their hair long, liked to do make-up, and enjoyed doing things that are typically associated with femininity, such as cooking and keeping house.

> I would say football, I loved but I was interested in everything. I was as comfortable cooking as I was playing sports or fighting. In school you have to take part in everything as nothing was optional. So I did crafts, needle work, cooking, sports. Though I didn't like craft, I liked sports.
>
> [Abhijit, 35 year old gay man talks about his schooling years]

Thus, there were those who followed their assigned gender script and many who transgressed that script, and then there were also narratives with a mix of conformity and non-conformity. I have highlighted the narratives of non-conformity to draw attention to the 'difference' that these participants experienced during their childhood and growing-up years. All these narratives are a stark reminder of the gendered nature of our private and public lives. Gender seems to determine everything from clothes, hair, jewellery, gait, and speech, to hobbies, play, and playmates. Rigid boundaries of what are seen as normative gender expressions, and the division of all gender expressions and roles into the binary of man and woman, were experienced by most participants as a major stressor in their growing-up years. Several of the participants discussed a sense of fear, confusion, and loneliness, due to the ways in which their gender expressions were read and responded to. Studies indicate that there may be a link between parental and peer rejection of childhood gender non-conformity, and long-term psychological consequences, including poor psychological well-being in adulthood (Landolt et al. 2004; Beard and Bakeman 2000).

## 3.3    Correction of Gender Non-conformity

The narratives reveal that transgressions from the gender normative script evoked '*corrective*' responses from several quarters. In childhood, most of the correction was targeted at gender non-conformity and after adolescence, with the emergence of sexual desires and increased moral pressure and surveillance around sexuality, correction efforts were targeted towards same-sex sexuality. Family, followed by school, emerged as the most normativizing force in the lives of the participants. The interplay of constant messages of 'you are not ok' from various sources from childhood onwards, meant that several of the participants engaged in self-correction behaviours believing themselves to be abnormal. In several instances, participants (usually as adolescents or young adults) themselves sought, or were taken to, professionals—doctors, psychiatrists, counsellors—for correction/cure of their 'abnormal' gender and sexual expressions.

- **Self-initiated correction of gender non-conformity and same-sex sexual attraction**

Self-initiated correction seems to be motivated by a psychic struggle between what feels like a comfortable, self-affirming, expression of one's gender and sexuality, and what society prescribes as normative and therefore, acceptable, gender and sexual expression. Under self-initiated correction, individuals who transgress norms of gender and sexuality may make an effort to 'correct', and hence 'fit in' with their assigned gender script and normative heterosexual interests. Self-initiated correction may be seen as being motivated by an internalization of negative messages regarding one's gender and sexual expression, and hence can be viewed as a form of internalized homonegativity/homophobia from a psychological perspective. On the other hand, from a structuralist lens—specifically the Foucauldian idea of governmentality (as discussed in Pyne 2014) that refers to a range of control techniques that fashion, shape, produce, normative gender and sexuality—self-initiated correction can be seen as a result of self-government. Self-government here implies governmentality reaching its ultimate form, wherein individuals begin to internalize the panoptic surveillance, or external eye, that moralizes and disciplines their behaviours, and in accordance alter/change/self-cure their deviance to achieve a better fit and be included.

Among the participants of this study, self-correction included attempts at correcting own mannerisms, gait, speech, choice of clothes, colour, and so on. At times, it also included efforts to 'hide' parts of themselves that they learnt could be labelled as gender transgressive and then there were also efforts to cover up their gender non-conformity and an attempt to 'pass' as 'normal'. Similarly, there were efforts at trying to find or fake sexual interest in the opposite sex, including going on dates and trying out a 'girlfriend-boyfriend' relationship in college. Research with LGBT adolescents states that a great deal of the psychic energy of LGBT youth is consumed in working out stigma-management strategies. This can negatively impact development and emotional well-being (Evans and Levine 1990).

> I made a lot of efforts to ensure that I behave like a boy. I practiced also a lot to walk like a boy. But when I walked, it used to be like a girl. My hips would sway like a girl. It was naturally that way…
>
> [Amol, 34 years, says about his teenage years]

Another participant described his motivation for self-correction:

> I was strongly effeminate before. I guess I did change stuff about myself. Because I was academically really good I would have friends, but in order to keep them, or then because people would laugh or then would talk in the corner, all that used to hurt me… that is why, I guess
>
> [Mansoor, 33 year old, says about his postgraduate college years]

'Straight acting' or 'passing' refers to concealing parts of one's self and life that one recognises as non-normative in terms of gender or sexuality. Paradoxically, while concealing one's stigmatising attribute is a coping mechanism, aimed at avoiding the negative consequences of stigma, this hiding can be extremely stressful (Miller and Major 2000). Smart and Wegner (2000) describe the cost of hiding in terms of the resultant cognitive burden involved in the constant preoccupation with hiding. The inner experience of the person who is hiding a concealable stigma has been described by them as "living in a private hell" (229). Strategies described in literature for 'passing' include: lying in order to be seen as heterosexual; covering, which involves censoring clues about one's self; being implicitly 'out' which involves telling the truth without using explicit language (Griffin 1992).

Participants in this study discussed different strategies of 'passing' such as watching straight pornography with friends and pretending to enjoy it, participating in talking about girls in a sexualized manner in all-male peer groups, trying out relationships with or pretending to be in a relationship with members of the opposite sex, feigning interest in sports or other macho activities, and so on.

> I might have held a bat, but it has never happened that I have hit a four or six (Laughs). I used to go to show the boys that you like cricket, and therefore, I also like cricket. But, I never liked it one bit (Laughs) I don't like playing or even watching those manly games. I used to go, just to show them… whenever I was in a group and if some girl passed by, they used to say, wow! What a girl! so, I also used to say, 'Wow! What a girl!'
>
> [Amol, 34 years old, says about his college years]

> I was 19 then and there was so much of peer pressure… I was inflicting so much pain on myself and then I thought that I should have a girl friend. So I was unnecessarily flirting with this one girl, which was then successful unfortunately! It was a very very confusing time…
>
> [Mansoor, 33 years, says this about his college years when he was 19]

Another aspect of 'passing', as described by one of the participants, is that of avoiding others who are like oneself: boys trying to 'fit in' and fighting the label of being 'sissy' may avoid other boys who are seen as effeminate. The motivation to do this comes from an internalization of society's negative attitudes towards gender transgressive persons and an attempt at distancing oneself from the very traits that may put one at risk of being labelled 'sissy' and effeminate.

> I consciously stayed away from boys who were effeminate… I used to be scared of these people because somewhere that concern is there na… You like to fit into people's standard only…There was a hijra in our chawl called Heera and her parents liked me a lot, but I never spoke to her in my life…
>
> [Mansoor, 33 years, says about his junior college, when he was about 17 years old]

This experience is, in fact, in stark opposition to the idea of 'finding community' and reduced isolation that I describe in chapter six, that many have referred to as an important step in developing a healthy and positive sense of self. It highlights the role of working through internalized homonegativity as well as resources—psychic, social, and political in nature—that individuals may gather as they grow up.

Finally, as stated by one of the lesbian women, several of the participants had learnt early in life that their gender inappropriate interests in make-up and dolls (for boys), outdoor and risk-taking games (for girls), as well as their interest, curiosity, and attraction to persons of the same sex was unacceptable in their social context. Hence, they learnt, at times, to deny themselves these or, at times, hide these.

> ... unfortunately somewhere you do have that recognition, that probably what you are doing, although it is very pleasurable and good fun and you are enjoying it very much, it is not correct, you know, you grow up believing that...
>
> [Pradnya, 33 years, about graduate college years, when she was about 18/19 years old]

- **Correction by parents**

Parental responses to gender non-conforming behaviours were described by several participants as confusing. Gender non-conformity in terms of wearing frocks, make-up, dancing and cooking among boys, and wearing shirts, climbing trees, and riding bikes among girls were initially encouraged by parents and other elders at home. However, as the children grew older the expectation of gender normative behaviours became stricter, and non-conformity evoked reprimanding responses. Several gay male participants stated that their 'cross dressing', make-up and putting up a dance show was in fact appreciated, even encouraged and often seen as 'cute' within their family and school, when they were younger. One of the participants stated that he recalls doing some of these activities with his other male cousins during vacation. However, as they were growing up, the cousins stopped playing with dolls or cross-dressing, but the participant wanted to continue. Many of the gay male participants reported a sense of confusion resulting from the ambivalent responses of parents towards their cross-dressing. Another participant stated that his interest in cooking was initially encouraged by his parents. However, as he was growing up, the pressure to play outdoor sports, make friends with other boys, and not spend too much time at home or the kitchen increased.

Research on parental responses to their gay or lesbian children has pointed out that same-sex parents often have greater difficulty in accepting their son or daughter's same-sex sexual orientation and gender non-conformity. Thus, fathers have a harder time dealing with their son's gayness, and mothers have a difficult time dealing with their lesbian daughters. This finding can be explained by the fact that usually it is the same-sex parent that blames themselves most for not imparting 'appropriate' gender roles and sexuality related messages to their child. According to tenets of both sexism and heterosexism, the traditional role expectation from mothers is to "pass the baton of traditional woman's role to her daughters" (Rosen 1992 in Ritter and Terndrup 2002, 305). It is the power of this precept that may cause a sense of 'personal failure' in the mother and make it challenging for her to be receptive of a gender-role discordant daughter, possibly causing lack of mutual empathy between a heterosexual mother and a lesbian daughter. With respect to fathers, Herek (1988) points out that attitudes of heterosexual males towards male homosexuality is often much more negative than that of heterosexual women. This is due to the fact that gender non-conformity in men tends to threaten core male gender identity, male roles, or heterosexual masculinity (Herek 1986).

In the present study, most gay men, who were labelled as 'sissy' or seen as effeminate, described their relationship with their fathers as strained. In an attempt to inculcate and reinforce masculine, macho behaviours in their sons, fathers used several methods including name calling, shouting, shaming, forcing their sons to play outdoor games, sending their son to a military school with the hope that the army discipline and role-modelling would change the child, reprimanding the child for playing with dolls or wearing lipstick, and so on.

> I was sent to a military school after 5th std. It was an only-boys school. I didn't like the environment there at all. There was extreme discipline there. We used to have a khaki dress, half pant and half shirt. I didn't like that. At St. Andrews (earlier school) it was ok to wear anything, even casuals…
>
> [Mansoor, 33 years about the time he was in 5th class in school]

> Almost every evening ya… I would dread him coming back from work because he would find me sitting there in front of the TV, munching on something or reading a book and he was like aaj bhi tum khelne nahi gaye? (you haven't gone out to play even today?)… what a disappointment you are!
>
> [Avinash, 28 years old, says about all his schooling years]

One of the participants described an incident with his father, after which he took a large dose of medicine meant for cold and cough in an attempt at self-harm;

> That was when my father had torn up all my photos of Madhuri Dixit. He tore all my photographs and he threw away my creams, my fair and lovely cream…
>
> [Ashok, 32 year old, says about the time when he was 12 years old]

Violent responses and surveillance by family members, of gender atypicality and same-sex sexuality in their children, has been documented in other studies in India as well (Fernandez and Gomathy 2003; Joseph 2005; Ghosh et al. 2011; CREA 2012; Shah et al. 2015).

In a few other situations, the fathers did not necessarily react in a violent manner. They were concerned and anxious about the future of their child and firmly believed that being effeminate or being attracted to other boys was abnormal and deviant and needed to be set right. One of the participants, who was effeminate since childhood and was often scared to interact with groups of boys and instead preferred to interact with girls, recalls his father's reaction when he came to know about his son's sexual preference. This father was very religious-minded and hence encouraged the son to pray for these traits to vanish or to be cured.

> They tell me to do naam smaran (chanting name of God). Do yoga and all so these thoughts will go… They say go to the Swami Samarth Math, go to the temple. There is Gondolekar Maharaj na, he asks me to listen to his pravachans (sermons), he tells me to chant shree ram jai ram and those feelings will go…
>
> [Sandip, 24 years old, a few months before the interview]

This form of correction is another example of power being used not in a coercive, brutal fashion, but instead as a productive one, aimed at shaping the behaviour of the son, with the ultimate goal of self-government as described earlier. Yet another example of this is that of mothers of lesbian women focusing on encouraging their daughters to look and act more feminine. Thus, there was emphasis on longer hair length, piercing ears and nose, wearing make-up, wearing *salwar kameez* and so on. There were a few instances where mothers discouraged their daughters from being friends with or engaging with other girls whose gender expression they read as masculine.

Disapproval by mothers and their way of communicating the same was often subtle, but it did have a deep impact on the participants. One participant recalls a time when her mother decided to give her a surprise visit at her hostel in undergraduate college. The participant, who now identifies as a lesbian, was sleeping with one of her girlfriends on the same bed in the hostel, when her mother arrived. On seeing them together, the participant's mother only made one comment, but this had a major impact on the participant.

> I still remember the expression on her face, when she saw that woman and me get out of bed. I remember she said only one thing… tu phar anga anga shi kartes (you stick to her too much). It has stayed with me, I mean I still remember it, I still remember the words and the way she looked at us.
>
> [Pradnya, 33 years, said about her hostel years in undergraduate college, when she was about 18 years old]

Gay men too recalled a few instances of correction of their gender non-conformity by their mothers. However, correction initiated by mothers was often less aggressive and usually was made as a suggestion. One of the participants described his shock and sense of despair when his mother commented on the way he swayed his hips and danced. He had never expected his mother to reprimand or disapprove of him. He said:

> I was doing some… not even dance, some dance like thing, and she sort of reacted for the first time. She said, 'that's not how guys behave'… I was like completely shocked that mom is saying that. *Duniya to thik hai,* but her? (World says it anyway, but her?) I remember crying like crazy. I was completely inconsolable
>
> [Vinay, 36 year old gay man said about the time when he was 13 years old]

Marriage as a solution to same-sex attractions as well as gender non-confirming behaviours was suggested by both parents, as well as siblings in some instances, to both gay men and lesbian women. For instance, the elder sister of one of the lesbian women interviewed in this study told her after her break-up with her girlfriend that "she should just forget about this girl, burn all her letters, and say yes to the next proposal and get married".

The theme of greater surveillance and regulation of gender and sexual expressions around puberty for both lesbian women and gay men repeatedly came up in the participant narratives. While control over sexuality of young women may be stricter, gender corrective responses of young men were equally harsh, particularly by fathers and other men in their lives. This overall prescriptive and corrective approach of sexuality and gender can be understood in the context of reinforcing the ideology of reproductive heteronormativity. The institution of the 'natural family', or family defined by 'blood ties', is the primary source of socialization for its young members and one of its major tasks is to reproduce existing social hierarchies and norms; these include compulsory endogamous and reproductive marriage for all and maintenance of the 'pure' lineage of the heterosexual family unit. Parental corrective responses need to be viewed in this context. Rao (2005) points out that the family, which is seen as a space of nurturance, care, emotion and affect, is simultaneously also a space of regulating emotion, intimacy, and self-expression; it is this regulatory function of the family that is being highlighted here under parental correction and so is the thwarting of the lesbian/gay child's expectation of parental approval and nurturance.

- **Medical correction of non-normative gender and sexual expression**

Pyne (2014) discusses problematization and normalization as two important tools of surveillance. It is through the problematization—producing a problem—of gender non-conformity, or homosexuality, that professionals would then proceed to create a solution for the problem: a clinical sub-specialty of experts dealing with deviance in gender and sexuality or at least a basket of interventions to address this problem. Normalization refers to regulating behaviours through norms (Foucault 1979). Pyne (2014) suggests that normalization "governs families with gender non-conforming children through the administration of shame and desire, drawing them into an enclosure of power relations with clinicians and producing an efficient form of *self-governance*" (87). There has been a long history within the medical and mental health sciences of medicalization and pathologization of behaviours that do not fit within the rigid boundaries of the gender binary and heterosexual sex, as well as treatments aimed at 'cure' and correction of the same (Narrain and Chandran 2015; also see discussion on medicalization of homosexuality in chapter one).

In this study, some of the participants themselves sought the help of experts to deal with their confusion, anxieties, and questions about being different. Some attempted self-correction, even sought a cure for their condition and made efforts at changing themselves. In several cases, participants were asked to try different kinds of cures. Apart from participants themselves seeking help from experts, parents, siblings, and friends, sought expert help to facilitate change in or find a cure for sexual and gender expression. The context of seeking professional help was, at times, parental shock on having learnt about their child's sexual orientation and, in some cases, the parents' belief that their child was abnormal and needed treatment.

> My father responded by saying, 'Just pray to god, everything will be fine'. He said, 'we will take you to the best psychiatrist, we will take you abroad if necessary, we will treat you, don't worry... just pray to god, have faith'
>
> [Vineet, 40 year old gay man, when he came out at the age of 29]

So what my father wanted then was that no matter what, I should be better and whatever it takes, pills or operation or whatever, will be done but I should become alright and I should get married...

[Ranjita, 26 year old lesbian woman, a year before the interview]

Friends, who were unsure and, at times, ignorant about LGBT issues suggested that the participant talk to a counsellor. For instance, one of the participants stated that her friends asked her to speak with the college in-house counsellor.

I kind of told a few friends and then they suggested that I go and talk to Father Fernandez. I told him I am here because my friends asked me to come and talk to you and he told me that don't be averse to guys, try your best to keep an open mind, maybe because you don't talk much to guys, maybe that's why...

[Jemsy, 30 year old lesbian woman talks about her undergraduate college experience, when she was 19 years old]

The husband of one of the participants who later self-identified as lesbian spoke to her gynaecologist that she was not being a good wife, that she had anger issues and that she was disinterested in sex. The gynaecologist then called the participant and the participant said:

I was angry that he went behind my back and talked about this. I frankly told the doctor that I was not in love with him and he does not satisfy me sexually. *Me maza me karun ghete* (I do it for myself/ satisfy myself sexually). The doctor than said, 'many women do this and you are one of them and almost 70-80% women do it (satisfy themselves). So it is really not a problem that way but just don't tell anyone'. She told me that I should do anything I like but I should keep it to myself...

[Sneha, 31 years old, says this at 28]

Responses from the doctors and counsellors varied. There were psychiatrists who referred the participant for a hormone test, believing that testosterone deficit was the cause of effeminate behaviours. There were others who suggested that participants watch straight/heterosexual pornography to cure themselves. However, there were also those who advised the participants' parents to seek counselling to get comfortable with their son/daughter's sexual orientation rather than trying to change/cure them.

When my mom had found out, she had taken me to the psychiatrist, in 8th Standard only... the doctor kept saying this is a western phenomenon. He said it doesn't happen here, so I was wondering, if this doesn't happen here, how come it happened with me? And he kept saying it is a phase...

[Parul, 34 year old talks about the time when she was in Class 8th]

One of the participants, who underwent testosterone test to detect the cause of his effeminate behaviours, said:

The tests came out all normal. I was then given medicines to reduce my thoughts about sex and suicide… I used to be very disturbed those days and would often think of ending my life. The doctor told my parents that if I wanted, I could be cured in 2 years and that I could get married. He also told me that if I wanted to, I could watch blue films, with men and women in it

[Sandip, 24 years, a few months before the interview]

Historically, homosexuality had been viewed as a sexual perversion and a form of mental disorder. However, since 1973, the American Psychiatric Association declassified homosexuality as a form of mental illness. Subsequently, the WHO did the same in 1992 and recently the Indian Psychiatric Society stated that homosexuality was a normal sexual variant and not in need of correction or treatment (Rao and Jacob 2012). Despite this international and national position of medical doctors, several health and mental health professionals continue varied practices aimed at 'curing' homosexuality (Ranade 2015; Kalra 2012).

- **School as a space for correction of non-normative gender and sexual expression**

Studies with LGBT youth suggest that school is a major site of homophobic name-calling, bullying and labelling (Equality Challenge Unit 2009; Poteat and Espelage 2005). Victimization of lesbian and gay youth has been identified across elementary school (Solomon 2004), high school (Thurlow 2001) and university (Janoff 2005) settings. Limited evidence suggests that sexual minority youth lack supportive family, friends, and teachers (Warwich et al. 2001; Williams et al. 2005) and experience more victimization and isolation within their families and in schools (Garofalo et al. 1998). A study from India, focussing on lived realities of queer persons, found schools to be both an escape from the hostile, and often violent, family environment, as well as a violently normativizing institution that enforced strict norms of gender and sexuality (Nevatia et al. 2012).

Most participants in my study stated that their gender transgressions or sexual interests were marked as inappropriate and they received messages of correction from various sources in the school. These included teachers, principals, matrons, sports coaches, and classmates/other students. Most of the messages were similar and therefore reinforced the ones given by parents at home. These centred on reinforcing and repeating the need to adhere to gender stereotypes in areas such as dress, gait, speech, interests and other mannerisms.

One of the participants stated that he had become friends with a few other effeminate boys in school after they all performed together in a school dance. He said that the principal of the school did not like this group of effeminate boys. In this context the participant said:

He (principal) used to call us to his office and he was like *'kadak bol! asa kai boltoy? marda sarkha bol! baki pora kai mantil'*… (talk like a man, what are you talking like this for?, what will the other boys say?)

[Mahesh, 30 year old talks about the time when he was in 6th Std.]

Another participant, who was studying in a boarding school at the time, recounts an occasion when she was undergoing a lot of stress and had harmed herself by slashing her wrist. This incident took place after she heard that her then girlfriend was being forced to get married. At this time, the matron of her hostel dorm was very sympathetic and asked her if there was any stress at home or any other problem. When the participant told her about her relationship with her girlfriend, the matron became very angry and beat her severely. After this, the participant was humiliated in front of the whole hostel by asking her to publicly pray for forgiveness for her same-sex desires.

> We had prayer meetings every night so the same matron called me from my room. She said come and attend the prayers and I went in my night dress and girls of the entire hostel were attending the prayer meeting. So when I came in she said, 'we have to tell you guys something'. So she was like 'girls, she wants to confess something, that she is in love with a girl and that's why her state is like this right now and she is going to let you know that this is never going to happen ever again and she is going to be normal like us…'
>
> [Leona, 33 years, talks about the time, when she was in 11<sup>th</sup> Std.]

There were other participants who reported that they managed to escape with minor reproach and warnings from teachers and other school staff. One of the participants, who stayed in a hostel, recalls that in their school there were strict rules about seniors and juniors not being allowed to mingle together. On one occasion, when it was a '*passing out*' party of their seniors and the seniors were all well dressed, the participant broke the rule and went to the party venue to click pictures of this senior, whom she had a crush on. Another participant reported that she and another girl were once caught kissing by a member of the school staff. On both these occasions, the participants did receive warnings and were reprimanded, but, according to them, these behaviours were also treated by the school authorities as part of growing up and adolescent experiments. Similarly, several participants talked about flirting, exchange of love notes and greeting cards with classmates and friends whom they had a crush on. Thus, school was a space which included strong heterosexual messages and strict surveillance of sexuality; at the same time, in some instances, it was also a space that could be manipulated to disrupt its disciplinary gaze and create spaces for exploration of the self, including the transgressive queer self.

Some of the participants reported that it was in the school space where they first met someone like themselves. This meeting another person/s who was also seen as being gender transgressive had multiple meanings for different participants. Some have talked about actively avoiding others like themselves because being seen with another person who is gender transgressive calls attention to one's own transgressions and makes one more vulnerable to bullying. One of the participants talked about becoming friends with other effeminate boys in school, which reduced the sense of isolation he felt at home. In fact, in the group, there was a sense of cohesion, and they had found out ways of looking out for each other in the face of bullying at school.

Classmates and peers in school often taunted, bullied, and teased effeminate boys. One of the participants recalls the bullying and teasing that he underwent in school from classmates and seniors at school. This bullying, according to the participant, was somewhat under check in the presence of the class teacher or the prefect of the class; however, the same class mates were also at the participant's tuition class, and he describes the helplessness he felt while facing this bullying at school and at tuition, and having no safe space to talk about it:

> All the time… this whole time, maybe from the 6th or 7th standard onwards, I was feeling alone because I could not talk to anyone about it. I wanted to come back home and tell because I was in tears so many times, I just wanted to tell that this is what was happening in school, can you help me?
>
> [Avinash, 28 year old gay man, when he was in 6th Std.]

Quite often, the girl/woman friends in college advised participants (who later self-identified as lesbian) to try out sex with boys/men:

> Many of my women friends would say, have you ever tried a male? I say no! They always advice me to try sex with a man and I am like why are you telling me to? I am happy with what I have but they are like you will know what you are missing only then
>
> [Salma, 30 year old lesbian woman talks about her undergraduate years when she was 21 years old]

Several of the lesbian participants reported that, while the pressure to have a boyfriend or try sex with them was not always obvious, it operated in many subtle ways. Being feminine, seen as desirable to men, having a boyfriend, were all factors that made one popular. One of the participants talked about how this subtle, understated, expectation of being sexually active with a man led her to experiment with boyfriends.

> When in college, I started exploring with men because I was like everyone has had sex but me. Without realising that I have had sex, just not peno-vaginal sex. So I decided, I want to experiment with men. I was comfortable but it was not like mind blowing…
>
> [Vidya, 35 years, in her postgraduate years, when she was 22 years old]

> In college, I went out a lot, mostly with men, drank a lot and had sex, though I didn't like it. I was comfortable with whatever was happening, but I knew something was wrong. I kept feeling that all the men I had been with were bad kissers and nothing about them turned me on (laughs)
>
> [Mithun, 35 years says this at 21 years]

## 3.4  Emergence of Sexuality and Sexual Exploration

Adolescence has been described as a period of 'storm and stress' implying major physical, emotional, personality changes and intense struggles to define one's sense of self, personal value system and an independent place in society (Erikson 1950). Adolescents explore their beliefs, attitudes, behaviours, and roles in a broad range of life areas, including sexuality and sexual orientation. Among heterosexual youth, the search for sexual identity is primarily focused on relationship issues: intimacy; finding sex partners; exploring sexual arousal; determining what is sexually pleasurable and desirable; and ultimately, establishing committed and mutually respectful relationships. Exploring whether or not one has a heterosexual orientation is seldom part of a heterosexual adolescent's identity search (Rotheram-Borus and Fernandez 1995). In contrast, the exploration of sexual orientation is highly salient for gay and lesbian youth. In the absence of affirmative images or language for LG sexuality, exploring one's sexual feelings, fantasy, and experience, and finding a language of pleasure, desire, and diversity, while fighting labels of abnormality and perversion, becomes critical in the journey of sexual exploration for LG adolescents. Unlike their heterosexual peers, gay and lesbian youth face tremendous social pressures to deny or reject their sexual feelings, actions, and thoughts.

In this study, the awakening of sexuality, or experiencing oneself as a sexual being occurred for participants at different ages and through different sources. Some describe becoming aware of their sexuality through fantasy and attraction towards the 'hero/heroine' in movies that they grew up on. Some stated that they felt drawn towards teachers in school or a friend or their school bench partner. Others talked about exploring own bodies, sexual fantasy, and masturbation. Participants talked about sexual exploration with a friend during sleepover nights or while spending time together studying, or with a cousin during vacation when all the children in the family were together.

> When I saw any scene related to sex in cinema, I used to get aroused and I used to get aroused seeing men in such an act. I did not see the woman in it. I remember this film Dharamveer, which had both Jeetandra and Dharmendra and strangely it was the villain who was having sex with his girlfriend. Pran I think. I was not exactly attracted to Pran but I think the male body, showed nude in the film attracted me
>
> [Mansoor, 33, says when in school, around 8-9th Std]

Sexual fantasy even before or in the absence of a sexual experience was described as crucial in awareness about one's sexuality. Participants talked about fantasizing about actors, sportsmen/women, models. Some of them talked about not having access to internet while growing up, nor having any access to gay/lesbian pornography. In this context, as stated by one of the participants, 'imagination associated with sexual arousal played an important role'. One of the participants talked of drawing sketches and learning painting as he was growing up.

> One of the major things that crystallised my identity for me and helped me to say that I seem to like guys was when I was sketching... I used to sketch and I was learning a bit of painting... I realised that I was sketching more male than female nudes.
>
> [Atul, 33 year old said about the time when he was 18 years old]

> My dad had this set of porn novels and I laid my hand on it. They were not too graphic and were written with no pictures. It was straight porn of course! I realized that I was excited at

the part about the guys undressing… Even in my fantasy, I used to fantasize about a man instead of a woman. I did not know that there was a term for it or anything. It was a new thing for me.

[Ajay, 32 years, when in class 9^{th}]

A lesbian participant spoke about her attraction for her teacher and fantasizing about her:

She was an English teacher. I was just crazy about her then. I used to fantasize about her at night and I fantasized touching her boobs and it was quite thrilling.

[Mithun, 35, when in class 10^{th}]

Sexual exploration with friends, relatives, cousins, boys in the neighbourhood, strangers, as well as exploration of one's own body, erogenous zones, and masturbation, were reported as significant in the process of developing awareness of one's sexuality. This exploration occurred while the participants met with their friends or school mates after school for completing homework, or during sleepover nights, while watching blue films with friends, in hostels, in trains, while discussing questions related to sex, nightfall, and masturbation, among peers and so on.

In college we (all guys) used to watch blue films together and then regularly shag together. It was a done thing. Once after a film this friend and me, we went to the terrace as we wanted to masturbate… that time I shagged him and it was raining and it was beautiful. I realized then that I wanted to have 'body sex' with him… before that I did not know that I am attracted to the male body…

[Shailesh, 35, when in undergraduate college, age 19]

Interestingly, the gay participants described experiences of sexual exploration in public spaces with known and unknown persons such as trains, buses, colleges, and hostel terraces. Access to these public spaces was a significant factor that shaped the trajectory of sexual explorations for several male participants. Many of them also talked about learning more about the 'gay cruising scene' in the city during these chance encounters with strangers in public spaces.

Once I started college, I had to travel by train from Vile Parle to Byculla [name of local train stations] everyday… I was introduced to the famous fondling that happens on Bombay local trains… I was this young boy, so people coming up to me and trying to touch me here and there… I never found it objectionable… I enjoyed other people doing things to me and in some time when I gathered some courage, I did things to other people as well…

[Atul, 33, at 18 years]

Several male participants also talked about experiences of violence, fear of being caught/seen, police blackmail while they accessed public spaces for sex. Thus, while there was access to public spaces, violence in cruising areas and on the streets, where one is openly being gay or is seen as being sexual with men and boys, was a threat that some participants discussed. Several reports describe accounts of violence in public spaces against gay men, MSM, *kothi*s, male sex workers (PUCL-K 2001; Voices Against 377 2005; Chakrapani et al. 2007).

Among lesbian women, most of the sexual encounters they described had been with known persons such as friends, someone in the neighbourhood, a senior at school, and the like, and all of this occurred within private spaces. This finding is in line with the social reality of lesser mobility, and restricted access to public spaces, for women in all aspects of their lives, and especially so when it comes to being sexual. Also research on early sexual exploration among sexual minority women indicates that, often the first same-sex sexual attraction and sexual contact for them is with close friends, and emotional intimacy and the 'friendship script' remain important themes in their choice of lovers even later in their lives (Rose et al. 1993; Savin-Williams and Diamond 2000).

In societies with strict gender segregation—with strict rules regarding socialization between men and women, wherein men and women mostly lead separate lives with very few common/shared spaces, in the public as well as the private sphere—homosociality, that is, more concentrated and intense socialization among members of the same sex, is high. This is described by participants in this study too. Participants stated that their intense involvement with a friend of the same sex often was not seen as sexual and hence did not receive much rebuttal but also remained hidden, not only from others but even from themselves. One of the participants stated that she had a girlfriend for three years in school and they would spend all their time together, in and after school; they would hold hands and even kiss. She recollects that they had even exchanged greeting cards to celebrate the anniversaries of their relationship. However, they never talked about it as a sexual/romantic relationship even among themselves. Another lesbian woman participant spoke about her relationship with her women friends:

I was attracted to women and this friend and I, we even started exploring each other's bodies... I think at that time I wasn't aware of what it was. But in college I started getting very possessive of my girl friends, who I really liked and I didn't understand why...

[Mehek, 28, when in college at 22]

While homosociality would explain the social acceptance to intense same-sex friendship bonds, research on adolescent same-sex friendships of lesbian, bisexual and unlabelled women by Diamond (2007) indicates that adolescent friendships among young girls often involve intense feelings and behaviours associated with romantic relationships, and may be indicative of the fact that women in general are more open to emotional and physical intimacy with other women while they are growing up. This may become a turning point for sexual minority women in particular and lead to questioning of their own sexuality.

With respect to same-sex sexuality in boys and men in India, literature points out that there is a complex relationship between sexual behaviours and sexual identity and, as discussed later in the chapter on relationships, sexual subjectivity may often not be equated with sexual identity. Literature on men who have sex with men refers to 'Masti' or 'fun between men' with no connotations of a non-heterosexual orientation (Khan 2001; Seabrook 1999).

A gay man described the confusion that he underwent while growing up with other boys, who would engage in a lot of physical activity with each other, but never see it as sexual. This participant said:

> …a lot of fooling around happens between guys in terms of massaging each other and putting your hand here and there, as long as it doesn't get overtly sexual. So that happened in school as well as in college. That was what others also would do but for me it provided me intense physical pleasure and others didn't know it, for them it was, I don't know, maybe some form of just cuddling

[Atul, 33, at age 19]

Most of the research that describes MSM sexual behaviours and *Masti* has been conducted in the context of sexual risk and HIV. Parallel data on women's sexual behaviours does not exist in India as sexual-minority women have never been among the high risk groups for HIV transmission.

Having a crush on a friend or someone in school was a common theme that emerged among both gay and lesbian participants. This 'crush' and its expression often involved staring at each other, giving compliments, trying to impress, writing letters/notes to each other, sending a greeting card, writing '*I love you*' on school bench and so on.

> When I was in 9th Std., this guy, who was sitting in the next bench, I had a crush on him (laughs). I don't know how much he understood or I understood, or what this was called, but he was trying to flatter me. We never had any physical experience. He used to touch me and used to stare at me, give me some compliments and nothing more than that...

[Sunil, 32, gay man, when he was in Class 9th]

> From the 5th or 6th Std. only, whenever I saw young and beautiful girls, I used to like teasing them, tyenchavar impression maraila avdaicha (I used to like to impress them). When I was in the 8th, I used to like one girl, who was in the next class in school and my friend and I used to trouble her a lot. We used to throw chalk pieces at her when she was in class (giggles). I got to know her during a trip and after that she started talking to me more and I remember she used to bring greeting cards for me and she used to tease me too… like how a husband and wife tease each other…

[Sneha, 31, lesbian woman, when she was in Class 5th]

> We had exchanged a few letters and then we used to get this half an hour break in school. So we used to sit next to each other that entire half an hour without talking a word and then when the bell rang, we would just walk back to the class. I never knew what exactly I was doing.

[Parul, 34, in 9th Std.]

For some of the participants, having a sexual experience with a person of the same sex was a moment of insight. It was after this that they had the clarity that they are primarily attracted to persons of the same sex. One of the participants stated that for a long time he thought that he was asexual or just someone for whom sex was not a priority. He thought he was just more interested in other things like studies, music, science, and so on as compared to his peers who were all talking about and fantasizing about girls. However, all this changed once he had a sexual experience with a male friend. This helped him to see clearly that he was not attracted to girls and since he was socialized into believing that being sexual meant being so with girls, he was uninterested.

A lesbian woman talked about her first sexual experience with a woman in college,

> We were all drinking and we always used to have conversation about same sex and my friends were all cool. I don't know how it happened but me and this person slept together that night and the next morning I woke up and it was like 'wow'! 'What did I miss all these years?' This was not only in terms of sexual experience but in terms of just saying the fact that I like women and I sleep with them. It was actually like a coming out... My coming out happened the next morning when I woke up...

> [Priti, 31, in her postgraduate college, at age 22]

A gay man, who was aware of his attraction for men and would engage in sexual fantasies about men, described his first sexual experience with a man:

> It was the first time that the images in my mind were personified. Earlier on it was just the organs or just the body that I would think of. This was the first time that I saw everything that I wanted in front of me... it just became clearer.

> [Soham, 33 year old gay man talks about his first sexual experience at 20]

Some participants described sexual initiation by an older person, often a relative or school teacher or a senior student at school. Participants described these experiences of sexual initiation in varied ways. Some of the participants viewed it as a pleasurable first sexual experience with someone who knew more and initiated them into this act, whereas there were several participants who experienced these as abusive and coercive. They talked about coercion including a sense of 'not knowing' what was happening to them, which was experienced as fearful and not as the excitement of the unknown that others talked about. Some of them also talked about the sexual act being done in absolute secrecy, with an explicit message that this was not to be talked about openly. There were implications of threat in some of these scenarios. For many of the participants, while they as adults reconstructed the narrative of sexual initiation in their childhood, there were mixed feelings. Some did not wish to label the experience as entirely that of abuse whereas others did. Some described it as pleasurable and desirable, for some it was accompanied with a sense of feeling out of control, wherein the when, what, and how of the sexual act was completely decided by the other person.

## 3.5 Unique Developmental Challenges for LG Young People

Experiences of young gay and lesbian persons show that, in addition to dealing with all that is part of the process of normative growing up, LG young people have more/extra work to do while growing up. In addition to negotiating changes within their bodies brought about by the surge of sexual energy, negotiating issues such as acceptance and popularity within peer spaces, negotiating conflicts with adults (parents, teachers, other authority figures) and figuring out vocational and career choices, they are also working out questions around their sexual identity, an identity which may seem like a given to their heterosexual peers. They seem to be doing this in a socio-cultural context of heterosexual hegemony and absence of affirmative LGBT language, symbols, images, relationships, and ways of being. Thus, young gay or lesbian persons have to do 'extra work' in the process of growing up as compared to their heterosexual counterparts. I would like to use the concept of sexual minority stress as described by Meyer (1995) to understand this extra work of LG young people. The core idea behind the concept of minority stress is that stigmatization, discrimination, and prejudice can cause psychological distress. Minority stressors are conceptualized by Meyer as internalized homophobia that relates to gay individuals directing negative societal attitudes towards the self, the stigma that relates to expectations of rejection and discrimination, along with actual experiences of discrimination and violence (Meyer 1995). A few defining features of minority stress are: (a) it is *unique* and hence 'additive' to the general stressors that everyone experiences and, in that sense, requires a response over and above the one required to cope with other life stressors; (b) it is *chronic*, implying that it is related to relatively persistent underlying social and cultural structures; and (c) it is *socially based* and stems from social processes, institutions, and structures that are beyond the individual (Meyer 2007). While employing the lens of minority stress to understand some of the unique developmental challenges faced by young gay and lesbian persons, I am not homogenizing gay/lesbian identities; I am merely suggesting, as is also pointed out by Herek (2000), that many gay/lesbian persons may share a similarity of experience related to prejudice, stigma, discrimination, rejection, and violence, across cultures and locales. It is in this context of sexual minority/gay-related stress that I discuss some of the developmental challenges unique to growing up gay/lesbian.

- **Isolation, confusion and questions about sexuality**

An increasing awareness of their sexuality meant that several uncomfortable questions about the same arose in the minds of the participants. Some of the commonest of these included: Is this a phase? Will it go away? Are there others like me? Is this unnatural and abnormal? What will be my future? What if someone finds out? Linked to these questions are two further themes that I discuss below: absence of language, images, symbols about sexual diversity, and a central, hegemonic presence of heterosexuality and associated institutions of marriage and family. Resulting from this is the theme of isolation—believing that there are only heterosexual persons in this world and that is the only legitimate form of relating, and hence, one will remain alone and isolated; invisibility and isolation are thus two sides of the same coin.

One of the participants summed up the impact of all the themes mentioned above. He described the sense of isolation that arises out of lack of visibility and knowledge about queer lives and the resulting struggle of queer persons to try and 'make sense' of their life within the heterosexual/visible framework.

> I had decided that I would be single only all my life. I did not know that gay men existed. I felt that there are hetero men and then there are men like me who love the hetero men. But then hetero men get married and so I would never get anybody, I used to feel like that about my life…It is a scary thought, now when I think of it (laughs)
>
> [Mansoor, 33, at age 18]

Another participant in a similar situation spoke about his resolve to find a way out of this isolation:

> …in my mind the thought was always there that in this wide world there must be someone who will be able to adjust their life according to my life. I began thinking, 'ok, now I have to start discovering my own world'. There must be someone who will love me and I will love him…
>
> [Kumar, 30, at age 20]

One of the participants described his process of making sense of his sexuality. He was sexually active since school and thought that talking to the people he was having sex with would help him to reduce his isolation and also give him some answers about his sexuality.

> During my 9th-10th Std, I would try to talk to the guys I was sleeping with, I would try to break the topic with them about how I think I am different. I am not sure what words I was using but basically trying to see whether they feel the same way but the responses I would get would be very negative. Like 'let's keep it hush-hush, let's keep it hidden, let's not talk about it, let's not even talk while we are having sex! Lets just do it and forget about it and lets do it at the first opportunity when there is nobody, this is just pleasure and how can you not get married'… this would then just shut me up
>
> [Vineet, 40 year old gay man]

Describing the struggle between experience of his body, mind, and self, as a sexual being and social/normative expectations, one of the participants stated:

> During college, there was a lot of turmoil, in the sense of 'what am I'? Because I was getting confusing signals… My mind wants to do something then it tells me to not do it, my body asks for something else… The people I am doing it with are saying something else altogether and all around I find images that people are doing it only with the opposite sex and apparently this desire I feel is abnormal… so why am I doing this? Why? And why am I like this? Why am I the only one who wants to be different when people have taken decisions to lead a normal life? So then why am I the only one?
>
> [Vineet, 40 says this about the time when he was 20]

- **Invisibility: Absence of language/images of sexual diversity**

Language is an important tool, not merely for social communication but also to construct meaning and give structure to experience that can then be communicated to others. The absence of terms/words to reflect the experiences of the participants was a major barrier in the construction of an affirmative sexual identity. As one of the participants stated: "until you learn and own the word 'gay' with all its positive and affirmative meanings, you are constantly wondering what is going on with you?"

Two of the lesbian women participants underscored the importance of affirmative language and images/role models in the process of self-recognition and acceptance as a queer person.

> … not having the language, not having the vocabulary and the words that you do know have such a derogatory connotation to it… Not just language, images also. I mean I was 23 and I had had sex with three women by then but it was only at 23 that I finally saw on screen what it looks like. So just no images, nothing positive, no role models. Newspaper articles about LGBT rights and all have come out now. When I was like 20, say 12 years back, nothing! Nothing on same sex ever in sex education, no visible images, no visible people, no language…
>
> [Pradnya, 33 year old lesbian woman]

> I mean we didn't have the language to kind of understand what we were even doing. The thing is that everything is in a heterosexual context you know. So somehow when I was doing it with this woman, I didn't think of it as sex! I didn't think I was having sex with her, because for me the image of what sex is, is between a man and a woman only.
>
> [Salma, 30 year old lesbian woman]

One of the participants, while discussing the importance of gay affirmative language, images and role models while growing up, stated that the overall social context in which one is growing up is significant. She said:

> I am sure if you grew up in Amsterdam it would be very different because it is much more open … you know you see people being affectionate on the street which we don't have here…and every fairy tale you hear is that the prince and princess lived happily ever after. Its never a princess and princess went to the sex toy shop (laughs) you don't hear stuff like that! So I think its the way we are brought up. We are just made to believe that a man and a woman is what's conventional and what's right. And over here you know let's face it, until a few years ago, you didn't really hear the word gay. There is a generation above us who know the word homosexual but they don't know the words gay and lesbian…
>
> [Mehek, 28 year old lesbian woman]

Leap (2007) describes the concept of self-initiated and self-managed gay socialization, which includes looking for library books, magazines, newspaper articles, motion pictures, television serials, talk shows, folklore, jokes, with gay affirmative themes or looking for role models/gay icons, supportive friends, and allies. This implies that, for most queer people, working through feelings of loneliness, isolation, and simultaneously managing self-initiated and motivated gay socialization against several odds is a major developmental challenge.

- **Denial, fear and internalized homophobia**

All the participants reported that at some point in their lives they were living with a sense of being different; different from their peers, siblings, and family members. This sense of difference was eventually recognized as a sexual difference, and it often caused anxiety, fear, and denial in many of the participants. Fear of 'being found out', people getting to know the well-guarded secret of same-sex attraction and the resulting stigma were common. Denial involved lack of readiness to acknowledge and accept one's sexuality. Internalized homophobia—internalizing and accepting society's devaluation of homosexuality—was often the foundation for both denial and fear. Fear can be the result of a homonegative and hostile environment as well where a queer person may fear abuse, violence, and discrimination merely because of their sexuality. In this context, however, I describe anticipated fear as a response to internalized homophobia. Thoits (1985) describes this as 'self-stigmatization', wherein even in the absence of any overt negative events and when one's minority status is successfully concealed, gay, and lesbian persons may still be harmed by directing negative social values towards themselves.

One of the participants describes her own homonegative response at the prospect of being seen as lesbian. The role of perceived stigma, homonegativity, and the lack of visibility and affirmation around same-sex sexuality, in maintaining internalized homophobia becomes clear in the following quote:

> You know how these hostels are.... one day we were having a late night session in the hostel and someone said something about lesbians and I remember cringing because by then I knew, that probably what I am doing with this woman is what would make me lesbian and I just didn't want it. So I remember cringing at the word and saying I hope I am not lesbian, though somewhere I knew it but I was like, I hope I am not lesbian! Or then I am different. You know that what I am doing with this woman is not dirty and not what lesbians do (laughs). Yeah, I remember that embarrassment, that cringing, that fear so clearly! I was so traumatized that I might just be lesbian...
>
> [Pradnya, 33 year old lesbian woman talks about her hostel experience at the age of 20]

Another participant, who was married for almost a decade and then later divorced her husband, spoke about her growing-up years, her attraction for girls and her denial of the same.

> I was too scared. I was this complete *darpoke*! Too scared to look at what I was feeling. I was so attracted to my friends. There was this girl in my group and I was really attracted to her but I never ever had the guts you know to tell her I like you. I didn't know what she would say if I told her. So, till I got married, all my fantasises were only about women... Ya and yet the marriage happened; because I was too scared to admit it or look at it or address it in any way
>
> [Claire, 41 year old lesbian woman talks about when she was 22 year old and decided to get married]

Another lesbian participant spoke about having a boyfriend in college, while she knew that she was only attracted to girls. She explained her thoughts at that time:

> ... at the end of it I think it was (pause) more denial than anything else (pause) How should I say it? I mean denial is one thing, but I think its more of being afraid, rather than just the denial. Ok denial can be for so many reasons, mine I think was more out of fear, fear of acknowledging that this is my reality...
>
> [Vidya, 35, says about a time when she was about 20 years old]

- **Why am I Like this? Working out Causation of Same-sex Sexuality and Working Through Popular Misconceptions**

Since same-sex sexuality development is seen by society and experienced by the individual as something out of the ordinary, there is a felt need by all involved to find an explanation for the same. This includes not just parents, siblings, teachers, friends of gay persons, but also gay persons themselves, who want to know the cause, the etiology, of their same-sex attraction. This is not to imply that all the participants in this study, as well as the significant persons in their lives, viewed homosexuality as necessarily 'abnormal', but sometimes there was a need felt, to understand the origin of this kind of an 'uncommon', 'out of the ordinary' sexuality.

In a society that devalues homosexuality, myths, misconceptions, and stereotypes about the cause of homosexuality are present in abundance. Some of these include: sexual abuse during childhood causes adult homosexuality; growing up among many sisters causes effeminacy among boys and that later leads to homosexuality; similarly, that growing up among many brothers causes girls to be 'tomboys' in their childhood and later lesbianism; distant father and over-involved mother causes homosexuality in boys; and so on. Working through some of these homonegative narratives becomes a major developmental milestone for several LG persons to develop a healthy and affirmative sense of sexuality.

Several participants in this study were sexually abused during their childhood. In fact, research on the incidence of childhood sexual abuse (CSA) in India indicates that as many as 53.22% ($n = 12,447$) children report having faced some form of sexual abuse (Ministry of WCD, GOI 2007). Often the perpetrators are known to the child and include family members. As a result, it is often difficult to talk about the abuse. Research on CSA indicates that children living in unhappy families, growing up with a sense of loneliness, or having inadequate sex education, are more vulnerable to CSA (Finkelhor et al. 1990). Further, research with children with gender non-conforming behaviours suggests that these children have poorer relationships with parents, experience more childhood rejection (Rieger et al. 2008), and are at greater risk for physical, psychological, and sexual abuse, and possibly at higher risk for post-traumatic stress disorder in their youth (Roberts et al. 2012). In the current study, many of the participants, especially children with gender non-conforming behaviours described growing up with a sense of alienation from parents and loneliness at home and among peers. Several young boys who were effeminate, described experiences of hostility and violence from their fathers. Did this make them more vulnerable to CSA? Did gender transgressions, especially among boys who were feminine in their gender expressions, make them more vulnerable to CSA? These are some of the questions that would need further exploration.

One of the participants spoke about being abused by his school teacher:

> …this teacher used to come and sit beside me and he would say you look very nice. I was very effeminate then… The school uniform was half-pant… He would stroke my thigh and all… and it went on like that and our relation stayed till the 10th. I used to be scared because

he used to come home also and I was worried that if he told anyone at home, then my studies will be stopped or then I used to be scared that I am the only one like this… He would call me to his home also in May vacation when his wife and children would go to their village.

[Akshay, 26 years talks about the time between 6th–10th Std.]

The participants in this study stated that they had to not just deal with the trauma of being sexually abused in their childhood, but also had to struggle with the history of sexual abuse while figuring out their sexual identity. Some of them reported experiencing doubts about whether their homosexuality was linked with and caused by their experiences of childhood sexual abuse; this was a question that they had to work through for themselves, and often were faced with when they came out to significant others. This involved a great deal of psychological struggle and sometimes posed a barrier in the person's own self-acceptance as well as acceptance by family members.

One of the participants narrated that he had been sexually active with one of his male cousins during their teenage years and that this sexual engagement which lasted over a couple of years had actually helped him to understand who he was. Despite this, he had chosen to get married under parental influence, while struggling with a lot of internalized homonegativity. However, he later divorced and chose to come out to his parents. In order to help his parents understand that his homosexuality had nothing to do with a failed marriage but, in fact, was the cause of it, he told them about his relationship with his cousin. On knowing this, the parents—especially the mother, who was a doctor by training—were convinced that their son had been sexually abused as a teenager and that it was childhood sexual abuse which had caused his homosexuality. It was only later, when a psychiatrist told them that homosexuality may have a biological basis and that a person's sexual orientation is decided at the embryo stage in the womb, that the mother stopped blaming herself for not having protected her son from sexual abuse and indirectly having caused his homosexuality.

A biological cause for homosexuality somehow lends a degree of validity to it because of the association of biological/inborn with that which is seen as 'natural'. When homosexuality is perceived as a trait one is born with, then the arguments of dysfunctional upbringing or abusive experiences lose ground. That is possibly the reason why several participants relied on using biological/'scientific' explanations for their sexuality, and this played an important role in consolidation of their identities.

## 3.6  Some Thoughts on Gay and Lesbian Childhoods

In the overall literature on childhood studies, but particularly research on childhood studies in India, the gay, lesbian, or queer child is invisible. Childhood studies often is dominated by a universal narrative of childhood: the child within the family unit, innocent and uncorrupted by society and within the private domain, cared for by the mother in the domestic sphere. Such a child is, then, seen as an adjunct of the family and, hence, the identity of the child is subsumed within the family unit and ethnic community. In contrast to this 'normal child' are the narratives of the 'other' children, those outside of the family unit and in need of state intervention and protection; those who are the objects of state welfare (Balakrishnan 2011). Multiple identities have been ascribed to such 'deviant' children within development literature as well as state policy; some examples of these include orphan children, children in conflict with law, trafficked children, child labourers, and so on. It is interesting to note that, despite sharing some commonalities with these 'deviant' children, such as facing neglect, abuse, violence within families, schools, colleges, and among peer groups (Shah et al. 2015; Ghosh et al. 2011; PUCL-K 2001), gay and lesbian children do not figure in the discourse around childhood vulnerabilities in India. In fact, silences surrounding the lived experiences of gay and lesbian children, as well as the all-pervading, universalist, assumptions of gender binarism and heterosexism, means that these experiences are inarticulable[2] and are rendered unintelligible. Foucault (1978) speaks of 'the grid of intelligibility of the social order' and states that to be outside of the grid of the stable male and female is to be subjected to multiple acts of aggression; the correction of gender and sexuality discussed in this chapter are examples of some of these. In fact, most examples of correction are not just instances of rejection and exclusion but are often efforts at monitoring, moulding, and shaping behaviours and persons into acceptable ways of inclusion. Butler notes about gender non-conforming persons, "…to be deemed one of the gender problematic, is to no longer be recognizable as human and to court 'social or literal death'" (Butler 2004, 8).

Another reason for absence of queer children from within the literature on childhood is possibly the assumption that sexuality emerges only after puberty and is a legitimate subject of enquiry only for adult lives. Research and literature on LGBTQ lives in India, too, primarily focus on the adult queer subject, and possibly suffer from the same bias. In this chapter, I have attempted to throw light on the unique struggles of LG children with their own minds and bodies that disobey socially prescribed norms of gender and sexuality. Early messages of 'you are not ok' from family, schools, peers, doctors can be damaging, and isolation, invisibility, silence, and hostile messages about same-sex sexuality in the environment, only add to the challenge of growing up.

# References

Allport, G. W. (1954). *The nature of prejudice*. Reading, MA: Addison-Wesley.
American Psychiatric Association (APA). (1973). Position statement on homosexuality. In B. J. Sadock & V. A. Kaplan (Eds.), *Comprehensive textbook of psychiatry* (7th ed., Vol. 1). Baltimore, MD: Lippincott Williams & Wilkins.

---

[2]In the absence of language (except for pathologizing terms) that can speak to and of these lived experiences, these experiences cannot be described or articulated. They simply fall through the cracks between language, experience, and representation.

Bailey, J. M., & Zucker, K. J. (1995). Childhood sex-typed behavior and sexual orientation: A conceptual analysis and quantitative review. *Developmental Psychology, 31*(1), 43.

Balakrishnan, V. (2011). *Growing up and away: Narratives of indian childhoods memory, history, identity*. New Delhi: Oxford University Press.

Beard, A., & Bakeman, R. (2000). Boyhood gender nonconformity: Reported parental behavior and the development of narcissistic issues. *Journal of Gay and Lesbian Psychotherapy, 4*, 81–97.

Bell, A. P., Weinberg, M. S., & Hammersmith, S. K. (1981). *Sexual preference: Its development in men and women*. New York: Simon & Schuster.

Butler, J. (2004). *Undoing gender*. New York: Routledge.

Chakrapani, V., Newman, P. A., Shunmugam, M., McLuckie, A., & Melwin, F. (2007). Structural violence against *Kothi*–identified men who have sex with men in Chennai, India: A qualitative investigation. *AIDS Education and Prevention, 19*(4), 346–364.

Coleman, E., & Remafedi, G. (1989). Gay, lesbian, and bisexual adolescents: A critical challenge to counsellors. *Journal of Counselling and Development, 68*(1), 36–40.

Creating Resources for Empowerment and Action (CREA). (2012). *Count Me In! Research Report on Violence against Disabled, Lesbian and Sex-Working Women in Bangladesh, India and Nepal*. New Delhi: CREA Publications. Retrieved July 15, 2017, from http://web.creaworld.org/files/cmir.pdf.

D'Augelli, A. R. (1996). Lesbian, gay and bisexual development during adolescence and young adulthood. In R. P. Cabaj & T. S. Stein (Eds.), *Textbook of homosexuality and mental health* (pp. 267–287). Washington, DC: American Psychiatric Association.

Diamond, L. M. (2007). "Having a girlfriend without knowing it": Intimate friendships among adolescent sexual-minority women. In K. E. Lovaas & M. M. Jenkins (Eds.), *Sexualities and communication in everyday life* (pp. 107–114). California: Sage

Equality Challenge Unit. (2009). The experience of lesbian, gay, bisexual and trans staff and students in higher education. Equality Challenge Unit. Retrieved from www.ecu.ac.uk/publications/?browse=subject&filter=sexual-orientation.

Erikson, E. (1950). *Childhood and society*. New York: Norton.

Evans, N., & Levine, H. (1990). Perspectives on sexual orientation. *New Directions for Student Services, 51*, 49–58.

Feinman, S. (1981). Why is cross-sex-role behavior more approved for girls than for boys? A status characteristic approach. *Sex Roles, 7*, 289–300.

Feinman, S. (1984). A status theory evaluation of sex-role behavior and age-role behavior. *Sex Roles, 10*, 445–456.

Fernandez, B., & Gomathy, N. B. (2003). The nature of violence faced by lesbian women in India. *Mumbai: Research Centre on Violence Against Women, Tata Institute of Social Sciences*. Retrieved from https://www.tiss.edu/uploads/files/8The_Nature_of_violence_faced_by_Lesbian_women_in_India.pdf, last accessed on 15th July, 2017.

Finkelhor, D., Hotaling, G., Lewis, I., & Smith, C. (1990). Sexual abuse in a national survey of adult men and women: prevalence, characteristics, and risk factors. *Child Abuse and Neglect, 14*(1), 19–28.

Foucault, M. (1978). *The history of sexuality: An introduction* (Vol. 1). Paris: Random House.

Foucault, M. (1979). *Discipline and punish: The birth of the prison*. New York: Vintage Books.

Garofalo, R. R., Wolf, C., Kessel, S., Palfrey, J., & DuRant, R. H. (1998). The association between health risk behaviours and sexual orientation among a school-based sample of adolescents. *Pediatrics, 101*(5), 895–902.

Ghosh, S., Bandyopadhyay, B. S., & Biswas, R. (2011). *Vio-map: documenting and mapping violence and rights violation taking place in the lives of sexually marginalized women to chart out effective advocacy strategies*. Kolkata: SAPPHO for Equality.

Green, R. (1985). Gender identity in childhood and later sexual orientation. *American Journal of Psychiatry, 142*, 339–341.

Griffin, P. (1992). From hiding out to coming out: Empowering lesbian and gay educators. In K. M. Harbeck (Ed.), *Coming out of the classroom closet* (pp. 167–196). Binghamton, NY: Harrington Park Press.

Herek, G. M. (1986). On heterosexual masculinity: Some psychical consequences of the social construction of gender and sexuality. *American Behavioral Scientist, 29*(5), 563–577.

Herek, G. M. (1988). Heterosexuals' attitudes towards lesbian and gay men: Correlates and gender differences. *Journal of Sex Research, 25*(4), 451–477.

Herek, G. M. (1994). Assessing attitudes toward lesbians and gay men: A review of empirical research with the ATLG scale. In B. Greene & G. M. Herek (Eds.), *Lesbian and gay psychology: Theory, research, and clinical applications* (pp. 206–228). Thousand Oaks, CA: Sage.

Herek, G. M. (2000). The psychology of sexual prejudice. *Current Directions in Psychological Science, 9*(1), 19–22.

Janoff, D. (2005). *Pink blood: Homophobic violence in Canada.* Toronto: University of Toronto Press.

Jensen, K. L. (1999). *Lesbian epiphanies: Women coming out in later life.* Binghamton, NY: Harrington Park Press.

Joseph, S. (2005). *Social work practice and men who have sex with men.* New Delhi: Sage.

Kalra, G. (2012). Breaking the ice: IJP on homosexuality. *Indian J Psychiatry, 54,* 299–300.

Khan, S. (2001). Culture, sexualities, and identities: Men who have sex with men in India. *Journal of Homosexuality, 40,* 99–115.

Landolt, M. A., Bartholomew, K., Saffrey, C., Oram, D., Perlman, D., & Bartholomew, K. (2004). Gender nonconformity, childhood rejection, and adult attachment: A study of gay men. *Archives of Sexual Behavior, 33,* 117–128.

Leap, W. (2007). Language, socialization, and silence in gay adolescence. In K. E. Lovaas & M. M. Jenkins (Eds.), *Sexualities and communication in everyday life.* California: Sage.

Mallon, G. (1998). Knowledge for practise with gay and lesbian persons. In G. P. Mallon (Ed.), *Foundations of social work practice with gay and lesbian persons.* Binghamton, NY: The Haworth Press.

Martin, A. D. (1982). Learning to hide: The socialisation of the gay adolescent. *Adolescent Psychiatry, 10,* 52–65.

Martin, C. L. (1990). Attitudes and expectations about children with non-traditional and traditional gender roles. *Sex Roles, 22*(3/4), 151–166.

McCreary, D. R. (1994). The male role and avoiding femininity. *Sex Roles, 31,* 517–531.

Meyer, I. H. (1995). Minority stress and mental health in gay men. *Journal of Health and Social Behavior,* 38–56.

Meyer, I. H. (2007). Prejudice and discrimination as social stressors. In I. H. Meyer & M. E. Northridge (Eds.), *The health of sexual minorities: Public health perspectives on lesbian, gay, bisexual and transgender populations* (pp. 242–267). Berlin: Springer.

Miller, C. T., & Major, B. (2000). Coping with stigma and prejudice. In T. F. Heatherton, R. E. Kleck, M. R. Hebl, & J. G. Hull (Eds.), *The social psychology of stigma* (pp. 243–272). New York: Guilford Press.

Ministry of Women and Child Development, Government of India. (2007). *Study on child abuse: India.* New Delhi: Kriti.

Narrain, A., & Chandran, V. (Eds.). (2015). *Nothing to fix: Medicalisation of sexual orientation and gender identity.* India: Sage/Yoda Publications.

Nevatia, S., Mahajan, S., & Shah, C. (2012). Bound by norms and out of bounds: Experiences of PAGFB (persons assigned gender female at birth) within the formal education system: Lesbians and Bisexuals in Action (LABIA). *Contemporary Education Dialogue, 9*(2), 173–196.

Philo, C. (2011). Foucault's children. In L. Holt, (ed). Geographies of children, youth and families: An international perspective.

Poteat, V. P., & Espelage, D. L. (2005). Exploring the relation between bullying and homophobic verbal content: The Homophobic Content Agent Target (HCAT) scale. *Violence and Victims, 20*(5), 513–528.

PUCL-K. (2001). Human rights violations against sexuality minorities in India: A PUCL-K fact finding report about Bangalore. Bengaluru: People's Union for Civil Liberties—Karnataka.

Pyne, J. (2014). The governance of gender non-conforming children: A dangerous enclosure. *Annual Review of Critical Psychology, 11,* 76–96.

Rao, T. S., & Jacob, K. S. (2012). Homosexuality and India. *Indian J Psychiatry, 54,* 1–3.

Rao, A. (2005). Sexuality and the family form. *Economic and Political Weekly,* 715–718.

Ranade, K. (2015). Medical response to male same-sex sexuality in Western India: An exploration of "conversion treatments" for homosexuality. In A. Narrain & V. Chandran (Eds.), *Nothing to fix: Medicalisation of sexual orientation and gender identity.* India: Sage/Yoda Publications.

Rieger, G., Linsenmeier, J. A., Gygax, L., & Bailey, J. M. (2008). Sexual orientation and childhood gender nonconformity: Evidence from home videos. *Developmental Psychology, 44*(1), 46.

Ritter, K., & Terndrup, A. I. (2002). Handbook of affirmative psychotherapy with lesbians and gay men. Guilford Press.

Roberts, A. L., Rosario, M., Corliss, H. L., Koenen, K. C., & Austin, S. B. (2012). Childhood gender nonconformity: A risk indicator for childhood abuse and posttraumatic stress in youth. *Pediatrics, 129*(3), 410–417.

Rose, N., & Miller, P. (2010). Political power beyond the state: Problematics of government. *British Journal of Sociology, 61*(s1), 271–303.

Rose, S., D. Z. & M. Cini. (1993). Lesbian courtship scripts. In D. Rothblum & K. A. Brehony (Eds.). Boston marriages: Romantic but asexual relationships among contemporary lesbians, pp. 70–85.

Rosen, W. B. (1992). On integration of sexuality: Lesbians and their Mothers,' quoted in K. Y. Ritter & A. I. Terndrup. In *Handbook of affirmative psychotherapy with lesbians and gay men* (p. 305, 2002) New York: Guilford Press.

Rosenkrantz, P. S., Vogel, S. R., Bee, H., Broverman, I. K., & Broverman, D. M. (1968). Sex-role stereotypes and self-concepts in college students. *Journal of Consulting and Clinical Psychology, 32,* 287–295.

Rotheram-Borus, M. J., & Fernandez, M. I. (1995). Sexual orientation and developmental challenges experienced by gay and lesbian youths. *Suicide Life Threat Behavior, 25* (Suppl: 26–34): discussion 35–39.

Savin-Williams, R. C., & Diamond, L. M. (2000). Sexual identity trajectories among sexual-minority youths: Gender comparisons. *Archives of Sexual Behavior, 29*(6), 607–627.

Savin-Williams, R. C. (1998). *"... and then I became gay": Young men's stories.* New York: Routledge.

Savin-Williams, R. C. (2005). *The new gay teenager.* London: Harvard University Press.

Seabrook, J. (1999). *Love in a different climate: Men who have sex with men in India.* London: Verso.

Shah, C., Merchant, R., Mahajan, S., & Nevatia, S. (2015). *No outlaws in the gender galaxy.* New Delhi: Zubaan.

Sirin, S. R., McCreary, D. R., & Mahalik, J. R. (2004). Differential reactions to men and women's gender role transgressions: Perceptions of social status, sexual orientation, and value dissimilarity. *The Journal of Men's Studies, 12*(2), 119–132.

Smart, L., & Wegner, D. M. (2000). The hidden costs of stigma. In T. F. Heatherton, R. E. Kleck, M. R. Hebl, & J. G. Hull (Eds.), *The social psychology of stigma* (pp. 220–242). New York: Guilford Press.

Solomon, S. (2004). Kids Say The Funniest Things...: anti-homophobia group work in the classroom. *Teaching Education, 15*(1), 103–106.

Thoits, P. (1985). Self-labeling processes in mental illness: The role of emotional deviance. *American Journal of Sociology, 91,* 221–249.

Thurlow, C. (2001). Naming the "Outsider Within": Homophobic pejoratives and the verbal abuse of lesbian, gay and bisexual high-school pupils. *Journal of Adolescence, 24,* 25–38.

Troiden, R. R. (1979). Becoming homosexual: A model of gay identity acquisition. *Psychiatry, 42,* 362–373.

Voices Against 377. (2005). Rights for all: Ending Discrimination Against Queer Desire Under Section 377, A Compilation By *Voices Against 377,* Delhi.

Warwich, I., Aggelton, P., & Douglas, N. (2001). Play it safe: Addressing the emotional and physical health of lesbian and gay pupils in the U.K. *Journal of Adolescence, 24,* 129–140.

Williams, T., Connolly, J., Pepler, D., & Craig, W. (2005). Peer victimization, social support, and psychosocial adjustment of sexual minority adolescents. *Journal of Youth and Adolescence, 34* (5), 471–482.

World Health Organization (WHO). (1992). *ICD-10 classification of mental and behavioural disorders.* Geneva: WHO.

# Chapter 4
# Exploring Identity Development and the Symbolic Meaning/s of 'Coming Out' in the Process of Identity Work

*Prelude*

*To tell or not to tell, that is the question!*

*narrative one:*

*this whole idea of coming out to parents and family is totally irrelevant in my life. matlab (i mean), we as a family are very distant, i mean emotionally. we are like a unit that shares gossip, social information, discuss political happenings, but we never really talk about ourselves. so my family has no idea for instance that i was taking anti-depressants at one point in my life or that i have been a smoker for over a decade now, so discussing with them who i have sex with or who i am emotionally close to or in a relationship with is just... well simply not relevant, you know.*

*now while this is true, it is also true that i have taken several of my boyfriends home. in fact i think, my parents have met all my partners, but not as partners of course! it is like a classic, 'don't ask, don't tell policy'. matlab (i mean), they will not ask "who is this friend? how come you spend so much time with him?", or "what happened to this other friend we had met last time? you would always talk about him all these years and you don't seem to meet him or talk about him anymore?" so when i was living with them and that was a long time ago, while i was finishing my undergrad studies, they have seen me go through break-ups... that whole natak (drama) about late night phone calls, fights, crying, banging the phone receiver... and they have never asked a single question.*

*what is interesting to me is that, though there are no conversations about any of this, my mother has known about all my ex's favourite foods (with one person, even food allergies), their likes/dislikes... similarly, they have seen me write on lgbtq issues, give interviews to magazines and TV shows, they have read interviews of my gay friend's mom who speaks to the media as a strong ally of the movement. they read, watch these, and even share with their friends with the tag line "our son works for the rights of these people". so you see coming out to family is irrelevant in this context. i live my life fully and they live theirs...*

© Springer Nature Singapore Pte Ltd. 2018
K. Ranade, *Growing Up Gay in Urban India*,
https://doi.org/10.1007/978-981-10-8366-2_4

*narrative two:*

*i cannot imagine a life of not sharing my joys, my sorrows, my dilemmas, my challenges, my gayness with my mother; cannot think of having to ever choose between my girlfriend and my mom by my side on birthdays, anniversaries, job promotion parties, shifting houses, buying a car, days of tooth extraction and other kinds of aches and losses; telling my mother about being in love… about s, who she is, how special she is, how she looks after me, makes the best biryani in the world, you know, little things like that…*

*i think an interesting thing about coming out to your parents is also about sharing and talking about your partner, your life together, your 'gay' life together. in some ways that makes it easy to talk about your gayness, the fact that you are in a relationship, you have someone who will look out for you… it in a way normalizes your gayness, almost gives it a kind of a respectability, makes it relatable. i think we as a society think of the world in pairs or groups, you know like couples and families… there is safety in it but also a sense of achievement and worthiness. also, i think, we are just terribly invested in the idea of everlasting romance and love. so if you were to come out and tell your parents, "mom, i am in love with so and so", it would be so much more palatable than just saying, "i am gay!" i think that the latter will evoke a barrage of questions like, "what would that mean for your life? who will you marry? who will look after you?" i think that the idea of singleness can evoke a sense of lack, anxiety, incompleteness*

*and i think it is anyway damned tough in our context to talk about sex with our parents, so in my coming out story, there have been lots of references to love but none to sex. it is like saying, you don't talk about your sex life with me, and i will not talk about mine with you (laughs). it would be nice though to be acknowledged as a couple, you know like mom-dad have a bedroom and my sister and her husband are given a separate room, when they visit, i would like that kind of treatment for me and s too… it's not just about what is said, but also what is unsaid…*

*narrative three:*

*i grew up surrounded by a lot of violence… there was my feminine side that led to massive bullying in school. i was commonly and regularly called 'sissy', 'faggot', 'bailya' (effeminate) as though i did not have a real name, then there was violence at home… there was violence that was happening in the city in which our small colony in mahim in what used to be called bombay was very much involved. the year was 1992 and the violence i refer to was unleashed in preparation for and after the demolition of the babri masjid in ayodhya, uttar pradesh. it is strange, how events occurring in a far flung land that you have never seen can affect the way you relate to your neighbours, your school mates… that's the magic of hate and violence, it can burn down anything and everything, known and unknown, in its wake.*

*in these times of hate, here i was, a class 10th student, a hindu, brahmin boy with my sissy self, specially marked in the face of all the machismo… boys and men alike, in service of a hindu rashtra, performing poojas and maha-aratis* (community prayers), *beating the drums and playing 'lezim'* (a drill performed with a hand instrument that has many cymbals) *with military precision.*

*so, for me, finding peace and happiness within myself, being ok with my gay self and feeling integrated from within is more about avoiding violence. it is about knowing that i will not lose my job or my house or i will not be publicly humiliated for being, who i am. in that sense, safety within my small world is much more important to me than coming out and telling the world...*

*i think that even in the gay world, we are sometimes so naïve... yaar (my friend) ask yourself, that at this moment in the country, who can really participate in this exercise of announcing with 'pride'? it's like they say, "garv se kaho...", that sentence can only end with "garv se kaho, hum hindu hai"* ("say it with pride; we are hindu"—a slogan used by hindu right wing groups and political parties). *this whole exercise of chest thumping and talking about 56 inch chest size* (used in the pre-election speeches by the current prime minister of india), *is about a certain kind of an indian. it cannot be a safe space to come out for a five feet one inch tall, effeminate gay boy and certainly not for a poor, non-hindu lesbian woman or transperson... you may say that it is a bit of a far-fetched thing to say, but i think there is a direct relationship between a functioning secular democracy and coming out as gay or queer with pride.*

*narrative four:*

*i think it is all about meeting the right kind of people at the right time. i mean, you have to feel ready within to embrace your sexuality and then at that time, you should be able to find good role models... people you can look up to, where you can say, "he is gay and happy, so can i be"... it's like seeing and knowing that this is possible, viable, ho sakta hai, can happen or rather, can be made to happen.*

*it's a journey, you know, from the time i first read the word 'gay' in a newspaper article and kept the cutting of that article in my wallet, to deciding to migrate to Mumbai to be able to live my life, to being part of a circle of gay friends, to having lots of fun, gay sex (laughs). telling friends, boss, colleagues then came as the next natural progression in the story. the real challenge was telling parents and i think i finally did that only to get them to stop fixing up these meetings with girls and sending me letters and pictures of girls.*

*because i was so 'normal' during my growing up years, did all the boy things in terms of rough play, fights, getting into trouble with school authorities, having female friends, who were seen by them as my girlfriends, an image i then encouraged as that served as a good cover for me till i left home—so they had no idea until i came out and told them. it was tough, but i realized that once i was out of home and out of the closet, going back in was just not an option for me.*

Stage models of gay, lesbian identity development described in the introductory chapter lay emphasis on 'coming out' as a significant stage in the development of a gay or lesbian identity. This process of coming out has been defined as disclosure to others that one is gay or lesbian (APA 2004), and inherent to this disclosure is the notion of coming out to oneself, or self-acknowledgement/self-acceptance of being lesbian or gay. Coming out is not a one-time occasion. Comfort with one's sexuality changes and is likely to grow with time and so are the chances of disclosure to more and more people. Coming out is thus often described as a life-long process that involves a widening circle of friends, family and acquaintances. Viewed from the perspective of the stage models of lesbian, gay, bisexual (LGB) identity development, coming out to oneself and to others is a cornerstone in the process of self-acceptance (Cass 1979; Troiden 1979).

Most stage models describe LG identity development as occurring across various stages. These stages usually start with the individual becoming aware of and often confused by same-sex attractions. This is accompanied by defences and attempts at denial and blocking personal feelings. While these defences may last a long time, individuals may eventually learn to tolerate their homosexual feelings; this may be followed by greater self-awareness, looking for information and meanings of homosexuality, having homosexual experiences, working through questions of natural/normal versus unnatural/abnormal, guilt, fear, and so on. As individuals become more comfortable with the possibility of being gay and begin to accept themselves, they are said to enter the stage of 'coming out' or what has been defined by the various stage model theorists as 'coming out, identity tolerance, identity acceptance' and so on (Cass 1979; Troiden 1988; Coleman 1982). Fassinger (1998) developed a four-stage model of lesbian identity development that described two strands or processes in identity development. These two strands refer to individual sexual identity development and group membership identity development relating to one's place in the gay/lesbian community. Both these strands include four stages of development: awareness (about oneself and others like oneself); exploration of one's feelings and attractions and relationship to the community; deepening and internalizing a sense of being gay or lesbian and committing to the lesbian and gay community; synthesis i.e. incorporating one's sexual identity in one's overall identity and internalizing a minority group identity across contexts. This model of identity development also emphasizes a need to come out and commit to a lesbian or gay identity. D'Augelli (1994) has proposed a lifespan approach to sexual identity development with emphasis on six developmental tasks: exiting heterosexual identity; developing a personal gay identity status; developing a gay social identity; becoming a gay offspring; developing a gay intimacy status; and, entering a gay community. Here, too, the second, third, and fourth tasks—of developing personal and social gay identity and becoming a gay offspring—are related to coming out to oneself and others, including one's parents.

One of the major assumptions in all of these models of identity development is that successful development of a lesbian or gay identity is about resolution of an internal conflict within the individual; it is about self-acceptance or rather individuals allowing themselves or giving themselves the permission to embrace their lesbian or gay self through the resolution of intra-psychic conflicts. In other words, stage models of identity development view gay or lesbian sexuality as something that is already there and the task of identity exploration, development, and acquisition, is about being able to work through difficulties to find and accept oneself. The other assumption underlying these models is that a healthy and well-adjusted lesbian or gay person is the one who, after successful resolution of internal conflicts, decides to come out to significant others including family, friends, and colleagues. In this chapter, I challenge both these assumptions by making an assertion that coming out as gay or lesbian may have much more to do with one's interpersonal and social contexts, and not necessarily to do with internal conflicts.

There are several other critiques of the stage models of LG identity development. One of the critiques is that the stage models tend to define sexual identity development in terms of a linear progression that starts, for the LG individual, with a negative, socially ascribed, heterosexual identity, and ends in becoming an 'out' and happy LG person. Thus, not only is development viewed as a linear process but there is value-attribution associated with moving up on the development ladder. Also, these models understate the importance of the social context within which the LG identity development occurs. Finally, they minimize the tremendous variation in experiences of LG individuals that is mediated by 'contexts' of social class, ethnicity, age, gender, and other background factors (Kaufman and Johnson 2004).

## 4.1  Symbolic Interactionism[1]: A Framework to Understand Identity Development and Disclosure Among Gay and Lesbian Individuals

Kaufman and Johnson (2004) suggest that in order to centre the role of social context and interaction between 'self and context' within the narrative of development and maintenance of a LG identity, symbolic interactionist literature on self and identity, to theorize gay and lesbian identity development, would be useful. They use Goffman's work (1963) 'Stigma–Notes on Management of a Spoiled Identity' to describe the process of individuals becoming aware of their sexual identity, becoming aware of social perceptions of the same and using various stigma management strategies and negotiations situated within their contexts.

Kaufman and Johnson (2004) argue that key concepts and theory from symbolic interactionism provide a more coherent theoretical framework to examine identity development and the situated complexity of identity negotiation and disclosure

---

[1]Symbolic Interactionism lies on the continuum of a range of theoretical positions within social psychology and micro-sociology that engage with the 'individual in context' frame. In this book, it is being used along with social constructionism and a critical psychosocial perspective. Read Billson (1994) for further discussion on relationship between psychology and symbolic interactionism.

among gay and lesbian individuals. The concept of reflected appraisals—individuals' perceptions of how others perceive them—is central in symbolic interactionist research on how social interaction impacts the self (Gecas and Burke 1995). In the case of gay and lesbian persons, as they begin to become aware of their same-sex attractions, they also become aware of society's negative evaluations of same-sex sexuality. Thus, as the identity standard (view of oneself) of a LG person develops, so does their awareness of negative reflected appraisals from society. In fact, the presence of hostile and negative reflected appraisal hinders the development of a strong identity standard. As discussed in the previous chapter, the initial identity standard of an LG person is likely to be negative as mediated by the negative reflected appraisals from others. However, research on reflected appraisal also points to the role of the active individual, who interprets, acts on, and may even refute, reflected appraisals (Gecas and Schwalbe 1983; Ichiyama 1993; Milkie 1999). Burke (1991) points out that individuals actively construct identity. Burke theorizes that individuals strive for consistency between their view of themselves (identity standard) and their perceptions of how others see them (reflected appraisals). When inconsistencies arise, individuals act in ways to bring the reflected appraisals more in line with the identity standard. In doing so, individuals may reject reflected appraisals that are not important to them or come from others they do not value, or they may look for objective information in the environment that may counter the reflected appraisals (Ichiyama 1993; Milkie 1999). They may engage in social movements to actively change the perceptions of their social group (Goffman 1963), may selectively associate with supportive others, and try to sustain an identity that is congruent with their self-concept (Snow and Anderson 1987). Some of these ideas, such as looking for and finding people like oneself, in the form of LGBTQ communities and other supportive allies, as well as engaging with LGBTQ groups and collectives for larger social change, are discussed in the next chapter.

The role of reflected appraisals from one's immediate environment, and the importance of individual agency in rejecting negative appraisals and looking for positive ones in consolidation of identity, can also be found in literature that compares experiences of sexual minorities with that of other marginalized and minority groups such as ethnic and religious minorities. Like other minority groups, sexual minorities are also characterized by group victimization, concern about group stigma, denial of membership, and aggression towards one's group (Allport 1954; Martin 1982). Thus, they too have to face the effects of negative appraisals. However, there exist several differences between other minorities and sexual minorities. One major difference, in the context of reflected appraisals and stigma, is that individuals who are gay or lesbian are usually born in heterosexual households and hence they do not get labelled as 'discredited' at the moment of birth itself. This 'discredited' status, which Goffman (1963) refers to as 'undesired differentness', is something that they become aware of as they are growing up. The undesired differentness, if and when it becomes known, would make the individual 'discredited'. Though there are obvious differences between ethnic or religious minorities and sexual minorities, I draw upon the work of a Dalit scholar describing the childhood experiences of a Dalit child in Maharashtra, India. Thorat (1979), in a chapter titled 'Passage to Adulthood: Perceptions from Below', describes the process of entry into a stigmatized identity, right from birth, of a Mahar/Dalit child in Maharashtra, India, and the possible exit from this identity by forming a new identity for oneself. Thorat states that an untouchable child, particularly one growing up in a village, receives guidance and messages from his parents, family, caste-mates, and caste Hindus regarding his identity, and it is this range of experiences and explanations that shape his attitude towards his stigmatized identity. Whether the child accepts or rejects this identity will depend on several factors, including: explanations given by parents, caste-mates, and caste Hindus about challenging or defending the stigma; whether there exists around him, in a visible way, social struggle against the caste system; and, whether the child is exposed to education and ideologies that are emancipatory or status-quoist in nature. Thus, the forming of a new identity, with an ideological base rooted in equality, would be dependent on several factors in the person's immediate as well as larger social context.

In the context of 'growing up gay', too, early experiences such as correction of one's gender and sexual expression by parents, doctors, teachers, and classmates, or experiences of homo-ignorance and negativity, throughout the growing-up years, would have an impact on the development of gay identity, as discussed in the previous chapter. Participants in this study have discussed their process of becoming aware of their same-sex attractions, and increasingly developing 'comfort' with who they are (identity standard). Along with this, all of them describe being aware of the negative reflected appraisals and working actively to seek out positive reflected appraisals, through looking for positive/affirmative information and depictions of LG individuals, looking for role-models, engaging with the queer community, making alliances with sympathetic others, and so on.

In the face of the invisibility of same-sexuality in public discourse, during the 1980s and 1990s when most of the participants were growing up in different cities of India, most participants talked about the importance of finding affirmative information about homosexuality, and meeting other people who were 'gay and ok with it'. Participants talked about finding the word 'gay' or 'homosexual' for the first time in a newspaper article, in the dictionary, on the internet, gay chat rooms, and so on.

Around the 9th Std., I knew it, but I would keep it to myself and I would read whatever information I would get and I think those days Ashok Rowkavi (one of the first gay man who came out on national television in the early 1990s) was quite famous. I wouldn't say he was my hero but then I used to read those articles by him or about him, cut them and keep them with me… it was during that time that I came out and said to myself, 'look this is the way I am, now I have a word for how I feel, so that's it!'

[Abhijit, 35 year old gay man]

I was exploring (on the internet) and then I came to a site called 'naughty chat' and I typed the word 'Gay' and entered a gay chat room and talked to the people there. So that time I was introduced to the concept of gay. It is through one of these sites that I spoke to the first Indian gay man who was there. He was 29 then and I was 19 and we used to talk a lot…

[Amit, 33 year old gay man]

Others described the importance of meeting gay and lesbian persons, support groups, or organizations working with LGBT persons.

at the age of 16 or 17, you don't know much and I think its necessary to meet someone else, who has figured this out… its like until someone uses the word, 'gay', 'lesbian', that flash bulb doesn't really go off in your head…

[Mehak, 28 year old lesbian woman]

One of the participants stated that she had her first girlfriend in her second year of post-graduation and that, once they were in a relationship, they both acknowledged for the first time that they could be lesbian. They then wanted to meet other people like themselves and know more about gay life in Bombay. She said:

So she (her girlfriend) decided to do a study on psychosocial aspects of coming out. And, she got in touch with the queer community in Bombay and Pune. And then I started getting the language, the confidence, the pride, you know the acceptance, when I met all these people, the queer community, the feminist women, then it worked for me

[Pradnya, 33 year old lesbian woman]

Another gay man, who first contacted a support group for gay men in Bombay, talked about his experience of volunteering for a gay rights conference in Bombay in 1998.

I happened to become part of one of the preparatory meetings for the conference, then I became part of the conference and as I told you, those three days were wonderful, lots of discussions happening, sharing stories and sharing experiences, meeting people from around the world with such different experiences… that I think really changed it for me, that helped me make the decision of coming out and deciding not to get married for sure and then to be involved in activism.

[Vineet, 40 year old gay man]

Thus, the shifting of reflected appraisals and seeking more positive reflected appraisals is an important step in strengthening one's identity standard. Participants played an active role in shifting the reflected appraisals to accurately match their identity standard. Goffman (1963) states that when the identity standard has not developed too strongly, individuals may find it difficult and may not seek to alter the negative reflected appraisals and instead may engage in the stigma management strategy of 'passing' as part of, or member of, the non-stigmatized group. However, when the identity standard is positive and strong, then the urge to come out and not hide anymore, as well as to work to alter the perception about one's group is strong too.

Reading Ek Madhavbag (*a play in Marathi depicting the coming out story of a gay son to his mother*) was a milestone for me and by that time I realized that it is futile to hide anything and whatever I am, I am… call it illness, call it anything but this is what I am and I also realized that if there is a debate between vikruti (perversion) and prakruti (nature), then for me, all this was so natural.

[Mansoor, 33 year old gay man]

Participant descriptions of joining support or activist groups, seeking safe, queer-friendly spaces and literature, is a reflection of individual agency in rejecting mainstream negative reflected appraisals and looking for positive ones. However, it is also a reflection of the structural and situational reality that such affirmative spaces have been created, since the early 1990s, in cities like Bombay, and continue to exist and support young queer persons in the face of a heterosexist public and institutional discourse in India.

While one underlines the importance of access to affirmative spaces in the process of the development of an affirmative LG identity, the subjective and the psychological experience of living with a stigmatized identity, and its impact on identity development as well as disclosure, cannot be ignored. In other words, while empowering and affirming social processes may enable stigmatized individuals to reject and alter negative reflected appraisals, the psyche needs to heal from the effects of stigma in order to engage with, and participate in, the empowering processes. This is illustrated in the following quote:

> My low self-esteem has got a lot to do with it. Me being compared to a girl... my girlishness, all this being socially unacceptable... The non-acceptance feature was there all the time and the experience of being ridiculed. These two factors were always in the picture. That is why I did not want to come out to people
>
> [Ajay, 32 year old gay man]

## 4.2 To Tell or Not: Situated Complexities of Disclosure/ Non-disclosure in Lives of LG Individuals

Stage models of LG identity development assume that once individuals become aware of their same-sex attractions and pass through the initial phase of denial, fear, and bargaining, and learn to tolerate their lesbian or gay identity, then the path is paved for self-acceptance and coming out to oneself and others. These models, thus, assume that every LG individual who has developed comfort with their identity and accepted themselves would come out to most people such as family, colleagues, and friends. In fact, non-disclosure is interpreted as failure to attain the later stages of LG identity development, such as gay pride and integration (Cass 1979). In making this assumption, what the stage models overlook is the role of the situational complexity of individual lives, and what they overemphasize is the impact of identity on behavioural choices of disclosure (Rust 1993; Parks 1999). Situational complexity may include several individual factors such as being stuck in a homophobic job environment or lack of availability of social and familial support. It is necessary to recognize that the individual 'self' is not merely a psychological reality; it is a collection of self-concepts and multiple identities that are essentially based within social positions (Stryker 1968) of class, caste, gender, age, and so on. Thus, choices of disclosure of sexual identity cannot be seen as merely being determined by levels of internalized homophobia or self-acceptance; several structural and contextual variables would play a significant part in these decisions.

Participants in this study discussed multiple factors that motivated them to come out, and also cited several processes and reasons to choose non-disclosure. In fact, the decision of disclosure, partial disclosure, or non-disclosure resembles the idea of a 'revolving door': of being in or out of the closet depending on the costs associated with disclosure (Schneider and Conrad 1980).

Being dependent on parents, living in the parental home while continuing studies, or not having a stable job with a regular income, were significant situational/contextual factors that motivated some of the participants to not disclose their sexuality to their parents. Fear of the worst kinds of responses from the family, based on the experiences of other LG individuals within the community, added to the apprehension of telling the family. Research studies, and other literature from human rights groups and NGOs in India, cites family as one of the main sources of violence and abuse in a LG person's life (particularly lesbian women), especially when their sexuality is known/ discovered by the family (Fernandez and Gomathy 2003; PUCL-K 2001). Non-disclosure to family, however, did not imply that the LG individual led a depressed, 'in the closet', lonely existence. Participants in this study talked about being part of the gay community, going for community events and parties, having sex, and having relationships, while they maintained a single status within their family homes.

One of the participants stated:

> No not yet because I am still dependent on them, even if I work... at least as of now I don't want to tell them. I go for parties and all and meet many people. At home, it is more like I went out with friends and got late coming back. They don't know I went for a gay party. Finally what is the end? Marriage! Marriage is the end. Till then if they don't come to know, its ok. When they start talking about that (marriage), then I will tell them... by then I will also be financially stable

> [Karan, 24 year old gay man]

Tan (2011) in his article titled, 'Go Home Gay Boy! Or why do Singaporean Gay Men prefer to "Go Home" and Not "Come Out"' argues that the Anglo-American ontologies, which posit that gay men should come out to match their outer selves with their inner ones, may be limiting in explaining the reality of gay persons in other parts of the world, particularly in the south-eastern context, where kinship and family ties play a central role in individual identities; familial concerns and filial duties are placed in high regard. Tan argues that gay men in Singapore couch their homosexuality in kinship terms and 'go home' with their boyfriends, and resist acts of coming out that are seen as causing hurt and bringing shame to one's family. Tan thus urges us to not uncritically accept the coming out ritual as the only way to lead an authentic life. Another dimension to this construction of self through family and kinship ties is proposed by the dialogical self theory (Hermans 2002). This position is conceptually very close to the social constructionists but different in that it does not lead us to dissolve the person in the social realm. It emphasises that the subjective 'I' is created within the inter-subjective experiences of 'being-with' (or 'being-against') others. Thus, the personal realm is bounded with the social realm, not as independent entities but as mutually defined (Hermans 2002). This implies that the 'going home' instead of 'coming out', as described by Tan, is as much about the interpersonal realm and the unique situations in every interpersonal dyad (e.g. parent-child) or triads (e.g. parent/grandparents-child-sibling) that influence/define one's self-concept, the expectations from the self, and ideas of 'appropriate/inappropriate' conduct. It is also as much about one's gender, birth order, one's status within the family, the family's status (or 'honour') within the community, and so on. Boyce (2006), based on his work with MSM in Kolkata, India, argues that, in the Indian context, among the large population of men who have sex with men, only a minority would 'identify' with same-sex sexuality and would take on an identity based on sexuality such as 'gay' or 'bisexual'. The default presentation of 'self' to family and society is a heterosexual one, and identity is constituted in social and community terms rather than individual ones. Privileging of family values, arranged marriage, and the obligation to marry, means that "same-sex sexual relationships have rarely been radically disassociated from heterosexuality" (Boyce 2006, 83). In fact, the centrality of heterosexual marriage is such that any sexual relations outside of it may often not be acknowledged. Thus, male to male sexual relationships can become problematic only when linked to claims for socially recognized sexual identities.

In a study by Thompson et al. (2013), the authors explore negative attitudes of *kothis* (effeminate men) from Karnataka, India, towards their sexuality and gender expressions. These attitudes include viewing their sexuality as a 'bad habit', an addiction, and viewing their lives (referring to their gender non-conformity and sexual attraction towards men) as 'spoiled'. The authors explore reasons for these self-depreciating attitudes and, in doing so, go beyond the explanation of internalized homonegativity, to explore a range of factors within the social contexts of these participants. Thompson et al. argue that negative self-evaluations of their participants are more connected to ideas of family dis/honour, shame, dis/loyalty than individual factors such as fear, rejection, pain, and so on. Several of the *kothi* participants talked about hiding their sexuality in order to protect their families from social stigmatization as well as from the fear of being disowned. Family disownment, in this context, does not merely refer to losing contact with one's nuclear family, but would constitute a form of 'social death' (Thompson et al. 2013, 1244), where the individual stands to lose virtually all connections with the wider kinship network and lose every form of social support. This would have material and financial implications, with the individual standing to lose any share of inheritance and access to familial resources in a patrilineal clan system. Thus, self-depreciating attitudes can be seen to be a result of continued experiences of stigma, discrimination, and violence from a society that values reproductive heteronormativity and dominant masculinity. It is in this context, of avoiding discrimination and violence, that several non-normative individuals try to construct a 'normal' identity and life for themselves through heterosexual marriage, children, and family.

Another one of Tan's arguments, that it is normative for grown up/adult men to live with their parents until the time they marry and buy their own house, combined with the fact that the real estate rates in Singapore make it difficult for young people to have their own place, applies directly to the situation of young people in India. In the Indian patriarchal and heteronormative society, mothers worry about their sons having to cook and clean and take care of themselves, and are ever willing to continue to take care of their adult unmarried sons. Thus, these sons can continue to live within the family home and, simultaneously, access freedoms and mobility that are available to men and sons in patriarchal societies, which in turn would allow for sexual exploration and living out one's sexuality to some extent. The analogy of 'going home' instead of 'coming out' is seen to be often working within the Indian context as well, at least for gay men. It is important, however, to note that, in such a society, the pressure of confirming to rigid standards of masculinity, heterosexual marriage, reproduction, and filial duties is high too. This implies that effeminate men, *kothi*s, who may not share the same cultural and social capital as 'masculine', (read in society as 'heterosexual') men, may not find it as easy to 'go home'.

One of the participants, Karan, states (see previous quote) that 'marriage is the end' implying that marriage is seen as compulsory in his context, and he expects that, at some point, the pressure to marry will begin to build up, when he would have to think about coming out to his parents. One of the other participants, also in the context of marriage, talked about avoiding disclosure to his family, friends, or colleagues. He said that, as an elder brother, he was responsible for his sister's marriage and could not think of coming out as it would affect her marriage prospects.

> I don't want it to affect my younger sister as she has to get married and I don't know how society and others would react to her. So I don't want it to affect anyone in my family.
>
> [Sunil, 32 year old gay man]

Tan's argument of 'going home' may not directly apply to all lesbian and gay lives and may be much more complicated, for instance, in the case of lesbian women. For most women, there are several restrictions placed upon their mobility, and access to resources and choices within the natal home. Control over their sexuality, the pressures of compulsory heterosexual marriage and reproduction are even stronger in their lives. Moreover, they do not have as much access to the social and cultural capital of community and family as their male counterparts. It is against this backdrop that lesbian women may choose other kinds of strategies to avoid violence, and manage stigma in their lives. Leaving family home and withdrawing from family, once they are independent, concealing their sexual identity and choosing whom, when, why to disclose to, are some of the stigma-management strategies that lesbian participants in this study reported. In fact, of the fifteen lesbian women interviewed in this study, only three were living with their natal families at the time.

One of the participants said that she was facing a lot of pressure from her parents for marriage and had been wondering about consequences of disclosure to parents. She said:

… but I can't tell my mom what I am. Because I am the only daughter and if I tell them, they will get a heart attack (laughs)… I know my mom very well, she will stop everything. She will throw my computer, she will throw my mobile because I am always online… She will think that this internet and my whole circle of online friends have spoilt me, so she will stop everything of mine…

[Salma, 30 year old lesbian woman]

Another participant spoke about leaving her parental home and migrating to another city; first, for her education, and now for a job. She said that her parents already had difficulty dealing with her choice of being away from home and making a career for herself, instead of choosing marriage. She spoke about not coming out to her parents:

I don't want to come out to them, not now for sure. They are still dealing with me not being there at home and working in another city. Then they think that I am living with a 'friend'. They know that I go out with her on little little holidays. I really don't know what they make of it… I wouldn't want to deal with repercussions of coming out right now.

[Priti, 31 year old lesbian woman]

Goffman (1963) describes the use of information-management strategies by those who are discreditable, that is, those individuals, whose stigma may not be visible and who can 'pass' as belonging to the group of non-stigmatized. However, they are 'discreditable' as they can be discredited with visibility. In the above quote, the participant seems to be managing the information that she provides to her parents about her living arrangement in the city. Though she tells them that she is living with a friend, who is a woman (an acceptable proposition), and that they take holidays together (more acceptable for a young unmarried woman than taking holidays with men), she chooses not to disclose the nature of her relationship with this friend (which would be a highly unacceptable proposition). In this sense, the participant is able to manage her identity as a 'good daughter', one who will not bring shame to the family, while being able to negotiate an independent life in another city, away from her parents and extended family.

Discussing the consequences of coming out, one of the lesbian participants, who came out of a heterosexual marriage and has two daughters, said that she would like to be able to talk to her daughters, about her sexuality and her woman partner, at some point in their life. However, she believes that her children have already undergone the trauma of parental divorce, and since that has caused a lot of insecurity, she does not want to further burden them by talking about her sexuality. Divorce has itself stigmatized and, in Goffman's words, 'discredited' this participant and her children; disclosure of her same-sex sexuality would mean dealing with an additional layer of stigma, both for her and her children.

I am still not out to her and I would like her to finish her 10th standard before I tell her. She is a little soft, she has taken a beating with a bad marriage, she has had to go through a lot of stress. She has so much to deal with; I don't want to add to her tension by telling her that her mom's a lesbian…

[Claire, 41 year old lesbian woman]

One of the participants recalled his college days and said that, while he was completely comfortable with who he was, the peer and college environment he was in was replete with ideas of heterosexual dating, romance, courting and there was total invisibility to same-sex desires. As a result, he said, he never really got a chance to come out. He said:

> I was reasonably good looking so there would be jokes and link ups depending on who they saw me speaking to… if I spoke to a girl who was absolutely ugly, they would say '*chee* (yuck) what a contrast' and if I spoke to a good looking girl, they would say '*achi jodi hai*' (you make a nice pair)… By this time I was very clear that I was a gay man who was in the closet and was taking things sportingly. In my entire batch or whoever I knew in college, I didn't see anybody who seemed gay or could be approached, so I just chose to keep it to myself.

> [Atul, 33 year old gay man]

Some of the participants who chose to not come out to parents cited interpersonal reasons, like lack of emotional closeness with parents, as reasons for the same. Since they did not discuss most aspects of their lives with their parents, disclosure about their sexual orientation seemed irrelevant. One participant said:

> My Aunt stays just down the road, I haven't met her for the last 8 months, my aunt and uncle call me and ask me to visit, I am like '*dekhengey*' (we'll see), I am quite apathetic to my father and my real mom. My step mom and I weirdly enough can talk now, but we are more like acquaintances…

> [Avinash, 28 year old gay man]

One of the participants talked about her strained relationship with her father:

> They don't even know about stupid things like I smoke! They don't want to confront anything, even something so stupid… Its pointless. And my father being my father, he couldn't accept me with short hair. I mean I cut my hair in the 3rd and he didn't talk to me till I was in 5th! I grew my hair long and I cut my hair again in the 11th Std. I cut it really short. My dad slapped me… and from that day till now he hasn't spoken to me.

> [Priya, 30 year old lesbian woman]

In addition to the lack of closeness with family, or even hostile relationships with family members, other participants stated that they knew their parents were conservative and hence were not likely to engage in a conversation about their sexuality or try to understand. Some said that they have just accepted that their parents belong to a different generation, and would have a hard time understanding this, so they have chosen not to disclose.

In the case of participants who chose to come out to their friends or family, most said that they wanted to share an important part of their lives with their loved ones, and wanted more authenticity in their relationships and did not want to hide anymore. Some participants stated that they knew that their parents had worries about them as they were not getting married, and coming out and discussing their relationships would be one way of addressing these concerns. Pressure of marriage was a common motivator and context to come out to parents, according to some participants.

...because they don't know me, a large part of me, that is the primary reason. I want to be able to share my life with them. Then there are some very practical things like they would be happy to know that I have a partner because currently they think that I am a single 33 year old man who has not gotten married till now and will probably not get married, will lead a solitary life...

[Atul, 33 year old gay man]

So that morning when the topic of my marriage came up, I said that I have to tell you something, I have decided not to get married.... Its a personal decision and I am very sure about it and there's nothing to discuss... even as I was saying it, I knew that this was the beginning of a coming out conversation...

[Shashank, 38 year old gay man]

Some of the participants stated that, now that they are independent and a few of them have steady partners, they were no longer fearful of the consequences of coming out and hence decided to disclose. Citing the ease of his life circumstances, one of the participants stated that, after the death of his father and marriage of his sister, he felt more confident in coming out to his mother:

The positive thing for me to come out was the fact that my father was no more because I don't think I could have ever told my father about me... then my sister got married. I had decided that I will tell my mother and then there was this play that I was reading, which was about a son coming out to his mother, I gave the script to my mom... that's how I came out to her.

[Mansoor, 33 year old gay man]

Thus, disclosure or non-disclosure of one's same-sex sexuality is not just a matter of achieving psychological comfort with oneself and coming to a point of self-acceptance after working through all the negative evaluations associated with same-sex sexuality in one's family, among friends, in school and colleges, at work place, in social contexts, media, and so on. It is, on the contrary, often a decision based on complex psychological, interpersonal, and social realities. Having access to gay affirmative language, literature, role models, support from the queer community, as well as straight allies, independence from one's parents/family, access to discrimination-free education, jobs, peers, protection from gay-related violence; all of these come together to create facilitative or debilitating environment/contexts that determines choices related to coming out.

## 4.3   Responses to Disclosure, and Its Impact on LG Identity Development and Maintenance

Coming out or disclosing one's same-sex sexual identity shifts an individual from the 'discreditable' stigmatized to the 'discredited' stigmatized. Hence, responses to coming out and its consequences, play a significant role in the identity development, consolidation, and maintenance of the LG identity. As described earlier, most LG individuals, even as they become aware of their identity and develop an identity standard, also become aware of the negative reflected appraisals associated with homosexuality. An important part of identity work, then, is to look for positive reflected appraisals and develop a positive self-view as a LG individual. These positive reflected appraisals may be available in one's natural environment (friends, family, co-workers), or one may have to look for the same in the form of support groups, activist collectives for LGBT, and so on. Examples of already existing positive appraisals would include: growing up in a liberal family, within a liberal neighbourhood, or going to a school that is affirmative of human diversity. Another example of a positive reflected appraisal is an accepting, affirming, or positive response, to coming out or disclosure of one's sexuality. Such a positive reflected appraisal, from persons who are significant in a LG individual's life, plays a crucial role in enhancing self-esteem and development of an affirmative LG identity.

> She took everything positively and supported me. I felt that since my mother has come to know about me and has accepted me the way I am, I need not fear anymore or hide my identity and in fact whom should I fear? My mother is with me and I need not think about the rest of the world. I really don't care.
>
> [Mansoor 33 year old gay man]

Several participants described their coming out experiences with their family members and friends. Gestures of support, unconditional love, assurance that the quality of relationship would remain intact post-disclosure, from mothers, siblings, and friends, were reported by participants.

> I am very fortunate with my people at home. They are quite accepting of most things… after I came out to my brother, he would tease me for a week and say, 'oh! you are so gay, so full of happiness!'
>
> [Abhijit, 35 year old gay man]

> I remember the night, when she (mother) asked me, if I have anything to tell her. I knew that it was time to just come out and say it and I was so scared. I started and then broke down and then in the middle of all that, did not want to tell at all. She was so worried that, she just said, 'whatever it is just tell me'. So I just said it and her first reaction was, 'thank god! I thought you were going to say something horrible like you are into drugs or in some trouble, this gay is fine, it is ok'…
>
> [Sahil, 25 year old gay man]

Some participants had come out at their work places as well and some were selectively out only in LGBT and/or other safe spaces. Goffman (1963) describes various stigma-management strategies used by stigmatized individuals to cope with negative reflected appraisals and to maintain a positive identity. Information management or selective disclosure of identity, depending on the individual's assessment of levels of hostility/safety that one expects, contexts, and relationships, is one such crucial stigma-management strategy.

As seen earlier, the decision to come out is mediated by several contextual and situational factors and not merely based on psychological preparedness or consolidation of one's identity. Similarly, according to a study of parental responses to same-sex sexuality in their children by Ranade et al. (2016), responses to coming out, too, are mediated by several factors, such as the extent of awareness, exposure, contact with LGBT persons, personal beliefs about sexuality, circumstances of coming out, and relationship with the LG person prior to the disclosure. Non-conformity by heterosexual parents in their own life choices—such as choices of marriage partners against wishes of the family or choosing to be in inter-caste, inter-religious, inter-regional marriages—mediated their responses to their children's transgressions. Among participants in the current study, too, several of these situational factors played an important role. For instance, one of the participants had gone to the UK as part of an exchange program while doing his post-graduate studies. Here he met and became friends with several people who were gay-friendly. One of his friends invited him to a wedding party of a gay couple. He recalls this event:

> I was shocked and surprised and of course happy. I was meeting a gay couple for the first time and that too, *ekdam direct lagnach* (directly at a gay wedding). I took lot of pictures and I still have them. I showed these wedding pictures to my mom when I came out to her. It was my way of saying that there are others like me and they can be happy too…

> [Mansoor, 33 year old gay man]

In the case of this study participant, a series of affirmative experiences during an exchange program helped his decision to come out to his mother. However, there can also be negative life events that may help with disclosure and mediate responses to disclosure. Another participant discussed her coming out to her mother, which had not gone well initially, and her mother had only cried in response and refused to talk to her about her sexuality after that. This participant said that a negative and stressful life event had actually helped her mother to acknowledge her sexuality and begin to engage with her about the same. The participant had had a difficult period in her relationship with her partner, where her partner attempted suicide and was admitted to the hospital. It was after this incident that the participant's mother came forward to support her daughter.

> After all the hospital stay and all, I went home to Pune, because I was so troubled, she (girlfriend) went to Meerut, her hometown. We stayed apart, dealt with it and later got back together… but all this helped with my mom and the barriers were broken. Then she started talking about my life, she started asking about her (girlfriend). So from July (time of first coming out) to April she didn't meet her at all and then she came to the hospital and saw her lying on the bed, really unwell and so she went and held her…

> [Pradnya, 33 year old lesbian woman]

Coming out, or making one's same-sex sexual orientation known, can also have the effect of *spoilage of one's social identity*. In Goffman's words, "it has the effect of cutting them off from society and from themselves so that they stand a discredited person facing an unaccepting world" (Goffman 1963, 19). Some of the participants in this study described homonegative, hostile and violent responses from their environment, responses which made their own journey of self-acceptance immensely challenging.

An illustrative example is that of Sandip, who first came out to his best friend who he was attracted to. The friend called his desire *gallicha* (disgusting), while also offering to help by taking him to doctors, who could cure him. Sandip recounts that all through his childhood he was effeminate and timid. He would find it difficult to make friends with boys and had faced severe corrective behaviours (described in the previous chapter) at home and school. This friend was his only support and hence he believed that the friend's effort at taking him to the doctor were well-intentioned. At the doctor's clinic, Sandip was asked to test his testosterone levels and then recommended testosterone injections (presumably to increase the male hormone in his body, in order to correct his effeminacy). Since the treatment was going to be expensive, Sandip's friend decided to tell his sister. When the sister was informed, she cried for a few days and stopped talking to Sandip. After a week, she gave him a newspaper article about homosexuality being curable with psychiatric help. At the psychiatrist's clinic, Sandip was offered counselling and anti-depressant medication. He was advised to watch 'straight pornography' (imagery of heterosexual sexual acts) at the clinic to enhance heterosexual desire. The doctors asked him to bring his parents to the clinic where they received counselling and they were informed that while the treatment may last for a long time (approximately 2 years), if Sandip had strong motivation, they could help him. The first response of the parents to this pathological presentation of their son's homosexuality was further pathologizing:

> My mother asked the doctor if *tyachi ji zaga ahey ti vyavastit ahey ki nahi?* (Whether his place down there/genitals were normal?), that was their first question. Then they asked if I had sex anywhere or if I had been raped because of which I had become like this…
>
> [Sandip, 24 year old gay man]

In addition to the clinically prescribed cures for homosexuality, Sandip was asked to try meditation, and *nama-smaran* (chanting of god/ godman's name) by different family members. Following these humiliating responses to his coming out, Sandip attempted suicide, believing that he was a pervert. At the hospital where he was admitted, he met a social worker, who gave him the phone number of a local LGBT support and rights group in Pune. Here, Sandip met people with diverse sexualities and gender expressions and this helped to reduce his isolation and his belief that 'he is the only one with such abnormal desires'. Sandip's narrative is an example of ways in which homo-ignorance, prejudice, familial and peer rejection, pathologization by experts, and experiences of systemic violence, can lead to a breakdown of the individual and may lead to what stage models of identity development have referred to as 'identity foreclosure'.

Highlighting the impact of negative appraisals and experiences of discrimination and violence in the lives of self-identified young *kothi*s in Karnataka, Thompson et al. (2013) state: "Some participants claimed that their experiences of discrimination had destroyed their sense of personal goodness and to manage these feelings of ruin, they tended to avoid certain places and people and were watchful for violence" (1243–44). Perry et al. (1956) describe a fatal deficiency of the self-system that results from social isolation as "the fear that others can disrespect a person because of something he shows means that he is always insecure in his contact with other people; and this insecurity arises, not from mysterious or somewhat disguised sources, but from something he knows he cannot fix" (145).

Achieving an affirmative identity or experiencing a 'spoiled identity' is a complex process that results from interaction between several factors, ranging from the intra-psychic to the social and political. This is illustrated in the narrative of another study participant. She describes how she processed her mother's response to her coming out. She says that, while she did feel sorry for all the pain and grief her mother was going through and the fact that she had let her down, this did not translate into her feeling sorry for being homosexual or directing the mother's anguish and pain towards herself in the form of self-imposed sanction.

> She read the letter (coming out letter written by the participant), and she started crying. She went out of the room and she howled and I think that was the worst sound I had heard in my entire life… I was so traumatized that I was giving her that kind of grief… Later at some point in the night, we all went to bed, but I couldn't sleep. I was alert and worried… was she still crying? because every time I would hear her cry, my heart would be like, shit man I have let her down so bad and at that point I was not upset that she had not understood or accepted me, I was just upset that she was so sad…

> [Pradnya, 33 year old lesbian woman]

Finally, having same-sex sexual experiences, relationships, and intimacies does not always translate into commitment to a same-sex sexual identity. Identifying or committing to a same-sex sexual identity does not automatically imply a public declaration or an 'out' status as a queer person. As seen in this chapter, identification, self-categorization, disclosure, non-disclosure, or partial disclosure, is mediated through a range of psychological, interpersonal, socio-cultural, and political factors, and should not be seen merely as a function of levels of self-acceptance. In fact, the idea of continuity or coherence of the self kept intact through the 'coming out' process, as described in American psychological literature on coming out, is challenged here. The need to view the self as being embedded in a familial, social, and cultural context, and as being an active agent negotiating these contexts is emphasized in this chapter.

# References

Allport, G. W. (1954). *The nature of prejudice*. Reading, MA: Addison-Wesley.

American Psychological Association (APA). (2004). *Assisting students with disclosure—The "Coming Out" process*. Washington DC: APA.

Billson, J. M. (1994). Society and self: A symbolic interactionist framework for sociological practice. *Clinical Sociology Review, 12*(1), 115–133.

Boyce, P. (2006). Moral ambivalence and irregular practices: Contextualizing male-to-male sexualities in Calcutta/India. *Feminist Review, 83*, 79–98.

Burke, P. J. (1991). Identity processes and social stress. *American Sociological Review*, 836–849.

Cass, V. C. (1979). Homosexuality identity formation: A theoretical model. *Journal of Homosexuality, 4*(3), 219–235.

Coleman, E. (1982). Developmental stages of the coming out process. *Journal of Homosexuality, 7* (2–3), 31–43.

D'Augelli, A. R. (1994). Identity development and sexual orientation: Toward a model of lesbian, gay, and bisexual development. In E. J. Trickett, R. J. Watts, & D. Birman (Eds.), *Human diversity: Perspectives on people in context* (pp. 312–333). San Francisco: Jossey-Bass.

Fassinger, R. E. (1998). Lesbian, gay, and bisexual identity and student development theory. In R. L. Sanlo (Ed.), *Working with lesbian, gay, bisexual, and transgender college students: A handbook for faculty and administrators* (pp. 13–22). Westport, CT: Greenwood Press.

Fernandez, B., & Gomathy, N. B. (2003). The nature of violence faced by lesbian women in India. *Mumbai: Research centre on violence against women, Tata Institute of Social Sciences.* Retrieved December 15, 2017 from https://www.tiss.edu/uploads/files/8The_Nature_of_violence_faced_by_Lesbian_women_in_India.pdf

Gecas, V., & Burke, P. J. (1995). Self and identity. *Sociological Perspectives on Social Psychology, 41*–67.

Gecas, V., & Schwalbe, M. L. (1983). Beyond the looking-glass self: Social structure and efficacy-based self-esteem. *Social Psychology Quarterly, 77*–88.

Goffman, E. (1963). *Stigma—notes on management of spoiled identity.* New Jersey: Prentice-Hall Inc.

Hermans, H. J. M. (2002). The dialogical self as society of mind: Introduction. *Theory and Psychology, 12,* 147–160.

Ichiyama, M. A. (1993). The reflected appraisal process in small-group interaction. *Social Psychology Quarterly, 56*(2), 87–99.

Kaufman, J. M., & Johnson, C. (2004). Stigmatized individuals and the process of identity. *The Sociological Quarterly, 45*(4), 807–833.

Martin, A. D. (1982). Learning to hide: The socialisation of the gay adolescent. *Adolescent Psychiatry, 10,* 52–65.

Milkie, M. A. (1999). Social comparisons, reflected appraisals, and mass media: The impact of pervasive beauty images on black and white girls' self-concepts. *Social Psychology Quarterly, 62*(2), 190–210.

Parks, C. A. (1999). Lesbian identity development: An examination of differences across generations. *American Journal of Orthopsychiatry, 69*(3), 347.

Perry, H. S., Gawel, M. L., & Gibbon, M. (Eds.). (1956). *Clinical studies in psychiatry.* New York: W.W. Norton & Co.

PUCL-K. (2001). *Human rights violations against sexuality minorities in India: A PUCL-K fact finding report about Bangalore.* Bengaluru, Karnataka: People's Union for Civil Liberties.

Ranade, K., Shah, C., & Chatterji, S. (2016). Making sense: Familial journeys towards acceptance of gay and lesbian family members in India. *Indian Journal of Social Work, Special Issue on Family Transitions and Emerging Forms, 77*(4), 437–458.

Rust, P. C. (1993). "Coming out" in the age of social constructionism: Sexual identity formation among lesbian and bisexual women. *Gender and Society, 7*(1), 50–77.

Schneider, J. W., & Conrad, P. (1980). In the closet with illness: Epilepsy, stigma potential and information control. *Social Problems, 28*(1), 32–44.

Snow, D. A., & Anderson, L. (1987). Identity work among the homeless: The verbal construction and avowal of personal identities. *American Journal of Sociology, 92*(6), 1336–1371.

Stryker, S. (1968). Identity salience and role performance: The relevance of symbolic interaction theory for family research. *Journal of Marriage and the Family, 50,* 558–564.

Tan, C. K. (2011). Go home, gay boy! Or, why do Singaporean gay men prefer to "go home" and not "come out"? *Journal of Homosexuality, 58*(6–7), 865–882.

Thompson, L. H., Khan, S., du Plessis, E., Lazarus, L., Reza-Paul, S., Hafeez Ur Rahman, S., et al. (2013). Beyond internalised stigma: Daily moralities and subjectivity among self-identified *kothi*s in Karnataka, South India. *Culture, Health and Sexuality, 15*(10), 1237–1251.

Thorat, S. K. (1979). Passage to adulthood: Perceptions from below. In S. Kakar (Ed.), *Identity and adulthood* (pp. 65–81). USA: Oxford University Press.

Troiden, R. (1979). Becoming homosexual: A model of gay identity acquisition. *Psychiatry, 42,* 362–373.

Troiden, R. (1988). *Gay and lesbian identity: A sociological analysis.* Dix Hills, NY: General Hall.

# Chapter 5
# Living Life as a Queer Person: Role of Intimate Relationships in Consolidation of Identity

*Prelude*

*Of love and relationships*

*narrative one:*

*i was in a relationship with a woman for more than eight years. she was in, what i call, 'a limbo married situation' for most of this time. she had not legally divorced her husband but about two years after we started seeing each other, she separated from him. the separation too was partial in the sense that he would control her in many ways primarily through their (at the time of separation) three-year-old son. her son and the custody battles she feared would ensue was her primary reason for not seeking legal divorce. at least, that was the stated reason. i think there is never any one reason that keeps married women in dead marriages from seeking divorce.*

*after her separation, she moved into a rented apartment and her son would stay with her on weekdays and with his father on weekends. so once she moved out, we had the place to ourselves during the weekends. i would visit every weekend and we would do the weekly chores together – buying veggies, groceries, school supplies, paying electricity and phone bills, watching films, drinks and dinner. so while we did as we liked, there was always a sense of watching over your shoulder... avoiding restaurants, cinema halls, where we were likely to run into the husband. if the phone rang, i could not pick it up as it could be her husband calling. i felt like i was always this person who needed to be hidden from her family and extended family with the apprehension that i, with my gender non-conforming appearance, would confirm something about her and her sexuality. she was convinced that he would probably hire a detective to take our pictures, which he could then use to blackmail her or take sole custody of the child.*

*i can't say for sure, whether for her all this was part of the violent consequences of defying the patriarchal institution of marriage and rebelling against the sacred*

© Springer Nature Singapore Pte Ltd. 2018
K. Ranade, *Growing Up Gay in Urban India*,
https://doi.org/10.1007/978-981-10-8366-2_5

*idea of full-time motherhood that is possible only within the institution of marriage or was this also about internalized homonegativity, shame, guilt… maybe it was a mix of all.*

*narrative two:*

*i have always wanted to see a bollywood style, three hour long film with lots of song and dance and locations in switzerland with two men, madly in love… people say, i am foolish, innocent, naïve for believing in that kind of a love story. i am just saying we need those kinds of larger than life, happy looking and pretty smelling images of gay love too. i think it's fine to be different and talk about that difference, assert that difference, and say f\*\*\* off to the world that undermines us for our difference, but to be able to do all that, it's also necessary to feel home somewhere…*

    *for me and p, our relationship has been that home for us for over a decade now. we have seen each other through that tumultuous phase of self-doubt about our sexuality, about dating women, dating men, reckless sleeping around, getting drunk and all that drama… we have also been together in taking decisions over career paths, jobs, illnesses, even a parental death. at the end of the day, when we hear about a young person being thrown out of their homes or someone giving up on the fight that life can be for most gay people, we know that we were saved because of each other.*

*narrative three:*

*among queer people when we talk about non-normative relationships, we usually mean 'open' relationships… like straight people when they talk about non-nor-mative relationships they usually mean 'live-in' relationships… come to think of it, what do these words mean? as if to suggest that people in normative relationships, what they do, their love, relating, their being is 'closed' and ours 'open' or that they 'live-out' instead of 'in' or 'with'… it's funny, isn't it? but i think there is a lot of stereotyping in both the gay and straight world about the normative/regular relationship as about the not-so-regular relationship.*

    *talking about the stereotype of 'open/non-monogamous' relationships, in the queer world, we see these as cool, radical… relationships that challenge patriar-chal and heterosexual norms of 'happily married forever' and all the oppression connected to that including staying on in violent marriages, guarding family 'izzat'* (honour) *to qualifying for inheritance of the 'family'* (read husband's/father's) *house that you have laboured in as much if not more, all your life. but when i think of my relationships with my lovers and partners, i do not see these as just political decisions taken to set alternative examples, models of other ways of living and loving… for me, initially, it was simply about being deeply attached to my partner of seven years, while having fallen in love, head over heels with another woman, someone who made my life richer, intellectually, emotionally, sexually… then it was about a lot of work, emotional work, i mean. it is about all of us consciously working on and dealing with our fears, insecurities, anxieties, jealousies—all those intense emotions that we experience, just as part of being human, but also because we have been conditioned all our lives to believe that we own, possess our partners and they are like our extensions in this world. so when we hear our partner say that they have fallen for someone, what we hear instead is that they have betrayed us, betrayed our trust, loyalty, years of togetherness… as if they owe their existence to us. it does not have to be like this… a conversation with your partner that starts with, "i think i may have fallen for someone…", can end or begin in multiple ways.*

*for me, it was about assuring my partner of seven years that she would always be a significant part of my life and we will continue to do the things that we did together as a couple, as a family and be part of each other's life projects. it also meant working a new equation with my new lover about how much time we could spend together and when i needed to be away. basically, a lot of work on boundaries and also figuring out alone time with myself, so that i nurtured myself as much as i did both my relationships. it got more complicated as more and more actors like friends and family got involved in our story, each with their own ideas of what is a good relationship… my therapist once said to me that resources of money, time and energy are finite… for me this is the bottom line and of course consent of all involved and other such questions of ethics but certainly not guilt and loyalty in deciding on having one, two, many partners, lovers, crushes, flings…*

Consolidation of one's identity as gay or lesbian is as much an interpersonal and social process as it is an intrapsychic one. In other words, recognizing 'difference' in various areas of life while growing up, making sense of this difference, finding the language for articulating this difference in terms of sexuality and gender expression, working through straitjacketed definitions of heterosexuality and homosexuality, are some of the intrapsychic (within the individual's psyche) battles that queer persons fight to reach a point of self-acceptance and celebration. However, in addition to this internal process, meeting other people like oneself, sharing life stories, forming community bonds, supporting each other's struggles (personal and political), and finding romantic/sexual partner/s, are important processes that are enabling for a gay or lesbian person. Thus, experiences with interpersonal and social interactions are as much significant in consolidation of a lesbian/gay identity as the psychic journey of navigating difference and understanding one's sexuality.

The previous chapters have focussed on non-normative gender and sexual expressions and 'making sense' of this non-normativity, while living within the normative frame of family, school, and peers. One chapter has explored the dynamic process of communicating this 'non-normative/difference' to the world around and making multiple choices of disclosure and non-disclosure while looking for affirmations of one's identity.

In this chapter, I explore the role of intimate relationships and meeting with the queer community as milestones in the process of identity development and affirmation. From 'being gay' to 'being gay with someone', that is, developing an intimate relationship with another same-sex adult, can often be an experience that further affirms one's identity. Similarly, meeting with, and being part of, a queer community enhances commitment to one's gay identity. In fact, many people initially access the queer community/s in their respective cities or across cities, and virtual or online communities, in the hope of finding a romantic/sexual partner. In that sense, meeting community and forming intimate relationships may be closely linked processes.

## 5.1  Same-Sex Relationships: Mirroring and Self-affirmation

Being in an intimate relationship with a person of the same sex can be an immensely affirming experience and can help crystallize one's own sense of self as a gay or lesbian person (Kaufman and Johnson 2004). Several participants echoed this sentiment with respect to some of their initial relationships.

> I was first involved with this woman who was a crack pot... she actually was so terrified by her sexuality. So after I left her, I met this other woman, who was pretty sure of herself. She was out and all... that relationship kind of gave me the strength to be confident about who I was. It gave me the courage.

> [Vidya, 35 year old lesbian woman]

… discussing with my partner, I gradually realized that this defense mechanism that I am using, saying that I am a bisexual and will get married one day is not right… because I haven't tried it and he encouraged me to try it and that's when I knew that it's not going to work and that I am hiding behind the label bisexual, when I am actually gay.

[Atul, 33 year old gay man talks about his first long-term relationship at age 26]

For many participants, being in a relationship for the first time was also their first experience of knowing another gay person closely. Hence, in addition to self-affirmation and joys of first love and sex (which may be comparable to the first relationship experiences of heterosexual couples as well), forming intimate relationships with a person of the same sex was also about the experience of reduced isolation, identification, shared experiences of 'becoming', and acknowledging one's gayness, learning more about gay life, and so on.

Karl was almost nine years elder to me, he spoke about a lot of things, not just about sex but he spoke about gay life, what homosexuality is and how it is not abnormal. He was very positive about himself and that helped me to feel very comfortable. I think that is why, I didn't have any problems with coming out.

[Amit, 33 year old gay man talks about his first relationship at 22]

In my second year of M.A., I fell in love with this woman. And she was the one who gave me the language… she said that if you and me are in love with each other, we are homosexual. And I was like ouch, No No!… she was like yes we are and I was like, its an ugly fucking name (laughing), but then we started with saying that ok we are probably lesbian…

[Pradnya, 33, says about her first relationship with a woman at 22]

A romantic relationship, especially the first one, as well as the initial few relationships for a gay or lesbian person are not just relationships but can be a mirror for validation of themselves, a gateway to reduced isolation and knowing more, meeting more gay persons, seeing more non-normative and queer ways of being and relating, and, possibly, also the beginnings of a political queer identity. Thus, queer relationships, in addition to being spaces for sexual exploration and emotional intimacy, can often play the role of what Leap (2007) describes as 'gay socialization', that which tends to be self-initiated and self-managed in a heterosexually constructed world.

Deaux (1993) suggests that identity is both defined internally by oneself and externally by others. This implies that identity is not just about self-definition (personal dimension of identity) but also about how one's identity is read or perceived by others. This external perception—the social nature of identity—is important in the construction of identity. Thus, while being in a same-sex relationship can be an empowering experience for the LG individual, the flip side can be increased visibility of the gay or lesbian identity. Kaufman and Johnson (2004) point out that being in a relationship makes the same-sex couple more visible to both family and society, and this visibility often implies heightened homo-negativity and prejudice. Also, being a gay or lesbian couple, rather than a LG individual (often read as a 'single' man or woman) adds another layer of negotiation to everyday interactions. Being in a gay relationship can shift the individual's status from 'discreditable' to 'discredited'[1] due to heightened visibility. While this observation is partly true for LG individuals in India, there are other cultural and social realities that mediate this.

## 5.2  Homosociality as Paradigm

In India, even in cities, we live in a highly gender-segregated society, which lays down strict rules and norms for interactions between men and women both in the public and the private domain. Furthermore, in traditional, patriarchal societies such as ours, there is a clear public–private divide, with women often expected to operate primarily within the domestic and private realm, while the public, economic, and political sphere is seen as a male domain. Thus, men engaging with each other on matters of intellectual and political concerns, and spending a lot of their time in the company of other men, is encouraged. Similarly, women sharing their domestic chores and concerns with each other is a norm. As a result, intimate relationships between members of the same sex are often interpreted in terms of 'friendship bonds' and deep emotional connections that are celebrated within the cultural context. Thus, in India, there exists a cultural script for homosociality, which refers to close social bonds between persons of the same sex.

One of the participants discusses ways in which she and her partner engage in 'PDA' (public display of affection) in public spaces without being severely reprimanded.

> It is a straight world *yaar*... So technically I and my girlfriend cannot hold hands in a mall or whatever, but we still do. I keep pecking her on the cheek or put my arm around her, basically we are our coochie cooing selves everywhere... and then if someone looks at me, I quickly call out to her, 'didu'! Its a thing, like didi or didu (meaning sister). So people around are like, 'oh they are like sisters'... I think you have to find your way out...
>
> [Priya, 30 year old lesbian woman]

Thus, having a same-sex relationship but couching it in homosocial/kinship terms can actually work as a strategy to counter the challenges thrown up by becoming a 'gay couple' that Kaufman and Johnson (2004) describe above. Employing the normative gender script of 'expressive' young girls, and articulating it through a familial language of 'sister', leads to the relationship being read/ interpreted as an emotional/intimate, but nonsexual one. However, acceptance to homosociality does not necessarily translate into acceptance of homosexuality. In fact, contrary to that, homosociality may invisibilize the sexual/erotic aspects of a relationship between persons of the same sex.

---

[1]Goffman (1963) uses the term 'discredited' to refer to those whose stigma is known/visible and 'discreditable' to refer to those whose stigma is unknown and concealed.

Literature on homosociality, particularly in the context of male bonding has focussed on ways in which men tend to build social bonds and closed teams with other men to construct power blocks and protect male territory and privilege. Traditional ideas of hegemonic masculinity emphasize a discontinuity between homosociality and homosexuality, resulting in a form of male bonding characterized by homosocial desire and intimacy but, at the same time, of homosexual panic and the need to confirm one's heterosexuality through displays of homonegativity, prejudice, and misogyny (Hammarén and Johansson 2014). However, there have also been queer readings of homosociality exploring the underlying continuum of desire and relationship (Janes 2012). Hammarén and Johansson (2014) argue that there can be a horizontal homosociality between men, characterized by emotional closeness, intimacy, and non-profitable forms of friendships. The idea of 'Bromance'—referring to a non-sexual love affair between men—is an example of this kind of an inclusive masculinity that is possible only through undermining of the traditional rigid gender binary system (Svenska Dagbladet, quoted in Hammarén and Johansson 2014). Homosociality among women, on the other hand, has been seen as a continuum between homosocial and homosexual: women caring for each other, promoting each other's interests, women's friendships and bonds, and women loving women (Sedgwick 1985).

Apart from the lens of homosociality, culture studies scholars have noted that, to understand same-sex sexual relationships in India, such as among men having sex with men, it is important to note that their sexual subjectivity and practices may have little to do with claiming explicit identities or rights and these may not be neatly aligned to any kind of a uniform, "globally intelligible gay liberatory" narrative (Boyce 2006, 85). Thus, men who have sex with men in India may appropriate the term 'gay' in their own way to talk about themselves, but the use of this term may not mean the gay identity as defined in the western gay liberation discourse. Also, many MSM may use other kinship, or community, notions to talk about their self and identity, and may not see some of their sexual practices as linked explicitly with an identity label. Thus, as described in Boyce (2006, 90), "sex between men may not be differentiated from heterosexual practices in expected ways". As argued earlier, the idea of the self itself can be viewed from a familial and relational lens, and is constituted through a matrix of social/familial duties and responsibilities, that are determined by the institution of marriage/family and kinship.

Some of the participants talked about their intimate relationships with people who did not identify as gay or bisexual, who may be referred to as described by Boyce (2006) as 'non-identified sexual subjects'. These relationships included expressions of love, concern, and affection, at times even jealousy. In a few instances, these also included sexual expression. However, it was never articulated or labelled as sexual or romantic. Participants in this study described these relationships as having happened at a younger age and were part of their initial exploration. At times, these relationships existed over several years, but without any explicit articulation of a sexual/romantic nature.

We used to share everything. We used to tell each other everything. He doesn't know I am gay or that I have sexual contacts with men or that I am so feminine. Many of his friends told him that this guy behaves like this but he fought with them and told them that its ok, he is still my friend. He would tell me that he will not get married and stay with me only. Then last year he went back to Nashik for a job and we both cried a lot… whenever he comes to Pune, he meets me. We still feel a lot for each other but we don't say anything. I feel that if I tell him how I feel about him, then whatever is there, will also go away.

[Karan, 24 year old gay man]

I kind of kissed her and got physical with her once when we both were really drunk. I don't remember it very clearly but ya that kind of started it. She is essentially straight. But she didn't stop it, it's not like I forced myself on her or anything. So it kind of continued over the years… Whether she was attracted, not attracted, whether it was experimentation for her, I have no idea. But I was definitely attracted to her.

[Aditi, 31 year old lesbian woman]

There was this really handsome guy in my batch during my internship. We had this intense *Dosti* (friendship), like male bonding, which in Indian society is very common. We clicked right at the first moment. And then he kept on calling. Calling as in keep calling and all those lovey-dovey things… then we happened to go for an outstation audit together. There I remember we slept like hugging each other for the whole night. We didn't do anything more… It kept on growing. I knew that he is not gay. Although emotionally, he was reciprocating, very much and that physical thing is happening I mean whatever hugging tightly and all that. But, there was no genital contact as such. Then one day I decided to come out to him and he was not negative at all but he said the same things like try looking at girls and then I decided to stop all this with him. He was still very keen and would call and the hugs and all that, but I lost interest…

[Salil, 28 year old gay man]

These descriptions of intimate relationships with same-sex friends is an example of the homosocial–homosexual continuum described earlier. Same-sex friendships and same-sex intimacies, which border on the homoerotic, have been discussed as being common to Indian culture/s (Vanita and Kidwai 2000). It may not be labelled as odd or abnormal and may be seen as part of male bonding, or as part of the overly emotional nature of women's friendships. Diamond's (2002) research with eighty lesbian, bisexual, and unlabelled women, in the age group of 18–25 years revealed that their closest adolescent friendships with girls involved possessiveness of the friend's time and attention, fascination and preoccupation with friend's appearance and behaviours, and gestures of intimacy such as massages, back rubs, playing with each other's hair, holding hands, and so on. These accounts indicate that the same-sex adolescent friendships contained many feelings and behaviours typically associated with romantic relationships. Similarly, literature in India on sexual behaviours between men, often referred to as *masti* (friends having fun), includes descriptions of mutual masturbation, group masturbation, relieving each other's body tension, and so on (Khan 2001). This is often viewed as a 'natural' part of the development of masculine sexuality, as well as an acceptable form of sexual expression for men (Singh et al. 2012). Yet another way would be to view these relationships as a *queering of normative sexual relationships*—straight or gay, where being sexual (read genital sexual contact) is essential for a relationship to count as romantic/sexual; similarly, romance and love is seen as necessary for a sexual relationship. However, queer relationships could be about non-sexual romance, non-romantic sex, and multiple other expressions, outside of the matrix of sex and romance.

## 5.3  Centrality of Marriage

Another socio-cultural aspect, to be considered in the context of relationships, is that of marriage, (read heterosexual) which is seen both as compulsory for all and as a duty (Kakar 1978). The Indian family severely limits experimentation in the choice of partners by adhering to the practice of arranged marriage (Beteille 1993). Marriage (read endogamous marriage) and procreation are necessary to establish one's social status within one's family and larger clan/community. Even with respect to inter-caste marriage, often the structural distance between members of the two castes that intermarry is not too much in terms of the local or regional caste ranking (Kolenda 2003). Thus, the compulsory nature of marriage and rules about who can marry whom are quite rigidly defined. Vanita observes, "In India, most people have been, and many continue to be, married off at a very young age. Hence exclusive same-sex relationships are necessarily rare" (Vanita 2002, 3). Because of the great emphasis on marriage as a marker of adulthood, consolidation of sexuality around ideas of individuated sexuality is less entrenched. In fact, marriage is seen as a bond between two families and not individuals. "The legal and social validity enjoyed by marriage makes it the unquestionable foundation of families and kinship formation... The family is looked upon as the foremost bonding, that is, as if inherently, by definition, capable of ensuring one's physical-material security, interpersonal growth..." (Biswas 2011, 417). As a result of this primacy given to the institution of marriage-family-kinship, relationships that fall outside of marriage and, by extension, outside of the family and community network are unthinkable for many.

The centrality of the institution of marriage and family in social life in India can be understood from one more perspective. With the Indian state steadily withdrawing investments in social security (reflection of a trend world over), and disinvesting in education and health care, the task of care for the vulnerable, ill, disabled, and old has been entirely shifted onto the family unit. One has to then exclusively depend on family support for any needs including support to get through college, having a roof over one's head, and any crisis such as loss of job, ill health, accidents, disability, and so on. Thus, the state, by outsourcing the care function to the family, makes the family the default care unit, thereby enhancing its power of surveillance and regulation (LABIA 2016).

As a result of this centrality and almost compulsory nature of heterosexual marriage in adult lives, I see two kinds of trends with respect to same-sex relationships that have emerged from my conversations with the study participants.

First, almost all participants faced pressure for heterosexual marriage mostly from 'concerned' family members. In some instances, forcible marriages were conducted by family members; in others, emotional blackmail strategies—such as refusing to eat, crying, not sleeping—were used to pressurize the lesbian/gay child to get married. From among the forty participants in this study, five were in heterosexual marriages at some point; of these, two continued to be married. In addition, several participants reported instances of their partners having been forced into or pressurized into marriages. Also, some of the participants were currently in a relationship with married men/women. This implies that pressure for heterosexual marriage, despite knowing about one's sexual orientation is a serious concern in the lives of several LG individuals.

> He came out to his parents about four months ago and their reaction was adverse... in terms of crying, not eating, asking him to change, asking him to cut off relations with me... in fact he promised her (mother) that he will change and get married. Then he comes up to me the next day and says, 'I won't be able to keep my promise with you, if I want to keep my promise with them...'
>
> [Vineet, 40 year old gay man]

> She had to get married... there was too much pressure. I was still studying and neither of us had a job or money or a place to stay. We lived in the same building and so I could not even bring her home. Our parents, mine and hers, would have killed each other if that had happened. So she got married and she called me on her first or second night and told me, she did not like that man, she did not like his looks, the way he touched her. At that time, she was in Amritsar and I was in Panchgani at boarding school... I knew I couldn't do anything.
>
> [Leona, 33, talks about her forced separation from her first lover at 18]

> Right after college, my then girlfriend wrote a letter to me one day saying that this entire thing between us is a sin and it is abnormal and she has decided to get married and I should do the same. Pressure for marriage was high in my family too... you will not believe it, I said yes to the first man who came to see me at my father's place for that *baghnyacha karyakram* (ritual of boy's family coming to see the girl in an arranged marriage)...
>
> [Sayali, 31, lesbian, currently in a heterosexual marriage with a 3 year old child talks about the time when she was 21]

All of the above responses indicate a complex web of factors including the power (in a specific context) of family members to emotionally blackmail or decide their child's future but also the structural power of the institution of marriage and family that are naturalized, universalized and seen as the only official/legal framework for love, sex or intimacy. In addition, a range of material realties such as lack of access to resources—the job, money, shelter that Leona talks about in the quote above—as well as other material resources, such as inheritance and property that is tied in with loyalty to one's biological/blood family, are also important factors that render queer relationships (un)viable. Internalized homonegativity, isolation, and the lack of support hinted at in the quotes of Vineet and Sayali are other intrapsychic and interpersonal factors that affect the (im)possibilities of queer relationships.

Second, in a few instances where family members did engage with their lesbian/ gay son/daughter's life and relationships, they viewed these relationships/ partnerships in terms of, or with reference to, a heterosexual marriage. Two of the participants recount that it was when their mothers interacted with their partners, and saw the support and nurturance of these relationships, that they were able to accept and respect their sexuality. They often equated these relationships with marriage and that made the relationship and, by extension, the individual's sexuality, more valid and respectable. It also alleviated parents' anxieties about their LG children's future. One of the participants talked about his mother's acceptance of his sexuality as a result of being seen to be in what may be termed as a 'stable, respectable' relationship with a man from a 'good family'.

> I think it's our relationship and how she perceives it. She is very happy that I have somebody, who is always by my side no matter what happens… he is an inseparable part of my life and its a mature relationship. It's not like two boys coming together and having sex every night. So it's more than that and she knows that he is from a good family background. So I guess it is the image of our relationship that has helped her, since now it has become more of a social relationship and the same thing has happened to many of our friends… they kind of look up to us and want to be like us. It was unintentional but it has helped us also. It's a kind of a moral boost for us and we take it as a compliment.
>
> [Atul, 33 year old gay man]

This response of parental acceptance and validation of their son's sexuality on seeing him as having 'settled down', being in a 'marriage-like' relationship, can be understood in multiple ways. One explanation that stands out the most is that of 'respectability' being accorded to a relationship that is long-term, monogamous, marriage-like, among equals (social class, caste: among boys from 'good family'), albeit breaking one rule, that of gender/sexuality, but holding onto other rules of the 'charmed circle' (see Rubin 1984 for description of sexuality and the charmed circle). Thus, respectability, which can be described as a central pillar of the normativity discourse, makes this transgression seem somehow acceptable. Also, while same-sex relationships challenge the practice of heterosexuality, a married/ marriage-like same-sex relationship that maintains class, community, and caste boundaries may not be seen as much of a threat to the heteronormative institution of marriage and family.

The other way to read this is in terms of the anxieties of heterosexual parents, who have been only exposed to a heteronormative world, about the future of their gay son/daughter. A qualitative study on parental responses to their gay and lesbian children in Mumbai states that parents worried about their children's future and care during old age, and this is often a barrier to accepting what are seen as their children's choices around their sexuality. However, if parents, especially mothers, see that there is a 'marriage-like', stable, committed, nurturing relationship, although with a person of the same-sex, then the worry and resistance is likely to reduce (Ranade et al. 2016).

## 5.4  Living Within and Outside the Heterosexual Script

The heterosexual script in the Indian context is tied in with marriage. Marriage in India is endogamous and there is a high social and institutional commitment in ensuring that marriages take place within-caste or castes that are of similar stature in the social hierarchy, as well as within same social class and religion (Kolenda 2003). In addition, marriages are expected to be procreative and monogamous and the pressure is especially high for women. Same-sex relationships, by definition, fall outside of these marital norms and prescriptions and yet, by being lived out in a heterosexual world, may often emulate them, but also challenge and resist them, and create a range of diverse intimate partnerships.

The aspirations and experiences of same-sex relationships that participants in this study shared, can be broadly clubbed under two main themes. There were those who wanted everything that their parents, siblings, or friends had in their relationships and marriages. In this sense, while they transgressed boundaries of normative sexuality, they wanted to access all heterosexual institutions and practices, and did not envision any change in these institutions except that they should be able to access them as freely and openly as their heterosexual counterparts. These responses can be broadly described under the umbrella term 'marriage equality'; that is, all relationships, irrespective of straight or gay, should have the same status and rights in the eyes of law, state, religion, family, etc.

Some of these participants talked about the need for a long term, committed relationship. One of the participants described the time when he first met his current boyfriend. He said:

> I always believed that I am never going to have a LTR (long term relationship) and I am not made for that but I don't know how things changed and they changed for good... but in the meantime I had a lot of doubts. I even went and slept with three different men in that period of six months before committing to him as I was not sure, but there came a point when I wanted us to be exclusive, monogamous...

> [Atul, 33 year old gay man]

Another participant said:

> Because I have a twenty four hour broadband connection, I am just sitting late at night, checking out profiles, sending messages, receiving messages, meeting guys for sex and that just felt very sleazy after a point. I did not like it. I just wanted to settle down with someone who has a similar family background, similar values, with who I can share my life...

> [Avinash, 28 year old gay man]

Both these responses imply the need for a monogamous, stable, relationship after having spent some time on sexual exploration. The second participant also describes the need for a similar family background and shared values in their long term partner. This is similar to some of the matching of class, caste, religion, and other background factors, that are taken into consideration while arranging a heterosexual marriage. As mentioned earlier, seeking a relationship like a marriage may be linked with notions of respectability, acceptance, and leading a 'normal' life, and this can be seen as seeking normative privilege and yet it can be more. It can be about internalizing social morality, as described in the quote above, using terms such as 'feeling sleazy'; it can be about changing needs of a changing self, changes in intimacy needs, emotional dependence/independence, changes in experience and knowledge of possibilities, changes in meanings of what it means to be queer, and also changes in one's political understanding and positions. It can also be about structural realities, wherein, increasingly, the state is disinvesting in social sectors and withdrawing support from any care and welfare and relegating these functions to the 'family'.[2] Who would be this family in the life of a queer person? For many, with rejecting and violent natal families, the need to have a marriage-like/recognized, monogamous, and stable relationship may be expressed strongly; is this, then, as much about angst and the exigencies of living, as about emulating a heterosexual norm?

Some of the male participants talked about their initiation into gay sex, cruising, relationships, and their surprise and shock at the many ways in which these differed from the mainstream notions of love, marriage, romance. They talked about the many ways in which their ideas of love and sex were rooted within heterosexual and often Bollywood-promoted depictions of romance and marriage.

I remember the first gay man I met online. We chatted for a few weeks and then met at Deccan (a place in Pune city). I remember looking at him and thinking how handsome he is... I thought I found my husband! ... you know like it is in hindi movies... that time I did not know anything about casual sex and all that. Initially I found it very difficult to adjust to all this.

[Mihir, 30 year old gay man talks about the time when he was 21]

A lot of people have different definitions of what a partner is. Some people want to live together, some want to meet only on Saturday-Sunday, like a weekend relationship, some want to meet only for pleasure, some people, actually two men I met just wanted care-takers, someone to talk to and take care of them, if they are upset or down... it took me a while to make sense of all this.

[Sunil, 32 year old gay man]

The second theme that emerged in response to relationships is that of a critical stance towards hetero-patriarchy, and is mostly from participants who identified as queer and feminist, or who had affiliations with groups that had a critical political stance towards not just issues related to gender and sexuality, but all issues pertaining to hegemonic power in social life. These responses are not merely rooted in a sexual desire and identity that is non-normative, but refer to the radical potential that queer forms of relating have to challenge norms and structures related to hetero-patriarchal institutions of power. Kingston (2009) describes, in his essay 'Foucault on Homosexuality and Social Experimentation', that homosexual

---

[2]This idea was discussed in the context of a possible demand for gay marriage in India, at the National Seminar on Feminist Queer Organizing, a two-day meeting organized by LABIA, a queer feminist LBT collective and Center for Health and Mental Health, TISS on 19th and 20th December, 2015.

relationships cannot derive from the existing norms and hence necessitate experimentation with ways of relating that can be seen as localized resistances to social normalization, and those, in turn, often serve to challenge excessive normalization of relationships on a societal level. Some of the themes that participants described were non-monogamy or open relationships, challenging the idea of everlasting love/ one true love. They also talked about queering the idea of family, and talking about families of choice as opposed to families through biological or kinship bonds. In fact, expressions of lesbian and gay adult relationships, often in the form of families composed of non-biologic kin and non-traditional configurations of sexual and emotional intimacy, receive little, if any, social valuation, and are unsupported by law or public policy (Cohler and Galatzer-Levy 1990). These queer networks, consisting of lovers, ex-lovers, non-sexual romantic partners, biological and non-biological parents, have the potential to challenge every norm of the institutions of marriage, family, and state. As Foucault (1996) comments in an interview on 'Friendship as a Way of Life', "homosexuality threatens people as a 'way of life' rather than as a way of having sex" (310).

The following two participants question the idea of fidelity and monogamy as necessary and prescribed as compulsory to two individuals who are in love with each other. Both of them make different choices and reach different conclusions to the process of questioning.

> I had an affair with a woman when she (partner) was out of town and it was supposed to be a fling but it carried on for some time and I really hurt her (partner's) feelings and then she also got into a relationship and then we were contemplating a non monogamous relationship because we could see that we are attracted to other people and then we were questioning whether you can be with one person all your life... but we kind of realised that we do care about each other a lot and somehow, we can't really see each other with other people... so I think we are right now open to having friends, lots of friends but we are essentially monogamous
>
> [Joanna, 40 year old lesbian woman]

> One year back we discussed about our relationship and we decided that we should explore other relationships too. Now she has a friend who is bisexual and we are in an open relation. Now I am also seeing someone for last two months.
>
> [Mithun, 35 year old lesbian woman]

The idea of 'family of choice', or what has been referred to as 'personal communities' (Pahl and Spencer 2003), questions the notion that family can be defined only in terms of blood relationships or through an alliance of marriage. One of the participants said:

> I don't understand this primacy given to a sexual relationship or blood relation in defining family. I have multiple people in my life who are as important as the person I am sexually and romantically involved with. These include my ex-lovers, my friends, comrades within the movement, my sister, who is extremely supportive of all my life choices, and I access each one of them in a significant way for different things in life...
>
> [Pradnya, 33 year old lesbian woman]

Another participant was married for several years and has two daughters. She came out to herself and then got out of her marriage three years ago. She has come out to her eldest daughter, who is a teenager now, but not yet to her second daughter. She currently lives with her parents and her daughters and has been seeing a woman for almost two years now. She described her living arrangements and relationship as well as family status,

> ... for the past two years this has been going on. I have been seeing K and I have been spending all my weekends with her, whenever the kids have holiday I go for a little time more, during the week sometimes... K has also started coming over now slowly... I mean for her it was a big thing because she was not used to being around so many people but there was a little adjusting time. My mom still doesn't look at her as a daughter in law kind of thing, she still treats her as my friend, but at least she treats her well. It's not that she invisibilises what we share. She acknowledges her as a part of my life. And my elder one knows about us and treats her very well. The younger one is also very fond of her and K also makes the effort na...

> [Claire, 41 year old lesbian woman]

Apart from dealing with the stigma of breaking social and familial norms of love and relationships due to one's sexual orientation, there were other complications that participants described. For instance, one of the participants, who is a sex worker, described his apprehensions about intimate partner relationships and once again raised the question of 'who can be in 'respectable', monogamous relationships'?:

> Since I am a sex worker, I fear that tomorrow if we have a fight, he will say *'arey tu tar paisa gheun dhanda kartos, tula kai re majhi kimmat'* (you take money to have sex, how will you know my worth). So I am scared. Its best to not get so emotionally involved with anyone. I have seen many people getting wasted because of this love addiction

> [Akshay, 26 year old gay man]

Same-sex relationships, thus, need to be understood on the backdrop of patriarchal institutions of marriage and family. Despite this, same-sex relationships play an important role in validation of the queer/lesbian/gay self of an individual and also open up several possibilities and negotiations for the individual to live out their queerness.

## 5.5 Challenges in Relationships: Some Issues Unique to Marginalized Sexualities

In this section, I discuss same-sex relationships to understand the role of these in the process of the individual's identity journey, consolidation, and negotiation. Thus, as in previous sections, I don't discuss here the nature, quality, and other particularities of same-sex relationships; instead, I discuss the context, and the ways in which same-sex relationships may be lived out, and its impact on the gay and lesbian individual as they are growing up and negotiating their lives.

## *Continuum of Loneliness, Isolation, Break-Ups, Depression, and Self Harm*

The trope of isolation while growing up gay—thinking that one is all alone in this world—is a common one, and has been described earlier in this book. In Chap. 3, Mansoor says, "I had decided that I would be single only all my life. I did not know that gay men existed. I felt that there are hetero men and then there are men like me who love the hetero men. But then hetero men get married and so I would never get anybody..." (Chap. 3, 87). Battling with this sense of loneliness and trying to meet others like oneself—for friendship, for sex, for romance, for love, for camaraderie—has been reported to be a common experience. This experience of developing a bond, a relationship, an engagement, irrespective of the label given to the relationship, has been both an empowering experience for many of the participants, but also an experience of heightened vulnerability.

As one of the participants said,

> ... it's like you are desperate to stay afloat amidst the ocean. You want to swim against the tide and thrive, but you do need and are looking for even the slightest bit of support and then when you find that one relationship, you hold onto it with dear life! I think it is the desperation because of the isolation that makes you extra vulnerable to exploitation in relationships and makes break-ups really hard.

> [Vinay, 36 year old gay man]

Same-sex relationships, particularly sexual and romantic relationships play an important role in self-affirmation of one's sexuality. The experience of this affirmation, against the backdrop of an otherwise alienating, bullying, regulating environment while growing up, can feel like a solace, but may also add to vulnerabilities as suggested by the above quote. Several participants talked about experiencing relationship break-ups, especially while they were younger with almost no back-up/ support systems, as being devastating. One of the participants, who had migrated to the USA in the late 1990s to be able to live as a more open gay person, realized with a shock that the small university town that he had shifted to was not the cosmopolitan, liberal, America that he had dreamt of. He, instead, had to face isolation born, not just out of his gayness, but also his brownness. He described his difficulties in finding a boyfriend and then the experience of depression after the break-up,

> I wouldn't say I totally lost it that time, but I would drink every single day. I won't say alcoholism but I drank a lot. I was quite depressed after the break-up. I was this close to buying a gun but because of the paper work issue, I didn't... I had to go onto meds [short form for medicine] for a while.

> [Abhijit, 35 year old gay man talks about his early 20s]

> After the break-up, I was totally messed up. I dropped out of college and then later joined a call center to somehow keep myself afloat. Also it's such a small community in this city na... everyone knows everyone and so there was always this fear of running into her at community events when I wasn't ready to see her, so I kinda isolated myself from everyone... that's what happens. It's just very hard.

> [Priya, 30 talks about the time when she was 20]

Several of the participants talked about varying degrees of self harm and suicide attempts in response to relationship related stress and violence. Sandip's narrative discussed earlier in Chap. 4 (114), is an example of a suicide attempt that is directly linked with homonegativity and prejudice, in Sandip's case from his friend as well as family. Similarly, Ashok describes an incident where he had a fight with his boyfriend and his boyfriend publicly humiliated him resulting in an impulsive act of attempted suicide by Ashok.

> In front of all the guys there he started saying, eh gud! eh mamu! (swear words implying effeminate man). He started shouting. These guys all knew that we were like husband and wife and they used to earlier humiliate me but had stopped after they knew about us. He was kind of powerful in that area. So that day when he called me all those names, I just went home and took all the pills that were there. When my mother came to wake me up for dinner, she saw that I had vomited all over. Then they took me to Sion (hospital) and then Rajawadi (hospital)… it was a police case.
>
> [Ashok, 32 year old gay man talks about the time when he was about 18 years of age]

Research on LGBT mental health worldwide suggests that LGBT youth are more at risk for suicide, depression, and substance abuse. A few studies done in India too suggest a link between stigma, violence, depression, and suicide attempts, among persons with non-normative sexual and gender expressions (see Chap. 1 for this discussion). As discussed in Chap. 1, sexual minority stress model (Meyer 1995, 2007) helps to understand the links between stigma, prejudice, chronic stress, lack of support systems, and poor mental health outcomes. Social suffering as described by Kleinman et al. (1997) can be another framework to understand suicides, distress, and trauma of marginalized groups, that are a result of what socio-political, economic, and institutional power does to people. The social suffering model, which highlights the social violence underlying lesbian couple suicides, transgender youth suicides and self harm among *kothis* (effeminate men), is a useful one in that it frames the problem not in terms of individual pathology but in terms of systems that discriminate (Ranade 2016).

## Negotiating Gay-Related Relationship Stress and Support in a Heterosexual World

Since gay relationships exist outside of the heterosexual script of dating, falling in love, everlasting marriage, procreation, and so on, gay partners often have the task of figuring out whether they would like to copy the heterosexual script exactly, or make changes to it, or write one afresh for themselves. In a relational sense, this is complicated by further questions: Are two or more people in an intimate relationship on the same page with respect to the new script/s? Is this something that people think through together? How does power operate there? Is someone always trying to catch up with the other/s? Does this agreed-upon script hold true for a certain time period? Can one change one's mind? In a social/structural sense, issues of resources, mobility, familial responsibilities, and many such issues often place limitations on the many ways in which relationships can be imagined and lived. All of this clearly involves work—intrapsychic, interpersonal, as well as social—and often this work can be taxing in the context of the fact that ideas about good/true/real/moral love are not only pervasively present but enjoy a great deal of legitimacy in our society. Hence, the task of scripting and communicating the same to significant others—including lovers/partners but also friends, colleagues, family members—can be very stressful.

The range of stressors and challenges associated with same-sex relationships are many and diverse and would depend on other social locations of the same-sex partners/lovers. For instance, for a couple thrown out of their natal home or having run away from their homes and having meagre resources, finding a safe shelter, and a steady job can become immediate challenges that decide the viability of their relationship. This is not to imply that their only challenges are with respect to '*roti, kapda, aur makan*' (food, clothing, and shelter), or that, once these are sorted, all else will be well. Similarly, the idea of re-scripting one's life and relationship, which I mention above, does not apply only to couples who have sorted out the questions of basic survival. Several of these challenges may co-exist and will affect and be affected by personal journeys, resources, and negotiations of partners with regard to their sexuality. I highlight in this section a few examples of ways in which gay relationships have to negotiate with a heterosexually constructed world, particularly while dealing with crises and accessing support.

One of the participants spoke about a stressful time in her relationship, when she and her girlfriend were trying to figure out the boundaries of their relationship and were working out issues such as whether they want to open their relationship up. It was in the middle of this turbulent time that the participant's girlfriend overdosed on some pills and had to be admitted to the hospital. The participant reported insensitivity of their straight friends (who knew about this relationship), and their inability to understand what the problem was, and be supportive. Instead, for their friends, since they were considering opening up their relationship, this relationship was over, and hence they wanted the participant to leave her girlfriend alone. They also believed that it was the participant who was to 'blame' for this suicide attempt. This participant said,

> I kept sensing that they just weren't willing to recognize that the bond between us was real and very strong. I remember telling this guy… he was like, come, I will drop you home? So I looked at him and said that if your wife was sleeping there, having taken those pills, would you have left the hospital? and he suddenly stopped and said ok I'm not saying anything. You know, so it had not even occurred to these people that it could have been that important to me. So that's what happened with my straight friends. They didn't understand what it meant to the two of us, especially since we were going through this thing of opening it up and all… so in a monogamous, mainstream way, they thought that ok, then it is finishing…

> [Pradnya, 33, talked about the time when she was 24]

There were other crisis situations, such as diagnosis of a terminal illness of a parent, the sudden death of a parent, the accident of a partner, or economic losses, all of which compounded the stresses of a same-sex relationship. These crisis events can be a strain on any couple relationship. However, for most socially acknowledged relationships, these can also be opportunities of bonding and enhancing family cohesion. Many of the study participants, who were in furtive relationships, had not come out to their families or friends, and did not have familial acceptance and social support; this added a layer of difficulty to the existing crisis. For instance, one of the participants shared that he was going through a difficult break up with his partner, when he first heard that his father had been diagnosed with cancer. He said:

> I did not know what had hit me. I had just broken up and was barely managing to keep my job and keep it all together… none of my friends and colleagues knew about us and about our break up, so I was pretty much on my own. And then when dad said, he has cancer and will be starting his chemo soon, I was just… don't have the words. I would come to Bombay every weekend and go with dad for his treatment… I just lived through that time completely numb.

[Salil, 28 year old gay man]

An additional stressor in gay relationships that some of the participants talked about, was that of partners figuring out their sexuality and not knowing whether both partners are on the same page with regard to their sexuality. Some of the participants narrated the stress of being in relationships with people who did not identify as gay or lesbian. Some narrated experiences of rejection and jealousy when their partners told them that they would like to explore by being with other people including people of the opposite sex. One of the participants said:

> First of all, we didn't have a language, we didn't identify as gay, we didn't know what to call our relationship and then he went and fell in love with this girl and I was completely shattered, I didn't know where that left me? where that left us? Was our relationship just a phase for him? I was plagued by these questions…

[Mansoor, 33 year old gay man]

> She was meeting all these men in her work place and she had a couple of crushes and then she realised that actually she was more attracted to men but she was not really dealing with it as in she didn't talk about it but I could see it happening and so I confronted her a couple of times and she said, I was just being possessive and that she was only going out for coffee with them and I was like coffee doesn't go on till 3am in the morning… So we had lots of fights and then one night she spent the night at that guy's house and then I decided to break up with her. She still said that they had not done anything but I was like, it is clear that you are very attracted to him, then it is better that you acknowledge it and move on than to carry on in this place… She made me feel really guilty for breaking up with her. It's only two-three years ago that she called and apologised for all that.

[Joanna, 40 years old talks about her first relationship break-up at 24]

Relationships with people not identifying with a same-sex sexual orientation, with people who got married eventually, either by force or by choice, or with currently married people, posed a range of challenges in the life of the gay/lesbian individual. Some have talked about getting into relationships, as well as marriage, with persons of the opposite sex as a way to cope with partner rejection or the partner deciding to get married. Some have discussed that the partner continuing in their marriage, continuing to be in the closet, meant a barrier in the person's own journey of being out and open and, as one participant said, *due to her homophobia and fears, it was like, I felt that I was being pushed back into the closet*.

## Targeted Violence

Violence targeted at individuals and couples because of their sexual identity, by family members, friends, strangers, work place colleagues, and ways in which this affects self-perception as a queer/lesbian/gay person, is an area that I explore here. Narratives of forced separation of same-sex couples by family, extended family, and community, are very common in the Indian context (PUCL-K 2001; Fernandez and Gomathy 2003; Ghosh et al. 2011; CREA 2012; Shah et al. 2015). This enforced separation may take the form of forcibly locking up the person at home, or strict monitoring of mobility: going to college accompanied by some male member of the family, confiscation of the mobile phone, denying access to phone, threats to the other person/lover, scrutiny of every activity, control over pocket money, and so on. These are mostly imposed on women; the threat of forced heterosexual marriage is common for all genders. An example of parental censure has been described by one participant:

> I was introduced to her mother on one of our trips to Pune. Her mom checked me out from top to bottom and thap!... she must have sensed that I was a dyke and she immediately declared that I was to be seen nowhere near her daughter again...
>
> [Joanna, 40 year old lesbian woman]

Blackmail, threats, extortion, and sexual assault by strangers, related to the participants' sexuality, were also reported by some of the participants. In one instance, one of the neighbours of the study participant's girlfriend knew about their relationship and he decided to blackmail them.

> At some point he stole photographs of us and started blackmailing us about it and I refused to pay him. So he and two of his friends went to the police station and told them that these two are a couple. Luckily the officer there was my dad's patient, so he contacted the psychiatrist in our hospital and he got in touch with my father. This was when I was in Goa with her. My father called me up and said that we are getting calls that we will tell about your daughter and lodge a complaint against her or else give us 10 lakhs... when we got back the police conducted a raid in her [girl friend's] house and did not find anything of course, but they were tapping our phones and all. This was about 2002-03 and that whole 377 thing was still hanging over our heads...
>
> [Payal, 28 year old lesbian woman about her girl friend's neighbour]

In another incident, Sunil reported that he was attacked at his own residence by two strangers, who blindfolded him, tied him up, and tortured him for details of his then boyfriend, whom he had met through an online chat room. Sunil refused to divulge the details and was raped and tortured. He had no idea about who the strangers were. Sunil was terrified about going to the police as this was the year 2005, and the positive developments that later happened regarding Section 377 were not yet heard of. Sunil's boyfriend claimed that he did not know who these men could have been and slowly distanced himself from Sunil. Being unable to seek justice, or share his trauma with his family or friends, Sunil merely had the support of a gay rights group in his city through whom he met a counsellor. This incident, while not a common occurrence, is also not extremely rare. There have been reports of sexual assault and rape, including custodial rape, of persons marginalized on the grounds of gender and sexuality (PUCL-K 2001). This incident not only highlights the vulnerabilities of LGBT persons to targeted violence, it also underscores the absence of institutional mechanisms for appeal to justice. Moreover, stigma and fear of further discrimination leads to silencing of such gruesome violence and absence of support to the suffering individual.

There have also been other types of violence: one of the gay men reported that his sexual partner, who does not identify with any sexual identity label, insisted that they could go home and meet the wife of this gay man and that he would sexually satisfy both of them. Another woman reported that the husband of her lover found out about the two of them and suggested a threesome between them. These were experienced by the gay individuals, in both these instances, as acts of violence due to their sexuality, and they believed that had they been heterosexual, they were unlikely to face such indignity and violence.

Invisibility of one's romantic and sexual relationship, among friends and at the work place, was described by another participant as a covert form of denial and hence violence.

> I would love to be out and tell everyone. She would love to tell her straight friends that see we are seeing each other, come over to our place for dinner. Or that we are celebrating our anniversary, come over. And if her office friends would have said we would like you to come for a party... as in just recently she was supposed to go for this outing, but she just couldn't say that my girlfriend is at home waiting for me so she said I am not feeling well. So we would just love to come out and tell people...

> [Priya, 30 year old lesbian woman]

In concluding this chapter, I would like to reiterate that being in an intimate same-sex relationship—short-term, long-term, casual, or any of the descriptors that have been used to describe relationships—leads to a further deepening of the gay or lesbian identity of the individual. Being in a relationship exposes the individual to many more experiences and questions relating to their queer/gay identity. Being in a relationship can be both affirming and challenging as it can promote well-being as well as cause distress.

# References

Beteille, A. (1993). The family and the reproduction of inequality. In P. Uberoi (Ed.), *Family, kinship and marriage in India* (pp. 435–451).

Biswas, R. (2011). Of love, marriage and kinship: Queering the family. In S. Sen, R. Biswas, & N. Dhawan (Eds.), *Intimate others: Marriage and sexualities in India.* Stree: Kolkata.

Boyce, P. (2006). Moral ambivalence and irregular practices: Contextualizing male-to-male sexualities in Calcutta/India. *Feminist Review, Sexual Moralities, 83,* 79–98.

Cohler, B., & Galatzer-Levy, R. (1990). Self, meaning, and morale across the second half of life. In R. A. Nemiroff & C. A. Colarusso (Eds.), *New dimensions in adult development* (pp. 214–220). New York: Basic Books.

CREA (Creating Resources for Empowerment and Action). (2012). *Count Me In! Research Report on Violence against Disabled, Lesbian and Sex-Working Women in Bangladesh, India and Nepal.* New Delhi: CREA Publications. Retrieved July 15, 2017 from http://www.creaworld. org/sites/default/files/TheCountMeIn%21ResearchReport.pdf.

Deaux, K. (1993). Reconstructing social identity. *Personality and Social Psychology Bulletin, 19,* 4–12.

Diamond, L. M. (2002). Having a girlfriend without knowing it—Intimate friendships among adolescent sexual-minority women. *Journal of lesbian studies, 6*(1), 5–16.

Fernandez, B. & Gomathy, N. B. (2003). *The nature of violence faced by lesbian women in India.* Mumbai: Research Centre on Violence Against Women, Tata Institute of Social Sciences. Retrieved December 15, 2017 from https://www.tiss.edu/uploads/files/8The_Nature_of_ violence_faced_by_Lesbian_women_in_India.pdf.

Foucault, M. (1996). Friendship as a way of life. In S. Lotringer (Ed.), *Foucault live: Collected interviews, 1961–1984* (pp. 304–312). New York: Semiotext (e).

Ghosh, S., Bandyopadhyay, B. S., & Biswas, R. (2011). *Vio-map: documenting and mapping violence and rights violation taking place in the lives of sexually marginalized women to chart out effective advocacy strategies.* Kolkata: SAPPHO for Equality.

Goffman, E. (1963). *Stigma – notes on management of spoiled identity.* New Jersey: Prentice-Hall Inc.

Hammarén, N., & Johansson, T. (2014). Homosociality in between power and intimacy. *SAGE Open, 4*(1), 2158244013518057.

Janes, D. (2012). Homosociality and homoeroticism in the leading British educational magazine for children, look and learn (1962–1982). *Continuum: Journal of Media and Cultural Studies, 26,* 897–910.

Kakar, S. (1978). *The inner world: A psycho-analytic study of childhood and society in India.* India: Oxford University Press.

Kaufman, J. M., & Johnson, C. (2004). Stigmatized individuals and the process of identity. *The Sociological Quarterly, 45*(4), 807–833.

Khan, S. (2001). Culture, sexualities, and identities: Men who have sex with men in India. *Journal of Homosexuality, 40,* 99–115.

Kingston, M. (2009). Subversive friendships: Foucault on homosexuality and social experimentation. *Foucault Studies, 7,* 7–17.

Kleinman, A., Das, V., & Lock, M. M. (Eds.). (1997). *Social suffering.* Univ of California Press.

Kolenda, P. (2003). *Caste, marriage and inequality—Studies from North and South India.* Jaipur: Rawat Publications.

LABIA. (2016). *Report of the national seminar on feminist queer organising in India* (Unpublished).

Leap, W. (2007). Language, socialization, and silence in gay adolescence. In K. E. Lovaas & M. M. Jenkins (Eds.), *Sexualities and communication in everyday life* (pp. 27–54). California/UK: Sage Publications London/Routledge.

Meyer, I. H. (1995). Minority stress and mental health in gay men. *Journal of Health and Social Behavior,* 38–56.

Meyer, I. H. (2007). Prejudice and discrimination as social stressors. In I. H. Meyer, & M. E. Northridge (Eds.), *The health of sexual minorities: Public health perspectives on lesbian, gay, bisexual and transgender populations* (pp. 242–267). Springer Science + Business Media, LLC.

Pahl, R. & Spencer, L. (2003, March). *Personal communities: Not simply families of 'Fate' or 'Choice'*. Working Papers of the Institute for Social and Economic Research, Paper 2003-4. Colchester: University of Essex.

PUCL-K. (2001). *Human rights violations against sexuality minorities in India: A PUCL-K fact finding report about Bangalore*. Bengaluru, People's Union for Civil Liberties—Karnataka.

Ranade, K. (2016). *Suicide, self-harm and pre mature deaths of transgender and gender queer persons*. Presented at the People's Hearing on the NALSA Judgment, at JNU, New Delhi, on November 2, 2016.

Ranade, K., Shah, C., & Chatterji, S. (2016). Making sense: Familial journeys towards acceptance of gay and lesbian family members in India. *Indian Journal of Social Work (IJSW), Special Issue on Family Transitions and Emerging Forms, 77*(4), 437–458.

Sedgwick, E. K. (1985). *Between men: English literature and homosocial desire*. New York, NY: Columbia University Press.

Shah, C., Merchant, R., Mahajan, S., & Nevatia, S. (2015). *No outlaws in the gender galaxy*. Zubaan.

Singh, S., Dasgupta, S., Patankar, P., Hiremath, V., Chhabra, V., & Claeson, M. (2012). *Charting a programmatic road map for sexual minority groups in India*. Discussion Paper Series, Report No. 55, South Asia Human Development Sector, World Bank.

Svenska Dagbladet. (The Swedish Daily). (2014). *Bromance för en kramigare manlighet* [Bromance for an Intimate Manhood]. In N. Hammarén & T. Johansson (Eds.), Homosociality: In between power and intimacy. *SAGE Open, 4*(1), 2158244013518057.

Vanita, R. (2002). Introduction. In R. Vanita (Ed.), *Queering India: Same-sex love and eroticism in Indian culture and society*. New York: Routledge.

Vanita, R., & Kidwai, S. (Eds.). (2000). *Same-sex love in India: Readings from literature and history*. New Delhi: Macmillan.

# Chapter 6
# Living Life as a Queer Person: Role of Queer Community/s in Consolidation of Identity

*Prelude*

*narrative one:*

*being able to recognize yourself... like seeing someone or something and saying, yes that's who i am or that is what i am like. i think most of us struggle with this until we meet others like ourselves, find queer friends, lovers and what we call the queer community!*

*this may not be a big deal for some of the young kids today, at least for those in cities like Bombay where every other post on your newsfeed in social media is about queer rights, every other film festival or party you go to has some gay content in it, celebrities are standing up for your rights and it's almost become cool to be gay or at least gay friendly (laughs)... it was very different when i was young. back in early '90s, we would have to struggle to meet our own kind. i recently read in some archival type material, that there were these guys who wanted to start meetings for gay men way back in the '80s and early '90s in delhi and decided to meet at a public park. as a way of identifying themselves only for their potential participants without being too conspicuous to general public, they said that they would carry a red rose as a marker of this invisible minority... can you imagine the invisibility in those days!*

*for me, this recognition began with the britannica encyclopaedia, where i first looked up words like men's sexual desires, homosexual... then came a newspaper article about a gay rights activist, but the most defining moment for me, where i saw for myself, who i could be, what my life could look like, came much later at a new year's party.*

© Springer Nature Singapore Pte Ltd. 2018
K. Ranade, *Growing Up Gay in Urban India*,
https://doi.org/10.1007/978-981-10-8366-2_6

*i had recently mustered the courage to call a helpline number that i had found in a magazine for gay men. i sat on this number for two months before finally calling... i had all kinds of apprehensions about the phone being tapped and then my call being used to blackmail me, of meeting strange people... all sorts of stuff that i later recognized to be my own internalized homophobia. the other reason for the apprehension was (this i realized later is common for many gay people) that for most of us middle-class boys, our world is really shaped by our families, neighbourhoods, work or educational places. so when we meet any new people, it is always with reference to these relationships... like cousin's friend or father's colleague or neighbour's distant relative or then there are friends and colleagues from college or work... when this has been your socialization history, how do you suddenly call a phone line and say that you want to meet men who like other men. it just seemed like now you had to do something that was not only outside your regular experience but something deeply secretive, like meeting someone from another world. it never occurred to me back then that in the gay community, i could still possibly meet that cousin's friend or that father's colleague... despite of all these apprehensions, i did make that phone call and i am so glad that i did, it just changed my life. no, i did not meet my dad's colleague, thankfully (laughs) but it just opened up a world to me.*

*it did take some time to meet people i could be friends with but then came this party invite. someone at the drop-in-centre of the NGO that was managing the phone line told me about this private party and said i could go with him. just before reaching, i was told that it was at this couple's house who had recently bought a place of their own. the excitement of going to a gay household!... i can't put it in words. in fact, the whole evening felt a bit like a dream sequence. not because it was anything extraordinary, it was the ordinariness of the lives of this couple and all their friends who had gathered to celebrate their togetherness, their new house and the new year... the affection, friendship in the air and the attention paid to me, the new comer, it all felt like a big warm hug. i was introduced to well, at least thirty gay men, men from different professions, different educational backgrounds, communities, religions, age groups, single men, couples, some married men too... some who had known each other or their hosts for a few hours or weeks and some who had been in the same city, been part of each other's lives for years... each one of them and their stories inspiring in me the numerous possibilities for my own life...*

In this chapter, I explore two facets of discovering the queer community. These include learning about queer lives and, through this, learning about the possibilities and viabilities of one's own life as a queer person; this facet is related to the idea of 'Gay Socialization' discussed in the previous chapter. Another aspect of discovering the queer community that is discussed here is related to consolidation of a collective identity or, as described by Simon and Klandermans (2001), "knowing one's place in the social world" (320). It is in discussion of the development and consolidation of collective identity as a queer person that I discuss the affective elements of collective identity, attachment and a sense of belongingness, experienced by the lesbian/gay individual with other gay/lesbian/queer individuals; as well as a political consciousness relating to one's position, power/powerlessness, priviledge in a highly stratified society, and collective action resulting from this consciousness.

## 6.1  Discovering Community: Gay Socialization

The motivation to meet others like oneself and feel part of a community of people is as much about asserting a collective sense of identity as it is about an opportunity to make queer friends and meet potential romantic/sexual partners. Leap (2007) uses the term 'gay socialization' as distinct from other socialization that takes place during the life course, that largely involves transmission and reproduction of heteronormative conventions and practices through institutions such as the family, peer group, educational system, and so on. Leap states that, on the other hand, gay socialization is self-initiated and self-managed and, while supportive allies or affirmative information that helps in the process may be present, their presence cannot be presumed or relied upon. In this sense, Leap focuses on the active agency of the gay individual in retrieving gay messages in newspapers, magazines, films, or books while growing up. It is through this process of discovering community that young gay people move from a life of secrecy and suffering, to survival, recovery, and politics (Plummer 1995). Leap summarizes this self-managed gay socialization as, "… narrators may find homosexuality to be disruptive, painful, and isolating, yet they search out ways to define a gay identity to their own satisfaction…" (103).

In the following sections, I first discuss the social context of invisibility, specific to the time and the cities in which the participants were growing up, and the ways in which they navigated their own gay socialization. I then discuss the journeys of *retrieving gay messages* within a heterosexually constructed world and the process of discovering gay communities.

- **Context of Invisibility and Silence of Same-Sex Sexuality**

For almost a decade now, especially after the historic judgment of the Delhi High Court in 2009 decriminalizing homosexuality, there has been a lot of visibility of the LGBTQ community in India. There have been many more books written about queer lives, many more interviews of queer people published in newspapers, magazines, many more films made about our lived realities, many more online and street based campaigns and pride marches that talk about LGBTQ rights. In fact, the Supreme Court judgment on Section 377, in December 2013, that re-criminalized homosexuality, received strong resistance not just from the queer community in India and globally but also from straight allies and progressive activists/allies and intellectuals across the globe. Thus, while instances of violence against the LGBTQ community and a sense of fear of the law among the most marginalized within the queer community has increased, the overall visibility to the cause has been high. However, this visibility and slogans of 'No Going Back' (in response to the Supreme Court judgment on 377) and '*Bekhauf Aazadi*' (Freedom without fear) from the queer community in India has been an occurrence of recent times; the struggles have been age-old.

Historical accounts of LGBTQ collectivizing in India, specifically Mumbai, tell us that there were a handful of initiatives by gay and lesbian activists to talk about LGBTQ issues in Bombay city in the decade of the 1990s. These included publication of *Bombay Dost*, the first gay magazine that was brought out in 1990 in Bombay, when there existed close to nothing in the form of gay literature in India. Later, in 1998, *Scripts*, a magazine that focused on issues of lesbian and bisexual women was started by Stree Sangam in Bombay. A few organizations such as Humsafar Trust and Gay Bombay that work with gay men, and Stree Sangam (later named LABIA) that works with lesbian, bisexual women and trans persons were started in Bombay in the mid-1990s, and continue to function even now. Some other initiatives in the cities of Bombay and Pune in late 1990s and early 2000s include 'Aanchal', a helpline and support group for lesbian and bisexual women that started in 1999 in Bombay. 'Humjinsi', a phone line, support group, and crisis centre for lesbian and bisexual women, was started in the mid-2000s under a broader human rights organization, India Centre for Human Rights and Law. In Pune, initiatives on LGBTQ issues started only in 1999/early 2000s. Olava (Organized Lesbian Alliance for Visibility and Action), working on lesbian and bisexual women's concerns, was started in early 2000 under the aegis of MASUM (Mahila Sarvangeen Utkarsha Mandal), an NGO working on women's health issues. Samapathik Trust, Pune, a men's sexual health organization was started in 2002 to work with gay, bisexual men, MSM, transgender persons, and *hijras*. Some of these organizations/initiatives, especially those working on issues of LB women, shut down within a few years of starting.

As discussed in the introductory chapter of this book, there have been several forces, events, and processes that have played a significant role in the collectivization as well as visibility of the queer community in India in the last three or more decades. The HIV/AIDS epidemic, and the public health response to the same, made conversations about sexuality, safety, and risk much more possible. It also meant an increasing recognition that there exists a wide variety of sexual practices within and outside heterosexual marriages. In fact, HIV-related research, program interventions, large-scale funding from international sources, and increasing involvement of the state and civil society nationally, and their recognition of MSM, Transgender persons, and Sex workers as 'high risk/vulnerable' groups also provided a platform for these groups to collectivize (Ramasubban 2008). Several NGOs, community-based organizations, and groups working on HIV, and also on rights of sexual and gender minorities, were formed with the help of the state and international agencies throughout the country in the 1990s and 2000s. Similarly, the campaign against Section 377 of the Indian Penal Code, which criminalizes 'sexual acts against the order of nature' and which is often used to harass and blackmail members of the LGBTQ community, has been an important process in the history of LGBTQ movement/s in the country. Nationally, groups working with non-normative genders and sexualities as well as straight allies, such as parents of LGBTQ, mental health professionals, media personalities, writers, and activists from other progressive movements, have joined hands in this campaign, lending the issues of LGBTQ visibility and solidarity. Finally, as discussed in Chapter One of this book, the autonomous women's movement/s of the country have been extending solidarity to queer rights, and have been discussing issues of women's sexual choices that are not restricted to marital heterosexuality, of violence against lesbian women, of lesbian suicides, of the rights of trans persons, and so on. Some of the other milestones include a Supreme Court Judgment in April 2014 that granted legal recognition to all transgender persons and allowed for self-identification of gender under the categories male, female, or transgender. It also recognized the historical injustices towards transgender persons and held that they be recognized as socially and educationally backward classes, and be provided with affirmative schemes in education, housing, employment, and health care (NALSA 2014). This judgment has been followed by several policy discussions and action at the level of various state governments in the country. Thus, the current vibrant and visible nature of the queer movement/s in India needs to be viewed within this historical context.

Participants in the study that I refer to in this book, were mostly growing up during the late 1980s and 1990s (the average age of study participants is 33 years, and data was collected in two phases, 2007–08 and again between late 2011 and early 2013), when this kind of visibility to same-sex sexuality was unheard of. Organizations and collectives on LGBTQ issues were only beginning to form in most parts of the country in mid- to late 1990s. Thus, participants in this study were mostly growing up in social contexts where queer sexuality was largely invisible in the public domain. Since it was the early beginnings of LGBTQ organizing in the country, with only some spaces in the form of group meetings, social events like party spaces, some film screenings, and a few newsletters existed, but were often closeted, and hence access to these spaces was restricted. The advent of technology such as the internet and mobile phones, its growing popularity, and cheaper/easy access through the decade of 2000–10 has immensely changed the nature of networking among the LGBTQ community; this, in addition to a shift from silence to assertion and pride around queer sexuality, has made accessing the LGBTQ community/ies much easier today.

In the following section, participants describe their pathways to discovering and meeting with the LGBTQ community/ies and the impact it has had on their lives as queer people. Participants describe their extent of identification with, and participation in, community activities and events, and ways in which these engagements with the queer communities shape their own self, identity, and life choices.

- **Reading About Ourselves: Newspapers, Magazines, Agony Aunt Columns**

Several participants stated that they heard the terms 'gay' or 'homosexual' for the first time in newspaper articles, a one-off interview of an 'out' gay man in a magazine, or even in the agony aunt or 'ask the (s)expert' section of newspapers. While several participants stated that their first exposure to the term 'homosexuality' was often in the context of 'disease/abnormality', some also said that the articles they read mentioned the name of an organization working with LGBT persons and their contact details. This became a gateway for many participants to get in touch with the larger LGBT community.

> I used to read this magazine called *Just Like That* and there was this help section in it, where a girl had asked a question, 'I am in love with my best friend, who is a girl'. So I was like, ya man, this is my story. They had given a number in that and said that you can contact a gay helpline, which is located at Santa Cruz in Bombay. I quickly took that number and thought about calling for like five months. When I finally called them, they told me about Aanchal and Humjinsi helplines that worked with lesbian women.
>
> [Priya, 30, says this at 19 when she first contacted a gay helpline]

Another participant talked about reading a book in Marathi, about the lives of lesbian women, when she was 29 years old and had been married for a few years with a three-year-old child. Reading this book helped her to make sense of the multiple sexual attractions towards women that she had felt all through her growing-up years. She now had a word, a term, for her relationship with her best friend in college, and her current attraction for her sister-in-law. After reading this book, she contacted a gay rights organization in Pune and also tried to get in touch with women whose stories the book had depicted.

A gay man described an article he read in the context of HIV/AIDS and in this article got information of an NGO working on gay rights.

> Then I read an article which came on the AIDS day. It was an article about Gay Bombay and then there was information of Humsafar Trust, but no contact details. There was only an e-mail id of the author of the article. After this I remember, I opened an e-mail account and wrote to the author. He put me in touch with someone, who told me about G Pune, Gay Pune and I enrolled my name there… I think this was in FY (first year of graduation) when I was just becoming net friendly.
>
> [Mihir, 30, says about the time he was 19 years old]

A lesbian woman described her attempt to access information about LGBT issues. She said:

> My brother, who really likes books, had once taken me to a bookshop and so we were reading and there I saw Bombay Dost. It was written, 'gay magazine' on the cover and since I had been reading the dictionary again and again (to understand the meaning of the term homosexual), I had read the word gay. So I remembered where this shop was in Khar and

after two days I collected some money, went back, picked up the book and as if someone was watching me, I reached Khar station, went to the loo and read the whole thing.

[Parul, 34 year old lesbian woman talks about the time when she was 18 years old]

This shows the extent of invisibility and inaccessibility of information or any kind of images related to same-sex sexuality, as well as the need to hide, keep secret, and the implied fear and stigma experienced by this participant in accessing information related to same-sex desires. The same participant further points out that, while she was growing up, even within the limited availability of materials and spaces to talk about same-sex sexuality, there were stark gender differences with lesbian women and their issues being rendered even more invisible among the already marginal space for sexual and gender minorities.

I read the whole thing (issue of Bombay Dost) but I could see that there was nothing for women, everything was for men. I also remember around that time, Mid Day brought out some anniversary issue and Ashok Row Kavi was there on the front page and his interview said something about he staying with his boyfriend and his mother being ok with it... much later I heard about Gay Bombay and while their parties are open for lesbian women as well, some of us started talking about creating separate social and party spaces for just us women...

[Parul, 34 year old lesbian woman talks of early 2000s in Bombay]

As discussed earlier in Chapter Three with regard to the unique developmental challenges faced by young LG persons, affirmative literature and materials plays a central role in helping young LG persons work through feelings of isolation, alienation, emptiness, loneliness, and thinking of oneself as abnormal. However, this information about gay life and experience is not readily available and the individual has to actively look for this in managing what I refer to above as self-initiated 'gay socialization' (Leap 2007). This reiterates the role of the active individual seeking to consolidate and manage their queer identity. In fact, the words of Parul, quoted above, indicate that this goes beyond finding affirmative spaces and people, to creating such spaces along with others in the community.

- **Internet and Chat Rooms**

For many of the participants, the discovery of the world of the internet coincided with their discovery of the queer world. Several participants described that when they had just been introduced to the internet and had learnt to surf the net, they came upon websites with information about LGBT issues, organizations, gay chat rooms, and dating sites. One of the participants summarized the importance of the internet for the queer community in the following manner. She said:

... the internet is a blessing for all gay people in India... Honestly ... Because our society is so closeted.

[Mehak, 28 year old lesbian woman]

I would normally chat on some site and then came to know that there are some rooms which are gay rooms and so I thought lets go and figure out and then I came to know that there are people like me, even in Bombay, not somewhere in the world, but right here!

[Sahil, 25 year old gay man]

Thus, for some study participants, the internet became a space to meet other gay people, make friends, as well as find sexual partners. One of them talks about being shocked when he found out that one could meet people online to have sex. Until then, though he was aware of his same-sex feelings and had a couple of 'flings' in college, he was only aware of the respectable heterosexual script of dating, falling in love, proposing marriage, as being the only route to have sex. He said:

As part of my course work in web designing, I learnt to use the internet and learnt to chat on the net as well. I once chanced upon a gay chat room and found out that there are many people, who meet here and chat, I was not aware of this at all. I can say it was shocking for me that this happens... this was the first time that I realized, that you can meet people online just for sex. Later on I got to know that it is called a one night stand... then I got to know about dating and that there are these categories like 'top', 'bottom', and 'versatile' (refers to preference in sexual acts) that people talk about on the net and based on this make choices of sexual partners...

[Sunil, 32 year old gay man talks about the time when he was 20 years old]

Online, I was pretty brave. I gave out my identity which is not advisable but most of the times, my trust was reciprocated and I met decent guys... I strictly avoided the 'a/s/l – age/sex/location' kind of guys or the 'coffee, tea or me' kind of guys, those corny lines... or 'your place or mine'. I made some very good friends too.

[Ajay, 32 year old gay man]

One of the lesbian women said that, the internet became her first point of contact with the lesbian community, which she says was largely invisible to her in the city of Bombay. When she first came out to herself, she started looking for other lesbian women online.

So I started looking on all these websites. I started registering everywhere... And in Indiatimes, I met someone. She was a married woman and so close to my age. So I was like, 'Wow!'... We started chatting and we met up a couple of times. She started introducing me to a lot of things and gave me a lot of information. We started talking about friends we met online, about whether they were genuine... Then she told me about this support group called Aanchal. She was the first one who actually brought me out slowly and she introduced me to another e-list called SIP, Symphony In Pink, which had about 50 members at the time. I was just overjoyed to know that there are so many lesbian women in Mumbai.

[Claire, 41 talks about her initial coming out around 2005]

Another aspect of discovering a global community through the internet, and ways in which that impacted his aspirations and dreams, is highlighted by one of the participants. He describes himself as net savvy and had an internet connection at home while growing up. This helped him to get in touch with a virtual community of queer persons across the globe, which, in turn, exposed him to the lives of LGBT persons in other countries and cultures. He said:

You know, you would read about people... how homosexuals live in other countries and at that point, I was very internet savvy and I would read about Canada and Scandinavia, South Africa and the kind of access that homosexuals had there to rights. For me the US was the 'ideal' place. I thought I would go there, find a million dollar job, get a perfect boy friend, get married and live happily ever after (laughs)...

[Abhijit, 28 year old gay man talks of the time he was 18]

- **Meeting Another Gay Person**

Meeting another gay person who then becomes a link to the larger community, was reported by several participants. Some talked about hooking up with a stranger in the train, who introduced the participant to more cruising areas, party and social spaces, and organizations that work for LGBT. Others talked about meeting an 'out' gay man, or a dyke, through their work place, who opened up a whole new world— a gay world—to them.

One of the participants talked about being invited to a gay wedding during his stay in UK as part of an exchange program. Here, he met people who told him about the community in India.

> Jim told me that in India too we have NGOs (working on GLB issues) and he knew about Mumbai, about Gay Bombay. So I called up the people at Gay Bombay and went to meet them. Coincidentally the day when I went there, there was a meeting taking place. It was Sunday and I took part in that meet and that was my first coming out to a lot of people together. I told them about my story, got to know people present there and also about NGOs in Pune that work on gay issues.
>
> [Mansoor, 33 year old gay man talks about the time when he was 26]

Another participant stated that they had a group of friends since school, who were effeminate, would like to dance, dress up in girls' clothes some times, and who would use feminine pronouns for each other. He said:

> Once we were all sitting in a park and were addressing each other as *aga-tuga* (feminine pronouns) and gossiping and laughing and our gestures were effeminate only. That time this person, much older to us came there and asked, *'tu sadi ghaltos ka?'* (Do you wear a saree?). I was surprised. He was dressed in pant-shirt, but he then told us that there are many of them who cross dress, feel like women and like to have sex with men. He then introduced us to a lot of kothis and told us about parties in Pune where cross dressing happens...
>
> [Dilip, 24 years old talks about the time he was 20]

Many of the lesbian women in this study said that their first contact with a lesbian woman/activist was through a helpline number or at some conference or event and then they were invited to a party where they met others. Social events, especially a house party, where people went only by invitation, were cited by many participants as a space to meet other lesbian, bisexual women.

> ... best part of this community is that when a new person gets in touch, there is a gathering to meet this new person. So people gather and go out pubbing or just drinks and dinner or somebody's house or whatever. So the same thing happened to me and that's how I met all these people.
>
> [Leona, 33 about meeting other lesbian women at age 25]

> And then she threw a party and she said I am going to call all the lesbians I know in Bombay. So that is where I met so many people. I had been in this intense and closeted relationship and now I was coming out to this group of people, actually a full thriving community. That was an amazing feeling!
>
> [Joanna, 40 about her first time meeting community at age 30]

- **Doctors and Counsellors Referring to LGBT Organizations and Support
  Groups**

A few of the participants stated that when their parents found out about their
sexuality, they were taken to doctors, psychiatrists, or counsellors, for curing their
homosexuality and, in a few cases, after attempting cure and seeing that there was
no change in their same-sex desires, the mental health professionals themselves
referred clients to LGBT support groups. One such participant was severely
depressed and attempted suicide after failed attempts at conversion of his sexual
orientation. The social worker in the hospital where he was admitted gave him the
address of an NGO working with MSM and gay men. Another participant described
how his doctor gave him the phone number of a helpline for gay men and
encouraged him to call. He said:

> I thought I should try calling, maybe something will come out of it as the medicines that my
> doctor had given were not helping, but it was 10 and the timings on the card were till 8.
> I still decided to try and to my luck someone was there and he spoke to me and I
> immediately felt relaxed. He called me to office in the morning… I came here and I saw
> these photos of men together and I was like *'my god this is like a treasure I have found'*. It
> was such a relief.

> [Kumar, 30 year old gay man]

Ways of getting to know about, and pathways to meeting the community/ies has
been different and unique to each person's story of growing up. Similarly, what this
meant to each person is also different. It has meant education and learning more
about ways of being queer, reducing isolation, and unlearning the heterosexual script
as the only or compulsory script for adult life. For some, it also meant affirmation of
their gay identity and, with that, a consolidation of the 'gay liberation project', stated
by one of the participants in terms of 'a million dollar job, a boyfriend, marriage, and
happily ever after'. However, meeting community/ies had unique meanings for each
of the participants and so, for some, it also meant politicisation of the self and
formation of a political identity,[1] challenging the norm of relationships, sexuality,
and family; this I will describe in the last section of this chapter.

## 6.2  Collective Identity and Selfhood: Meeting Community
## and Meaning-Making for Personal Identity

Collective identity simply refers to an identity that is shared with a group of others,
who have some characteristics in common. Some elements of collective identity,
as discussed by Ashmore et al. (2004) are self-categorization, or identifying oneself

---

[1]This evocative formulation of politicisation of self and formation of political identity is by Basak,
P. (2018). Tracing the Local Histories of Political Organising: Locating the sex worker within and
beyond Developmental Initiatives, MPhil Dissertation submitted to the Tata Institute of Social
Sciences, Mumbai

as a member of a particular grouping (Deaux 1996). This self-categorization may not always be a simple, clear, 'yes or no' process but collective identities can sometimes be ambiguous because of the individual's subjective uncertainty on issues of identity (Mohr and Fassinger 2000). This uncertainty may be linked with a subjective experience of lack of goodness of fit with the category, uncertainty stemming from stigma, and social devaluation associated with certain identities. This is relevant particularly (discussed previously in Chaps. 4 and 5) for those who do not identify with a gay/lesbian identity, or for those gay and lesbian persons who are in heterosexual marriages, or for other reasons do not see themselves as fitting well with what they see as a representation of the LGBTQ community.

Other dimensions of collective identity include evaluation of the identity as positive or negative, importance and salience of the identity for the individual, social embeddedness, and behavioural involvement, or the degree to which the collective identity is implicated in one's everyday social contacts and relationships, and degree of engagement in actions that directly implicate the collective identity. There is also the dimension of attachment and affective commitment, which includes an emotional involvement with the group as well as a sense of interdependence, which is fostered by an awareness of a common or shared fate. Finally, the content and meaning of a collective identity includes ideology and group consciousness that refers to members' beliefs about the experiences, history, and social position of their group in society (Gurin and Townsend 1986). It also includes the individual-level collective identity element that denotes the individual's internally represented story about the collective/social group that they belong to. It is all these multiple meanings of collective identities that I work with in this chapter.

Here, it is necessary to point to the distinctions between personal and relational identity and collective identity as discussed in the identity literature (Ashmore et al. 2004). Personal identity refers to characteristics of the self that one believes to be unique to oneself. Relational self refers to the self as shaped and influenced by people with whom one is, or has been, emotionally invested and influenced by such as spouse, family, close friends, and so on (Andersen and Chen 2002). Closely linked to collective identity is the concept of social identity defined as 'that part of an individual's self-concept, which derives from knowledge of his membership of a social group…' (Tajfel 1978, 63). However, there has been a shift in literature to the language of collective identity (instead of social identity) to mark the difference from personal and relational identities that are also inherently social in nature (Ashmore et al. 2004). While all these aspects of identity such as personal, relational, collective, social identity, are not separate or distinct from one another and more like a continuum that are integrated within the individual, each one has a distinct meaning, and I refer to an interplay of all these in this chapter.

Theorists working on concepts related to selfhood, such as self-concept, esteem, and identity, describe the self as being born out of reflexive action or a result of a person's interactions with others. In this context, Mead describes two components of the self—the 'I', who is the knower and actor and forms the dynamic, spontaneous, part of self, and the 'Me', or object, which refers to one's ability to imagine oneself from the standpoint of another person, and includes all the learned perspectives a person takes towards oneself (Mead 1934). It is this second aspect of the self, which is 'self' as 'reflected by others', that is significant to this discussion on personal identity being influenced by community. Literature on internalized homophobia describes the mechanisms by which gay persons tend to internalize negative social attitudes towards homosexuality (Herek et al. 2009). Growing up in a homonegative/hostile society and being exposed to stereotypes, prejudices, and silences about same-sex sexuality from all significant institutions—family, religion, law, education, science—can significantly shape the 'Me' part of the queer self, leading to internalizing of homophobia and homo-negativity.

In this context, meeting with the queer community and seeing positive affirmations of oneself as mirrored/reflected by others can mean what self-psychology refers to as '*corrective emotional experiences*' that were lacking in one's families and missing from one's childhoods (Beard and Glickauf-Hughes 1994). Meeting a large number of people who are similar to oneself in their sexual and or gender expression can be an experience of 'coming home' for many. This is not to suggest that the LGBTQ community is one homogenous group. There is a lot of diversity within the LGBTQ community and hence, while one would identify with similarities, there also exist differences, especially based on other identities of religion, region, caste, class, gender, ability, and so on. Yet, engaging in collective thought and action, about the rights of the LGBTQ community, can both be an act of empowerment and assertion, as well as an attempt at changing society's attitude towards LGBTQ and, thereby, reducing stigma and gaining a better fit within society. The following section explores the various meanings and functions that engaging with the queer community serves in the lives of queer persons.

- **Sense of Belonging and Identification**

Isolation and loneliness are a common experience for many queer persons while growing up. As one of the participants stated:

> 'until you learn the word gay and meet someone who calls themselves that, you are pretty much on your own, figuring out what is going on with you...'

> [Mehak, 28 year old lesbian woman]

A sense of alienation from the heterosexual world—and its web of relationships within family, educational institutions, peer networks, work spaces—is almost a universal experience for all queer persons. Meeting and engaging with community can become an experience of identification and reducing isolation. Meeting community can mean many things: seeing someone like oneself in person, who does not easily fit into the gender binary of man and woman; hearing someone use the term 'gay', 'lesbian', or 'queer' to refer to themselves; meeting two women who are in love, and openly talking about it; seeing someone in drag; seeing photographs of men loving men; exchanging notes about cruising areas, and places to meet people for sex, love, or romance; knowing about queer-themed films, books, organizations working on LGBTQ rights, and so on.

One of the participants talked about her first experience of calling on a helpline that worked with lesbian, bisexual women.

> I was like, I think I am a lesbian and I think I would like to talk to you about it.... I thought she was a doctor... I really thought that and somehow we always feel that doctors are the only ones we can talk to about these things *na* and so I told her, 'I think I am a lesbian...' She said, 'you know what? You are talking to a lesbian right now'. I was like on the ninth sky or whatever you can say. I was so happy!
>
> [Priya, 30 year old lesbian woman]

Another gay man talked about his first experience of visiting a drop-in-centre for MSM, gay men, and transgender persons.

> Then I came here. I met so many people and I felt that I am not alone and I began feeling comfortable here. I came here and I saw these photos of men together and I was like, 'My God this is like a treasure I have found'.
>
> [Kumar, 30 year old gay man]

Two lesbian participants, who belong to a voluntary queer collective, talked about how this collective has become a space where they experience personal affirmation, understanding, and comfort, in contrast to a heteronormative world, which can often seem alienating.

> Over the years I have felt increasingly alienated from the mainstream world around me. The collective then becomes a place where what I say/feel/express is immediately understood. People just get it. They think the same way. I don't have to explain anything. Whether its feeling disillusioned about the right wing politics that the country is headed towards or feeling let down by family members because they invisibilise my queerness... I can rant about it here and it is understood. Even if something is not accepted, the arguments come from a place of being on the same page and that is very important to me.
>
> [Pradnya, 33, member of a voluntary queer collective]

> The collective is a place where one can share happy things... for example, my work on gender... be it a published report/paper/book is either looked down upon as 'not real work'... some stuff we crazy activist type people do... or its seen as too 'hi-fi' by family and friends alike. It is a similar story with any other sort of political organizing - be it around caste oppression or the Free Binayak Sen Campaign or this campaign we ran *Humari Zindagi, Humari Choice* (a campaign about right to love)...
>
> [Mithun, 35 years, member of a voluntary queer collective]

One of the participants, who was violently outed to his family and had been taken to many doctors for curing his homosexuality, and had subsequently attempted suicide, talked about the first time he met with peer educators of an NGO that worked with MSM and transgender persons on HIV prevention. He said:

> I can talk to them as in whatever feelings I have in my mind I can tell them. At home I cannot tell anyone. Even if I talk to any guy a little, my family members think that I am thinking differently (sexually) about him... After coming here, I have improved a little. Now I don't cry as much and my eating and sleep has improved. These people are different from me and their lives are very different from me, but I still feel understood here and don't have to feel ashamed of who I am.
>
> [Sandip, 24 year old gay man]

Interestingly, along with a sense of feeling understood and not judged, the participant also talks of 'difference'. Most of this difference is that of class, caste, education, and occupational background. The NGO peer educators that the participant refers to in the above quote were from poorer backgrounds than his, had lower education, having dropped out of school before completing their SSC, and many belonged to scheduled castes. Some of them are also engaged in sex work in addition to working as peer educators on a HIV-prevention program. It is important to note that, like every other individual, LGBTQ persons also have multiple identities, and being gay/lesbian is one kind of identity that, in intersection with other identities, has differing impacts on their lives. Thus, any discussion on community and especially identification and belongingness with a community would be incomplete without recognizing the intersectionality of multiple identities. Another illustrative example of this is described in the following quote of a married lesbian woman, who attended a party organized by a local queer group in Bombay.

> When I went there I saw all drinking and smoking and it was all about fashion. I went in a *punjabi dress* and I had my *mangalsutra* (necklace worn by most married Hindu women) on and I really felt very odd that time that I am the only one here who is like this. I felt that you have to look this way, only then will someone take interest in you. I really didn't like that place and left immediately.
>
> [Sayali, 31 year old lesbian woman]

This participant said that she had grown up in a lower middle class, Brahmin, Hindu, household, in a conservative locality in Pune. After her college girlfriend broke up with her, told her that what they were doing was sinful and that she wanted to marry a man, this participant, too decided to get married. She had never heard of the term 'gay' or 'lesbian' until one day, several years after marriage, she read about lesbian women and same-sex love in a book in Marathi. It is through this book and its author that she contacted a queer women's group in Bombay. From her quote above, it is clear that differences in marital status, class, region, language, age, exposure to cultures, and ways of living other than the one that one is born in, are some of the things that set this participant apart from the community of women that she interacted with, in this instance. Thus, an individual's identity includes a range of multiple identities and, while there may be a sense of identification with other queer persons on some aspects, there can be a marked sense of difference based on other identity positions that the individual may occupy. This will be discussed further in this chapter while looking at collectivization in the queer community to bring about social change.

- **Safe Spaces and Support**

Several participants discussed the need for physical spaces where they can be themselves, without judgment, reprimand, or punishment. As stated in the chapter on childhood and growing up, most queer persons were severely reprimanded as children for their 'inappropriate' gender non-conforming behaviours or their lack of interest in opposite sex or their unusual interest in same-sex persons. Physical spaces created by the LGBTQ community, in the form of social meeting spaces, party spaces, drop-in-centres, support group spaces, where members of the community do not have to hide who they are, or pretend to be someone they are not, have thus been described as vital by many participants.

One of the participants talked about the need for safe space, where one can party and have fun. Another participant spoke about the need for a safe space to have 'shameless fun'.

> The reason why we go to gay parties is because that's the one place where we could be our own self. We can drink and dance and be like Meena Kumari or Akshay Kumar and do whatever you want to do. If you hold hands and walk around or engage in 'PDA' (public display of affection) with your boyfriend, no one is going to mind...
>
> [Atul, 33 year old gay man]

> A queer space for me is a place to have shameless fun and laugh. For those of us assigned female at birth, there are so many restrictions... but in a queer space I can really let myself have fun. Drink, smoke, talk about sex, have sex, write erotica... basically all the morality that weighs down on me, I have been able to challenge personally by being within queer collective spaces. And then I can generalise to more settings. And that has been freeing. Unlearning shame is what I call it... safe, queer spaces have helped me do that!
>
> [Pradnya, 33 year old lesbian woman]

Another participant talked about the importance of 'Friday Workshops' at the NGO where he works. During these workshops, the office staff and others from the community get together for fun after office hours. He said:

> ... basically its free in the sense that what we can't do in our house we can do here in a room. If someone likes to wear a sari, he can't wear one and dance at home... here you can.
>
> [Amol, 34 year old gay man]

Participants who were from a lower socio-economic background, and often shared small houses with other members of their family, did not have enough privacy to live out their sexual and gender aspirations. Thus a 'Friday Workshop' space, drop-in-centre within the NGO, other community events, become the only occasions where these participants could be queer openly. Participants who were living on their own, with their partners or with parents, but with enough privacy, also talked about the need for affirmative social/public spaces, which are free from violence. They discussed the need for spaces where they can be with their partner/lover without being stared at, commented on, bullied, blackmailed, or beaten up. Thus, the social/party spaces created by LGBTQ groups, such as Gay Bombay in Mumbai, were seen as significant by most participants.

A lesbian woman underscored this point of need for more social/public spaces that are friendly towards queer people.

> I came out when I was studying in the US. There I could go to a lesbian coffee shop, lesbian book store, lesbian restaurants, lesbian clubs and lesbian health centers and then I went to a lesbian strip joint too... So I was really stressed when I was going to come back. I did not know anyone and anything queer in India. But then I met someone online and wrote to her and we met up when I got back and that was great. She and her partner had arranged a small party for newer dykes, who were really not part of the community. They got us introduced to other women...
>
> [Mithun, 35 year old lesbian woman]

Safe spaces do not always imply segregated physical spaces, where all queer persons, even those, who are not out can feel safe. Safe space can also be about accessing and claiming public spaces (which are often cis-male centric and heterosexist), and doing so with the strength and the power of the collective. It may also imply interpersonal, relational spaces that are safe and non-judgemental for all, irrespective of a person's gender expression, sexual preference, HIV status, ability, age, caste, class, and so on.

In a heterosexual world, family, both natal and marital, are seen as the primary source of support during all major life events. Life events in adult life itself are so centrally defined by one's sexuality and marital status: marriage, pregnancy, children, children's health, education, career achievements and so on. Life events in adult queer life are rarely discussed, for instance coming out to oneself, decisions about coming out to others in natal family, work places, friends, looking for partner/s in a heterosexual world, dealing with romantic relationships that fall outside heterosexual marital scripts, stresses and strains of 'invisible' and socially unsanctioned relationships, dealing with multiple losses of relationships, friendships after coming out, dealing with ill health, and hostile health care systems. The mainstream world often remains ignorant of these life events in queer lives and hence support during these times of difficulty from community members, queer friends, and families of choice (consisting of queer persons and allies), become significant.

One of the participants talked about support from queer friends as well as straight allies in the process of coming out to family.

… basically my gay friends spoke to my sister on the phone and told her. Even my straight friends rather my female friends who are straight, even they offered to speak to her. One of my friends Asha, her brother is gay, so she spoke to my sister and told her that its ok and she told her that even she was in denial for a long time and now she is fine… So all these people and my gay friends have played a very important role in my life

[Ajit, 24 year old gay man]

We always go to Nerul as one of my friends has a bungalow there and we always go there. As in generally dance the whole night, booze the whole night, so it is fun. Or then every weekend if this doesn't happen, we have these get-togethers, we meet for lunch. We have these two friends who are a couple and they live together so they invite us for lunch, they cook for us and so it is fun.

[Sahil, 25 year old gay man]

Thus, while one of the features of growing up gay is that of loneliness and isolation, it can also be an opportunity for affiliation, collective identification, social support, and coping (Miller and Major 2000). In fact, along with the idea of minority stress, that I have discussed elsewhere in this book, it's also important to point towards minority coping. Minority coping is conceptualized as a group level resource and refers to the group's ability to mount self-enhancing structures to counteract societal stigma (Meyer 2007).

- ## Community as a Collective for Social Change and Political Action

Community or a collective identity is a result of a sense of connection, 'we-ness', shared experiences, and a sense of shared destiny among individuals (Owens et al. 2010). In that sense, collective identity is based on common bonds and attachments to individual group members. However, Prentice et al. (1994) distinguish between identities based on attachments to individual group members, and those based on attachments directly to the group or category. It is the second kind of attachment that is essential to produce a collective identity. In other words, identity commitment to the experience of the category 'queer' or 'sexual minority' would be salient in the development of a collective identity. Most definitions of collective identity include a notion of identification, commonalities of interests, along with recognition of shared opportunities and constraints, that serve as a foundation for joint mobilization and action. Thus collective identities include the affective and relational elements of being a binding force, a social glue, which enables individuals to form a sense of collective self (Brewer and Gardner 1996), as well as an opportunity to collectivize for joint action and change.

While describing their experiences of being part of the queer community, participants in this study referred to the various implications of collective identities described above. For some participants, being a part of LGBTQ communities was about feeling a sense of belonging, of being in a safe space and accessing support. Many talked about the queer community as the network of gay friends that they had. Some viewed LGBTQ communities as a forum (irrespective of individual friendships) for coming together and articulating rights of queer persons as a group and working towards joint action for change. This change meant multiple things for different people, and the process of this change was articulated differently by different people. There were study participants who talked about being part of collective action, which in itself was empowering for them and brought about change in their own self-perception, self-confidence, and in their relationships. There were others who talked about change in terms of securing state attention through programs on HIV, health care, vocational training, and employment. There were those who wanted change in discriminatory laws and talked about instituting anti-discrimination mechanisms. For others, collective action included developing a critical analysis of an unequal heterosexist, patriarchal, capitalist society, and a demand for a just, equal society, not just for queer persons, but for women, oppressed castes, the poor, the disabled, and other marginalized sections. This position is based not merely on an understanding of oppression and privilege vis-a-vis sexuality and gender, but with respect to other oppressed identities too. Some of the responses below are indicative of the multiple meanings of change that participants talked about.

One of the participants talked about how he has been able to draw strength from the process of collectivization.

It is often exhausting to be queer in this heteronormative world. The unfairness really gets to you sometimes. That is when I feel I can draw strength from collective thought and action. Learn ways to cope, feel heard, feel comforted and even role model sometimes...

[Vineet, 40 year old gay man]

Another participant elaborated on the idea of the process involved in collectivization and what it meant to her. She stated:

What it means to me is using a non-hierarchical, consensus based approach to produce collaborative and collective work. Also, using feminist methodologies in work and allying with other groups fighting oppression/(s) and marginalisations... that is important to me.

[Mithun, 35 year old lesbian woman]

One of the participants elaborated on the position stated above, about the need to be critical of power structures such as hetero-patriarchy,

I am part of this collective not just to make friends or socialize... I come here because there is a queer perspective not just on your personal life and relationships but on the world around you. It is important to destabilise patriarchal institutions of marriage, family, religion... We are here to talk about that in our campaigns, research, our support work... I think if one is not doing this, then one is wasting the gift of being queer...

[Priti, 31 year old lesbian woman]

Another participant took this argument forward and suggested that not only is it necessary to be critical of heteronormativity, but it is necessary to be reflexive within our own communities and look at homonormativity as well. She said that even among LGBT communities, just like any other space, dominant ideologies of *caste, class, majoritarianism, nationalist jingoism* exist in plenty. She said:

There are oppressions germane to the LGBT community such as transphobia, butchphobia, biphobia, which need to be questioned. For example, a popular party organizer, after a few parties, decided to modify their rules for entry and listed that drag wasn't allowed (especially skirts above a certain length). MTF (male to female) transpersons were turned away. When pressed for an explanation the official line was that the club was owned by a family and transwomen dress skimpily. Unofficially, we know that gay men are bothered a lot by transwomen...

[Mithun, 35 year old lesbian woman]

These words by Mithun reiterates that, while collective identities foster a sense of 'we-ness' and a sense of shared destiny, collective identity of individuals as identifying with the LGBTQ community itself is mediated through a range of other relational and social identities. Hence, the need to understand identities—personal, relational, or collective—through a lens of intersectionality is a necessity. Mithun's words also draw attention to the issue of power and politics. It is necessary to understand that just because of one's marginal position in one location or because one may have thought about structures of oppression, does not automatically ensure empathy when one is occupying a location of power. In other words, political consciousness or collective consciousness is not just linked with occupying a marginal position with respect to some aspect of one's identity, but through a process of consciousness-raising about ways in which power, control, and oppression work through a complex web of social and relational locations.

While collective identity has an individual and group dimension to it, the collectivization itself occurs in a context. There are contexts that are more enabling or more oppressive for collective marginalized identities to be consolidated and asserted strongly. As stated earlier, the HIV/AIDS epidemic, the campaign against Section 377, and the Delhi High Court verdict of 2009 are some examples of contextual factors that have enabled the collectivizing of queer identities. One other such factor that, on the face of it, seemed an oppressive factor, was the (re) criminalization of homosexuality through the Indian Supreme Court judgement on 11th December 2013. This event led to both a sense of threat and fear, but also a further consolidation of the collective identity of being queer in India. The visibility to LGBTQ issues around this event and the support from across the globe from queer and straight allies was unprecedented. The Supreme Court verdict became a reference point for a renewed assertion of sexuality rights and freedom of expression among the queer communities in Mumbai and Pune. Several of us within the community, including some of the study participants, talked about being angry and outraged at this outright denial of justice. Some of the responses included collective action such as street protests, online campaigns under the banner, 'Global Day of Rage' with the slogan 'No Going Back on 377'. Many more conversations about sexuality, and the right to love, started taking place even outside of the queer collective spaces; within college campuses, work spaces and in mass media. Many more people decided to come out as queer and as queer allies in their personal spaces and even on national media as a response of both anger and assertion. Britt and Heise (2000) suggest that anger, outrage, which may be considered as negative emotions, are high in energy and potency, and can motivate individual participation in collective action. Participation in gay rights movement/s could include efforts to transform shame and fear to anger and pride in an effort to construct an energized collective identity. Collective action among the LGBTQ communities across the country after the Supreme Court judgement seems to be an example of this.

This chapter highlights the very important role of queer community/s in the lives of the participants of this study. The multiple meanings of 'community' for the participants ranging from self-transformation and affirmation to inspiration for social transformation have been explored in this chapter. There have been also experiences of 'difference' from the queer community/s that some participants shared and this difference has at times co-existed with a sense of belonging and collective intimacy.

# References

Andersen, S. M., & Chen, S. (2002). The relational self: An interpersonal social-cognitive theory. *Psychological Review, 109*(4), 619.

Ashmore, R. D., Deaux, K., & McLaughlin-Volpe, T. (2004). An organizing framework for collective identity: Articulation and significance of multidimensionality. *Psychological Bulletin, 130*(1), 80–114.

Beard, J., & Glickauf-Hughes, C. (1994). Gay identity and sense of self: Rethinking male homosexuality. *Journal of Gay & Lesbian Psychotherapy, 2*(2), 21–37.

Brewer, M. B., & Gardner, W. (1996). Who is this "We"? Levels of collective identity and self representations. *Journal of Personality and Social Psychology, 71*(1), 83.

Britt, L., & Heise, D. (2000). From shame to pride in identity politics. In S. Stryker, T. J. Owens, & R. W. White (Eds.), *Self, identity, and social movements* (Vol. 13, pp. 252–268). U of Minnesota Press.

Deaux, K. (1996). Social identification. In E. T. Higgins & A. W. Kruglanski (Eds.), *Social psychology: Handbook of basic principles* (pp. 777–798). New York: Guilford Press.

Gurin, P., & Townsend, A. (1986). Properties of gender identity and their implications for gender consciousness. *British Journal of Social Psychology, 25*(2), 139–148.

Herek, G. M., Gillis, J. R., & Cogan, J. C. (2009). Internalized stigma among sexual minority adults: Insights from a social psychological perspective. *Journal of Counseling Psychology, 56,* 32–43.

Leap, W. (2007). Language, socialization, and silence in gay adolescence. In K. E. Lovaas & M. M. Jenkins (Eds.), *Sexualities and communication in everyday life* (pp. 27–54). California/UK: Sage Publications London/Routledge.

Mead, G. H. (1934). *Mind, self, and society from the standpoint of a social behaviorist.* Chicago: Univ. Chicago Press.

Meyer, I. H. (2007). Prejudice and discrimination as social stressors. In I. H. Meyer & M. E. Northridge (Eds.), *The health of sexual minorities: Public health perspectives on lesbian, gay, bisexual and transgender populations* (pp. 242–267). Springer Science + Business Media, LLC.

Miller, C. T., & Major, B. (2000). Coping with stigma and prejudice. In T. F. Heatherton, R. E. Kleck, M. R. Hebl, & J. G. Hull (Eds.), *The social psychology of stigma* (pp. 243–272). New York: Guilford Press.

Mohr, J., & Fassinger, R. (2000). Measuring dimensions of lesbian and gay male experience. *Measurement and Evaluation in Counseling and Development, 33*(2), 66.

NALSA v/s Union of India. (2014). Supreme Court judgement on transgender rights. Retrieved July 15, 2017, from http://judis.nic.in/supremecourt/imgs1.aspx?filename=41411.

Owens, T. J., Robinson, D. T., & Smith-Lovin, L. (2010). Three faces of identity. *Sociology, 36*(1), 477.

Plummer, K. (1995). Telling sexual stories in a late modern world. *Studies in Symbolic Interaction, 18,* 101–120.

Prentice, D. A., Miller, D. T., & Lightdale, J. R. (1994). Asymmetries in attachments to groups and to their members: Distinguishing between common-identity and common-bond groups. *Personality and Social Psychology Bulletin, 20,* 484–493.

Ramasubban, R. (2008). Political intersections between HIV/AIDS, sexuality and human rights: A history of resistance to the anti-sodomy law in India. *Global Public Health, 3*(S2), 22–38.

Simon, B., & Klandermans, B. (2001). Politicized collective identity: A social psychological analysis. *American Psychologist, 56,* 319–331.

Tajfel, H. (1978). Social categorization, social identity, and social comparisons. *Differentiation Between Social Groups,* 61–76.

# Chapter 7
# Concluding Remarks

## 7.1 Some Propositions from Life Span Studies in the Study of Growing Up Gay

Applying principles of life span development to lives of lesbian and gay individuals, Savin-Williams (2001) has proposed four significant propositions that I have used and or reflected upon as guiding principles in this book:

*First: We are the same.* This implies that, even while studying lived experiences of gay and lesbian individuals amidst normative scripts of heterosexual development, we should bear in mind that there are several general characteristics and developmental processes in the lives of sexual minority individuals that are similar to those affecting all humans. For instance, regardless of sexual orientation and gender identity, all adolescents have growth spurts, menses, nocturnal emissions, acne, and all of them have to negotiate issues of autonomy, individuation, attachment, intimacy, and identity.

While the principal of commonality of experience may be a useful tool in understanding the process of human development, it is necessary to resist universalist assumptions that homogenize and erase the growing-up experiences of many people. All bodies may not follow a universal biological clock; for instance, all adolescents with intersex variations may not necessarily experience menses or nocturnal emissions. Similarly, young malnourished girls may experience delay or irregularity in menses due to anaemia. However, assuming menstruation to be the hallmark of the experience of development of adolescent girls, would be using a majority experience to speak for all experiences. The same argument can be made about able bodies seen as marker of physical/motor or cognitive development and invisibilizing experiences of disabled persons. Through highlighting the *difference* in development trajectories and growing-up experiences of young queer people, I have attempted to challenge the majoritarian (in this case heterosexual and gender

© Springer Nature Singapore Pte Ltd. 2018
K. Ranade, *Growing Up Gay in Urban India*,
https://doi.org/10.1007/978-981-10-8366-2_7

binary   dominant   ideas)   assumptions   that   underlie   an   essentialist-naturalized-universalist discourse in life span studies.

*Second: We are different.* This implies that, due to a marginalized sexuality, sexual minority individuals experience a substantially different life course than do heterosexuals. Experiences of stigma and discrimination, and an accompanying sense of alienation, affects the childhood, adolescence, adulthood, and entire life of gay and lesbian individuals. In fact, the 'social schedule/social clock', as described by Neugarten (1979) to refer to prescriptions of life transitions based on social age, is informed by ideas of heteronormativity (among other kinds of norms), and lesbian and gay individuals are often 'off schedule' by default.

This proposition is one of the central themes of this book. I have sought, throughout this book, to understand the ways in which being gay/lesbian is different from being heterosexual and the ways in which it impacts growing up and life experiences. In other words, are there experiences that gay children or adolescents have that are different from their heterosexual counterparts? In this book, I highlight, through experiential accounts, a sense of difference described by most study participants right from a young age. For most participants, this difference was experienced as not a good but a '*bad difference*', at least initially. Several participants described gender transgressions from as early as five or six years of age, in areas such as clothes, grooming, play, and preference of play mates. While gender transgressions were common for lesbian women and gay men, their impact and consequences were often different for men and women. Family, parents, friends, schools, and colleges emerged as normativizing institutions, reproducing social norms of 'appropriate' behaviours related to gender and sexuality. However, participant stories also include accounts wherein certain transgressions were tolerated through ignoring/invisibilizing/not seeing or acknowledging, as well as viewing these transgressions as situational, contained within a specific context or time period, not spilling over into 'normal' life. 'Growing up' 'gay' posed several challenges for the LG child/adolescent, which I argue, in Chap. 3, sets the developmental process of gay and lesbian individuals apart from their heterosexual counterparts. Being a minority even in one's family and among one's closest friends; finding one's self in the absence of any gay affirmative language, images, or role models; fighting socially internalized messages of abnormality and pathology; dealing with feelings of alienation and isolation; all of this, in the absence of external support and with only the internal resources of an adolescent or a young person, can be an overwhelming experience.

Just as there have been unique developmental challenges in growing up gay, which I discuss in Chap. 3, there are also facets and challenges that are unique to gay relationships that I discuss in Chap. 5. For instance, one of the propositions I make in Chap. 5 is that intimate/romantic same-sex relationships for many young gay/lesbian individuals are not just romantic relationships but often a gateway to reduced isolation and a beginning of gay socialization. Similarly, there are unique challenges facing same-sex couples who are attempting to fit in with normative (heterosexual) scripts of couple-hood, or trying to defy them, or rewriting relationship scripts outside of the normative. I use the framework of sexual minority stress (Meyer 2007) to understand the impact of these unique developmental challenges on the life journeys of gay and lesbian young people.

*Third: We differ among ourselves.* There exist enormous diversities among gay and lesbian individuals. Sexuality is one aspect of an individual's identity and it intersects with several other identities such as class, caste, gender, religion, and urban/rural background, to produce a range of diversities, not to mention diversities around sexual desires, practices, sub-cultures, language, and so on.

This proposition has been adequately acknowledged, but not fully considered and worked upon, in this book. While I have discussed frameworks that conceptualize identity and selfhood as constituting of multiple dimensions, I have kept a sharp focus on sexual identity and meaning/s of growing up and living as 'gay'. Thus, other identity markers such as class, caste, religion, region, ability, and their intersections with experiences of growing up gay, have not been primarily focused upon in this book. This is not to undermine their role, but it is only to *'freeze the frame'* or define the scope of this book, that I chose to primarily focus on, and seek to visibilize, *gay/lesbian* childhoods, adolescence, and young adulthood, about which we know so little in the Indian context. The intimate intersections of sexuality with gender are explicated through the life stories of gay men and lesbian women in this book. Other intersections, such as sexuality and socio-economic class, have been described when they have emerged in the data. For instance, class is inextricably linked with access to privacy that is so important while growing up, especially for someone with gender and sexuality transgressions. There is a need to have access to safe and private spaces to try out things that are highly stigmatized and forbidden, such as wearing lipstick for a young person assigned male gender at birth. Similarly, socio-economic class is a significant factor in a person being able to leave the natal home to escape marriage, or violence, or just to live independently and explore the possibilities of a life outside the normative familial/kinship heterosexual narrative. While these intersections have been noted at multiple points in the book, these have not been the primary focus of this inquiry. It is necessary to explore further the intersections of being and becoming gay with other social identities and locations and describe the range of diversities and differences in growing up as gay in India.

*Fourth: We are each unique.* This implies that every individual is unique and that, while there may be similarities of experiences and similar articulations about growing-up experiences, no two individuals are identical and any research using a development frame has to be aware of the same.

This proposition is a core tenet of the psychosocial approach that I use in this study. The psychosocial approach, while fully acknowledging and being appreciative of the role played by social structures and environment in the process of development, also emphasizes individual agency and action in shaping their own development. Thus, while all gay/lesbian persons growing up in the cities of Bombay or Pune in the late 1980s or 1990s may have faced similar environmental constraints in the form of invisibility, isolation, criminalization, or violence in private and public places (emanating from the dominant ideologies of heterosexism and gender binarism), the individual journeys of each participant of meaning-making, coping, and thriving, would be different. This difference may be partly explained not only by their other social identities, locations, access to resources, and support systems, but also by the unique way of each person of making sense, relating, and living.

To emphasize the unique developmental situation of each person and inter-individual differences in response to their environment, D'Augelli (1994) uses the concept of 'developmental plasticity', which refers to human responsiveness to environmental and biological changes. In fact, the model of lesbian, gay identity development of D'Augelli (1994), that sees identity processes as a result of three interconnected variables, is a good example of coming together of the subjective/ psychological, interpersonal and social/environmental processes. The three variables discussed by D'Augelli are: (a) personal subjectivities and action (how individuals feel about their sexual identities over their lives, their engagement in diverse sexual activities with different meanings, and their construction of their sexual lives and feelings); (b) interactive intimacies (influences of early parental/ familial socialization, peer and romantic relationship influences), and; (c) socio-historical connections (social norms, particularities of sub-culture/geographic communities, local and national social customs, laws, policies, cultural and historical continuities and discontinuities).

In addition to the four propositions proposed by Savin-Williams (2001) in the context of lesbian and gay identity development, I would like to add the dimension of time and space to the study of growing up gay. Socio-historical time and geographical space in which the life narrative of a gay person unfolds is a significant dimension to this study. The life course narratives and their analysis that I present in this book are replete with examples of a particular gay magazine, drop-in centre, helpline, doctor, counsellor, a party, a group, a collective that were significant in the growing-up journey of the individual. Similarly, some of the participants talked about visiting other spaces that impacted their experiences of growing up. For instance, one of the participants talks about attending a gay wedding in the U.K. during a student exchange program and how that affected his thought process. All of these refer to spatial (as well as temporal) specificities that are central to the life narrative. In other words, if one were to ask these very research questions in a village in India or another city or town, these narratives would perhaps be different. In terms of socio-historical time in a city, or a country, I suggest that the invisibility and isolation that participants described, even in cities of Bombay and Pune, are a reflection of the time in which they were growing up. After 2009 (Delhi High Court judgment decriminalizing homosexuality), for instance, most young people growing up in cities would not have to face the question, 'Am I the only one who is like this?' Similarly, at a time predating the colonial encounter, young people in this region probably did not ask questions about their sexuality in terms of an identity. Thus, temporal and spatial dimensions are significant in the study of human development. Here, I suggest that the idea of cohort effect that has been used traditionally within life span studies may be extended to the study of growing up gay.

## 7.2   Socio-cultural Realities as Context for Studying 'Growing Up Gay'

In describing and analyzing narratives of young gay and lesbian persons about coming out to oneself and others, meeting community, and forming intimate/romantic relationships, I locate these in certain aspects of socio-cultural life in India. These include: the presence of a strong cultural script for homosociality; compulsory nature of heterosexual, endogamous marriage, and; a social and relational nature of identity that may not neatly fit in with the western individuated, bounded nature of self and identity.

In a highly gender-segregated society there are strict rules and norms for interactions between men and women, both in the public and the private domain. Kumar (1992) in his essay, 'Growing Up Male' reflects on the role of the gender-segregated education system in institutionally legitimizing the 'purdah' (separation) system between boys and girls, leading to a complete lack of access to the world for girls/women, and this, in turn, leading to a certain kind of dehumanizing of girls. On the other hand, close engagement with members of one's own sex is encouraged as part of appropriate socialization and role modelling. Thus, homosociality—intimate engagement and social bonds among members of the same sex—is not just accepted but prescribed. As a result, intimate relationships between members of the same sex are often interpreted in the Indian context in terms of 'friendship bonds' and deep emotional connections that are celebrated within the cultural context. However, homosociality, especially among women as described by Sedgwick (1985), can often mean a continuum between homosocial and homosexual: women caring for each other, promoting each other's interests, women's friendships and bonds, and women loving women. In India, there exists a cultural script for homosociality or close bonds among men and among women. As suggested by D'Augelli (1994), cultural and historical continuities and discontinuities (such as same-sex imagery, narratives, poetry, literature, art, and myths, as documented by Vanita and Kidwai 2000) are important in the study of same-sex sexuality.

Marriage is seen in India both as compulsory for all and as a social duty. While modernization, urbanization, and related social phenomena—such as migration, increasing numbers of nuclear households, and changing gender roles—have led to some change in the form and shape of the institutions of marriage and family, the core ideas about 'who can marry whom' (dictated by dominant ideas of caste purity, community and kinship solidarity, strict gender roles) continue to hold strong. Vanita observes, "In India, most people have been, and many continue to be, married off at a very young age. Hence exclusive same-sex relationships are necessarily rare" (Vanita 2002, 3). In fact, the centrality of heterosexual marriage is such that any sexual relations outside of it (and by extension outside of the family and community network) are not acknowledged and are unthinkable for many. In this study, too, forced (overt or subtle) heterosexual marriage has been a reality in the lives of many of the participants or their partners. The all-pervasive nature of this ideology of compulsory marriage means that, often, gay and lesbian individuals aspire for, and see, their relationships, with heterosexual marriage as their reference point. Thus, the centrality of heterosexual marriage is a significant social reality that has to be kept in mind, while studying gay relationships.

One of the conceptualizations of the self, in a modern sense, is that of an individuated, bounded, autonomous self. But there are descriptions of the self as expressed in kinship, community, and relational terms, and identity is seen as informed by an interdependent view of the self. In such a context, familial concerns and filial duties are placed in high regard, and individuals are much more enmeshed in their social and familial relationships. The default presentation then of the self to the family or society is a heterosexual one, and identity is often expressed in social terms such as caste location of one's family, gender, or one's birth order in the family. Hence, disclosure or non-disclosure of one's sexual identity in social life, embracing a 'gay lifestyle' as defined by a western gay liberatory discourse, needs to be viewed in light of a familial/relational construction and expression of self and identity, wherein sexual subjectivities may not translate into an identity based on sexuality. It is due to these specificities of the socio-cultural context that growing up gay in urban India may be different from the development of a gay identity and a gay life trajectory as described in psychological, or even popular, LGBT literature within Euro-American contexts. While conceptions of the self in literature suggest a mutually exclusive, polar opposite composition of the *Eastern* (socially embedded) and *Western* (individuated and bounded) ideas of self, the reality is likely to be more hybrid, especially in multicultural, urban locations such as Bombay and Pune, where I conducted my study.

The study of growing up and the development of a gay or lesbian sexual identity that I attempt to undertake here is also to be viewed in the socio-cultural context of naturalized heterosexuality; every form of non-heterosexual possibility is rendered invisible through a powerful, enmeshed matrix of family, marriage and kinship ideologies. In fact, marginality due to sexual difference, and exclusionary practices that one is subjected to due to one's non-normative sexuality, are largely invisible and illegible, as opposed to other marginalized locations relating to caste, ethnicity, gender, and religion, that are determined by birth into a certain body, family, community, spatial location, or region, and enforced through practices of social segregation. However, this is not the case with exclusions based on sexuality, wherein neither its possibilities nor its prohibitions are explicated. Dave (2012) refers to this work, of making explicit, legible, and naming of this difference based on one's sexuality, as *politics of invention*. The narratives of growing up gay in this book do exactly this. While negotiating invisibility, they talk of inventing and articulating new forms of relationality, belonging, and ways of being gay in a heterosexually constructed world.

## 7.3  Why Study 'Growing Up Gay'?

Studying growing up processes of gay and lesbian individuals can often be confused with attempts at establishing an etiology or causation of homosexuality. In other words, trying to retrospectively understand experiences of childhood and growing up can be seen as motivated by a need to pin down the origin, or the cause, of this 'deviation' from the path of 'normal' development. Historically, such 'causation' research in medical/mental health sciences has been conducted with the motivation of knowing and removing the root cause of the 'abnormal' condition of homosexuality, or changing/converting of such perversion into 'normal' heterosexual functioning.

It is due to the dominance of ideas of heteronormativity and gender binarism (and pathologization of sexualities and gender expressions that fall outside of these), that most studies focused on children and adolescents in India assume all of them to conform to the socially assigned gender at birth and expect all of them to grow up to be heterosexual adults. As a result, there exists no literature on children and adolescents who transgress norms of gender and sexuality. Similarly, since sexuality is expected to emerge in adolescence, even the sparse literature that exists on emergence of gay or lesbian sexuality does not focus on childhood/s. This has resulted in invisibilizing of the childhoods of gay individuals, and more so in homogenizing childhood experiences by assuming everyone to be cisgender and heterosexual.

As argued in Chap. 3, childhood studies is dominated by a universal narrative of childhood: the child within the family unit, innocent, protected and cared for within the private domain. And then there are studies of the 'other' children; children and childhoods that are deviant from the normal child. Some examples of these within development literature, as well as state policy are, orphan children, children in conflict with law, trafficked children, child labourers, and so on. Despite sharing some commonalities with these 'deviant' children, such as facing neglect, abuse, violence within families, schools, colleges, among peer groups, running away from home, and facing violence in public spaces (Shah et al. 2015; Ghosh et al. 2011; PUCL-K 2001), gay and lesbian children do not figure in the discourse around childhood vulnerabilities in India.

This book is an attempt to start critical conversations within the disciplines of psychology, social work, childhood studies, and family studies in India and to think about exclusions inherent in these disciplines. It is an attempt to locate experiences of lesbian and gay individuals within a life course perspective, which includes their personal histories of childhood and growing-up years, experiences of institutionalized homonegativity within homes, schools, neighbourhoods, among friends, and their journeys of finding themselves and their communities. The motivation behind this book is to initiate inquiry and understanding about growing-up experiences of gay individuals in the Indian context, which would enable parents, families, teachers, child counsellors, activists, academics and policy makers to better understand, counsel, protect and plan relevant programmatic interventions, or tweak the existing ones to accommodate needs of young gay and lesbian individuals.

In this book, I also attempt a discussion about possible methodological considerations for studying gay and lesbian life span experiences/development. I suggest that a methodological approach with adequate attention to the intrapsychic and subjective experiences, while also laying out the context of institutionalized homonegativity and socio-cultural and historical dimension within which these experiences unfold, is necessary. While I have attempted to do this here, in the interest of a focused inquiry and narrative, I have left out other layers of social identity that need to be thought through in future work in this area. For instance, while describing 'growing up gay', I primarily focus on sexuality and do bring up other social locations of class and gender where possible, but I have not centrally focussed on ways in which being gay intersects with social locations of class, caste, region, gender, language, ethnicity, and so on. Similarly, in this book I talk about childhood, adolescence, and young adulthood of gay and lesbian persons living in the cities of Bombay and Pune. However, I stop at adulthood and adult relationships with partner/s and community, and do not look at experiences of older adults, as well as ageing, among gay and lesbian persons. These would be significant areas for further inquiry. I also do not address incremental effect: How do childhood experiences affect adolescence or later development? Nor do I discuss circularity of experience: How is the psychic/subjective experience of a gay person shaped by and in turn, how does it shape, interpersonal and community or social experience? I hope that some of these complexities will be addressed in future work on life span studies with lesbian and gay persons. Also, this is not a longitudinal study and instead studies experiences of over twenty to thirty years retrospectively of young gay and lesbian persons and, hence, limitations related to the research design, such as recall and recency effect, apply here too.

Longitudinal studies to understand psychosocial processes related to development of non-normative genders and sexual expressions/identities within a socio-historical context, and accounting for intersection with other social identities by forming multiple cohorts, would possibly be an ideal study design to develop further on this initial exploratory work. However, the current study, even with its design limitations, provides a base for an empathic understanding of growing up gay/lesbian. This can be used to develop interventions towards more inclusive familial and educational environments, to develop LG-informed and inclusive curricula for educationists, doctors, teachers, counsellors, social workers, and also to inform future research agenda in this area.

# References

D'Augelli, A. R. (1994). Identity development and sexual orientation: Toward a model of lesbian, gay, and bisexual development. In E. J. Trickett, R. J. Watts, & D. Birman (Eds.), *Human diversity: Perspectives on people in context* (pp. 312–333). San Francisco: Jossey-Bass.

Dave, N. N. (2012). *Queer activism in India: A story in the anthropology of ethics.* Duke University Press.

Ghosh, S., Bandyopadhyay, B. S., & Biswas, R. (2011). *Vio-map: Documenting and mapping violence and rights violation taking place in the lives of sexually marginalized women to chart out effective advocacy strategies.* Kolkata: SAPPHO for Equality.

Kumar, K. (1992). Growing up male. In K. Kumar (Ed.), *What is worth teaching?* (pp. 1–22). Hyderabad: Orient Longman.

Meyer, I. H. (2007). Prejudice and discrimination as social stressors. In I. H. Meyer, & M. E. Northridge (Eds.), *The health of sexual minorities: Public health perspectives on lesbian, gay, bisexual, and transgender populations* (pp. 242–267). Springer Science + Business Media.

Neugarten, B. L. (1979). Time, age, and the life cycle. *American Journal Psychiatry, 136*(7), 887–894.

PUCL-K. (2001). *Human rights violations against sexuality minorities in India: A PUCL-K fact finding report about Bangalore.* Bengaluru: People's Union for Civil Liberties—Karnataka.

Savin-Williams, R. C. (2001). *Mom, dad, I'm gay: How families negotiate coming out.* Washington DC: American Psychological Association.

Sedgwick, E. K. (1985). *Between men: English literature and homosocial desire.* New York, NY: Columbia University Press.

Shah, C., Merchant, R., Mahajan, S., & Nevatia, S. (2015). *No outlaws in the gender galaxy.* New Delhi: Zubaan.

Vanita, R. (2002). Introduction. In R. Vanita (Ed.), *Queering India: Same-sex love and eroticism in Indian culture and society.* New York: Routledge.

Vanita, R., & Kidwai, S. (Eds.). (2000). *Same-sex love in India: Readings from literature and history.* New Delhi: Macmillan.

Printed by Printforce, the Netherlands